The "I DON'T KNOW HOW TO COOK" BOOK

300 Great Recipes You Can't Mess Up

Mary-Lane Kamberg

ADAMS MEDIA
AVON, MASSACHUSETTS

For my daughters, Rebekka and Johanna
My everlasting gratitude to the Kansas City Writers Group

Published by
Adams Media, an F+W Publications Company
57 Littlefield Street, Avon, MA 02322. U.S.A.
www.adamsmedia.com

ISBN: 1-59337-009-1

Printed in the United States of America.

J I H G F E D

Library of Congress Cataloging-in-Publication Data
Kamberg, Mary-Lane
The I don't know how to cook book / Mary-Lane Kamberg.
p.   cm.
ISBN 1-59337-009-1
1. Cookery. I. Title.
TX7114.K1277   2004
641.5--dc22   2003023159

This publication is designed to provide accurate and authoritative information with
regard to the subject matter covered. It is sold with the understanding that the publish-
er is not engaged in rendering legal, accounting, or other professional advice. If legal
advice or other expert assistance is required, the services of a competent professional
person should be sought.
—From a *Declaration of Principles* jointly adopted by a Committee of the American Bar
Association and a Committee of Publishers and Associations

Many of the designations used by manufacturers and sellers to distinguish their products are claimed as trademarks. Where those designations appear in this book and
Adams Media was aware of a trademark claim, the designations have been printed with
initial capital letters.

Cover concept by Marion Bolognesi.
Cover illustration by Irena Roman.

This book is available at quantity discounts for bulk purchases.
For information, call 1-800-872-5627.

Contents

Acknowledgments

From the first instant I shared the idea for a cookbook for people who can't cook, dozens of friends and family members have encouraged and assisted me in the effort. Special thanks to my mother and research assistant, Jessie Ladewig; my husband, Ken Kamberg; my daughters, Rebekka Kamberg and Johanna Kamberg; my siblings, Brock Ladewig, Amy Phillips, and Ann White; and the rest of my extended family: cousins, in-laws, nieces, nephews, my dear friends, and the clerks at Dillons Store No. 69, my favorite supermarket.

Particular thanks go to Lucy Lauer, Chalise Miner, Sophia Myers, Candy Schock, and Robin Silverman for their help. And to these friends and family who offered their favorite easy-to-make recipes: Melody Aldrich, Beth Bailey, Barbara Bartocci, Marsha Bartsch, Josh Baze, Nina Bertilsdotter, Deborah Bundy, Kerri Fivecoat-Campbell, Ginger Carter, Meri Carter, Maril Crabtree, Judith Choice, Lance Clenard, Alberta Daw, Ruth Ann Falls, Ricki Gilbert, Lisa Waterman Gray, Jacqueline Guidry, Madeline Guidry, Carolyn Hall, Greg Hockett, Sally Jadlow, Judith Bader Jones, Joe Karroll, Heather Kiepura, Tami Kohler, Betsy Krusen, Hank Krusen, Lindsey Krusen, Mary Ladewig, Julie Laird, Michelle Langenberg, Sophia Myers, Joan Nietzchke, Jon Phillips, Jane Rogers, Rex Rogers, Larry Schilb, Marsha Schilb, Corrine Russell, Susan Shanaman, Niki Shepherd, Amelia Mendus, Deborah Shouse, Patty Sullivan, Janet Sunderland, Polly Swafford, Vicki Swartz, Pat Walkenhorst, Toni Watson, and Bette Willmeth. Thanks, too, to my able, efficient agents Mike and Susan Farris and my editor Danielle Chiotti.

Welcome to the Kitchen

id you grow up in the kitchen watching and learning basic cooking skills? Or were you outside skateboarding or shooting baskets? Up in your room reading or playing music? If the kitchen is new to you, you may want to learn a few things about the culinary arts.

Now that you're on your own, you've probably already realized that life has more to offer than drive-thru hamburgers, pizza delivery, and carryout Chinese food. Sooner or later, you might even venture into the kitchen and wonder what that stove is for. Of course, you've *seen* a stove before. Perhaps you've even boiled a hot dog or heated soup from a can. But the idea of actually cooking something may, up to now, have been beyond your grasp or inclination. Don't worry. If you can read (and follow directions), you can cook.

If you have never cooked *anything* before, or if you have basic kitchen knowledge but a limited culinary repertoire, *The I Don't Know How to Cook Book* is a great place to start.

All recipes in this cookbook were selected because they are easy to make. They are grouped according to difficulty within each chapter and identified by these symbols:

Easy. Preparation for these starter recipes for new cooks is so quick and easy, you'll feel like an expert.

Medium. These basic recipes require a few more steps than the Beginner ones, but they're still quite simple.

Hard. Here are cook-off challenge recipes to try after you've prepared a few of the easier recipes in this book. Generally, the advanced recipes contain more ingredients and require steps that are a bit more complicated. But don't shy away from them. They're delicious!

If you're a vegetarian, this cookbook has plenty of recipes to fit your style. Look for this symbol next to the recipe titles.

Vegetarian. This symbol means the recipe is vegetarian and contains no meat, fish, or poultry, although some include such animal products as butter, milk, or eggs. Recipes with the word *vegan* in the title contain neither meat nor dairy products.

Before you begin, a word about nutrition. The sad fact is that many foods that taste good aren't too good for you—especially sweet snacks and desserts. So go easy on them. Be sure to include fruits and vegetables in your meals. One good rule is to try to eat five servings of fruits and vegetables every day. You also need grains (breads, cereal, and pasta) and protein (soy products, nuts, meats, poultry, fish, and cheese). And you need some dietary fat—although experts caution against eating too much of it. Be sure to vary your menu so you get a mixture of essential vitamins, minerals, and other nutrients. Try not to eat the same foods day after day—no matter how much you like them.

Once every week or two, why not try something new? You won't like everything you try. But you'll open yourself to new taste adventures, as well as new cooking skills.

Ready? Let's get started.

Recipe for New Cooks

1. Before you begin, read the recipe all the way through. Assemble all ingredients. (The ingredients in the *I Don't Know How to Cook Book* are listed in the order of their appearance in the directions if you like order and want to line them up in a row—but you don't have to!)

2. Always wash your hands before and after handling food, especially meats and poultry, which may contain harmful bacteria that proper cooking kills.

3. Ovens and microwaves vary, so many recipes give a range of cooking times. In recipes that give a range of cooking times, such as 15 to 20 minutes, check the food after the first time listed. If the dish is not done, return to the heat source for the additional time.

4. No recipe is cast in stone. After you try a recipe for the first time, make notes to yourself in the cookbook's margin. Note cooking times for your oven or microwave, as well as measurements you would like to adjust to your personal taste.

Recipes sometimes include ingredients without specific measurements followed by the words *to taste*. Most often this phrase applies to salt or pepper. It means to add an amount that tastes good to you. Just pretend you are adding the ingredient to your own serving plate.

5. Sometimes you'll want to prepare fewer or more servings of a recipe. All you have to do is a little math. You can double a recipe by multiplying the measurement of each ingredient by 2. You can cut a recipe in half by dividing the measurement of each ingredient. But be careful.

Cooking times may vary—especially in microwaves that need more time to cook larger quantities of food. If you're doubling a recipe, do *not* double the cooking time. Cook it according to directions, but be aware that you may need a little more cooking time. The reverse may be true when cooking smaller amounts.

6. Plan menus. Eat different types of foods so you get a variety of nutrients. If you're new at meal planning, follow the school lunch menu, which often appears in local papers. Qualified dietitians plan the menus. Do what they do.

7. Nothing will dampen your enthusiasm for cooking more than a kitchen full of dirty pots, pans, and utensils when the food is done. Whenever possible, clean as you go. When you are finished with a pot, measuring cup, or mixing bowl, wash it while you're waiting for noodles to boil or during baking times. You can let the cooking utensils drip dry. Or, if you're really a neat freak, you can also dry them and put them away. (Nah!)

Bon Appétit!

Common Measurements

3 teaspoons	=	1 tablespoon
4 tablespoons	=	¼ cup
5 tablespoons, plus 1 teaspoon	=	⅓ cup
1 cup	=	½ pint
2 cups	=	1 pint
2 pints	=	1 quart
2 quarts	=	½ gallon
4 quarts	=	1 gallon

The I Don't Know How to Cook Book

Eye-Openers: Breakfast Foods to Start Your Day

Orange-Banana Smoothie

Wake up to this delicious breakfast in a glass, and get ready for a great day! Bananas are known to calm the mind and oranges are said to clear the mind. You'll be prepared to take on the world in just a few minutes. Use an electric blender or electric mixer.

Serves 4

What You Need:
1 banana
1 (6-ounce) can frozen orange juice concentrate
1 (6-ounce) can water
Ice, as needed (about 2 cups)

What You Do:
1. Peel and slice banana. Place the orange juice, water, and banana in an electric blender. Add enough ice to fill the blender. Blend until smooth.

2. If you don't have a blender, place orange juice, water, and banana in a medium-size mixing bowl. Use a spoon or electric mixer to stir rapidly until well blended. Place ice in glasses. Pour the banana mixture over the ice.

Breakfast Sundae

Fresh bananas, grapes, apples, berries, pears, or other fruits let you make this breakfast sundae a new way every time. Choose your favorites for a fun way to start a summer day or holiday. If using bananas, apples, or pears, sprinkle them with a few drops of lemon juice so they won't turn brown. This can be made the night before. Cover and refrigerate until morning.

Serves 4

What You Need:
4 cups fresh fruits
2 tablespoons brown sugar
1 cup sour cream
4 maraschino cherries

What You Do:
1. Rinse and peel the fruits. Cut into 1" to 2" cubes. Place in bowls, sundae dishes, or glasses. (You may want to layer the fruit or arrange them on dishes.)

2. When ready to serve, mix together the brown sugar and sour cream in a small mixing bowl. Pour over the top of the fruit. Top each serving with a cherry.

Variation:
Breakfast Sundae with Yogurt
Add 1 cup of frozen yogurt to each serving dish. Top with fruits and sour cream mixture.

Orange-Glazed Biscuits

Sweet and tangy, these breakfast biscuits will start your day with sunshine. Make orange juice from the leftover orange juice concentrate. Measure remaining concentrate and add 3 times as much water, then stir.

Yields 10 biscuits

What You Need:
½ cup butter *or* margarine
1 cup white granulated sugar
3 tablespoons frozen orange juice concentrate
1 (12-ounce) can refrigerated biscuits

What You Do:
1. Preheat oven to 375°. Melt the margarine in a saucepan over low heat. Stir in the sugar and orange juice concentrate. Dip the top of each biscuit in this mixture and place glazed-side down, side by side and touching the other biscuits in a greased tube pan, bundt pan, or round cake pan.

2. Pour the remaining sauce over the biscuits in the pan. Bake, uncovered, for 15 minutes. During baking, the glaze works its way to the bottom of the pan, so when serving, turn biscuits upside down on serving plate so the glaze will drizzle over the top for an attractive presentation. Serve warm.

Easy Coffee Cake

The aroma of cinnamon and freshly baked biscuit dough is an inviting way to start the day. You can substitute chopped walnuts for the pecans.

Serves 6

What You Need:

½ cup butter *or* margarine

½ firmly packed cup brown sugar

1 teaspoon cinnamon

1 (12-ounce) can refrigerator biscuits

2 tablespoons chopped pecans *or* walnuts

What You Do:

1. Preheat oven to 350°. Melt the margarine in a saucepan over low heat. Stir in the brown sugar and cinnamon.

2. Grease a 9" round cake pan or spray with nonstick cooking spray. One at a time, dip the top of each biscuit into the butter mixture. Place butter-side down in the pan, starting on the outer edge and overlapping the biscuits in a circle. Use remaining biscuits to fill the middle of the pan.

3. Add nuts to remaining butter mixture. Spoon the mixture onto the biscuits. Bake uncovered for 10 minutes.

> **Measuring Brown Sugar**
>
> Some recipes that call for brown sugar specify the measurement should be firmly packed. To measure, put the brown sugar in the measuring cup and use the back of a spoon to pack it down. Keep tightly pressing it into the measuring cup until you have the amount asked for. This method results in more brown sugar than you would get using the usual measuring method—and that's what the recipe writer intends.

Makin' Bacon

There's nothing like the sound and smell of bacon sizzling in the pan to start your day. Bacon is a favorite with eggs, pancakes, and French Toast (page 16). You can also use cooked bacon in tossed salads and on sandwiches.

Method 1: Pan-Fried

1. One at a time, lay strips of bacon side-by-side in a cold skillet. Turn on heat to medium-high. As the bacon cooks, use a fork to move the slices often to avoid sticking. When each slice is brown on the first side, use a fork or tongs to turn it over.

2. Cook on the second side until the bacon is as crisp as you like it. Use a fork or tongs to remove each slice from the pan. Drain on several sheets of paper towel.

Method 2: Microwaved

1. Place 2 thicknesses of paper towels on a microwave-safe plate. Place strips of bacon on the paper towels. Cover with another layer of 2 paper towels.

2. Microwave for 5 to 10 minutes. Keep an eye on it. Check after 5 minutes and again every 2 minutes until done.

Method 3: Baked

Preheat oven to 400°. Separate pieces of bacon and lay across the rack of a broiler pan. The slots in the broiler lid will let bacon fat drip into the lower part of the pan. If you don't have a broiler pan, use a shallow ovenproof baking dish. Bake on a middle oven rack for about 10 minutes. No need to turn.

Poached Egg

Poached eggs are cooked in steam. You can make them in a frying pan that has a lid, or you'll need a poaching pan, an electric egg poacher, or a microwave egg poacher. Poached eggs are especially good served on toast, with a somewhat runny yolk soaking into the bread. Yum.

🍴 Serves 1 🍴

What You Need:
About 1 teaspoon butter, margarine, vegetable oil, *or* nonstick cooking spray
1 egg
Water

What You Do:
1. Lightly coat a frying pan with butter (or alternative).

2. Break the egg into the pan. Add ½ teaspoon water (for each egg). Cover tightly.

3. Cook for about 5 minutes or until the egg is as firm as you like.

Oops! There's Eggshell in My Eggs!

If a bit of eggshell ends up in your mixture, removing it is easy—if you know this trick. The best way to get hold of a piece of eggshell is *with* a piece of eggshell. (That's why you don't want to be too quick to toss the shells into the trash or stuff them down the garbage disposal.) Pick up a big piece of shell and use it to scoop out its offending cousin. The substance inside the shell helps the pieces stick to each other for easy removal.

Fried Egg

All you need to fry an egg is a frying pan—or a hot sidewalk—and some type of fat, like butter, margarine, or vegetable oil. You can also use nonstick cooking spray instead of fat. For added flavor, use saved bacon grease or the drippings from freshly cooked breakfast sausage.

Serves 1

What You Need:
2 to 3 tablespoons butter, margarine, bacon fat, *or* vegetable oil
1 egg

What You Do:
1. Melt the butter (or alternative) in a frying pan over medium heat. When melted, crack the egg into the frying pan.

2. For "sunny-side up," cook until the yolk is done according to your preference. For "over easy," let cook until the white is almost done. Flip with a pancake turner. Immediately flip over onto serving plate. "Basted" eggs look like "over easy" eggs, but you don't flip them over. Instead, as the egg cooks, spoon hot fat from the frying pan on top of the egg. The top will cook, but you won't risk breaking the yolk during the flipping process.

Variation:
Fried Egg and Cheese

When the egg white is cooked, or immediately after flipping over the egg, add a slice of your favorite cheese. Cook until the cheese melts.

Boiled Egg

Both soft-boiled and hard-boiled eggs are cooked the same way. The only difference is the cooking time. Start with an egg at room temperature.

E

Serves 1

What You Need:
1 egg
Water as needed to cover the egg

What You Do:
1. Place the egg in a saucepan (for many eggs at once, you can use a Dutch oven but don't stack on top of each other). Cover with water. Bring to a boil over medium-high to high heat.

2. When the water boils, cover tightly. Remove from heat. For a soft-boiled egg, let cook for 2 to 4 minutes, depending on your preferred firmness. For a hard-boiled egg, let stand 20 minutes.

3. Rinse the egg in cold water to stop the cooking process and to make it easier to remove the shell.

Boiling Water

Boiling water means to heat it enough that it turns to steam. Heat the water in a saucepan or microwave-safe dish on high until big bubbles break on the surface. Boiling water is an important cooking method for eggs, hot dogs, vegetables, and even some meat. Water boils faster if you cover the pan with a lid. Don't let the pan boil dry.

Scrambled Eggs

You can eat scrambled eggs alone or with cheese or other added ingredients, such as chopped bell pepper, chopped onion (or dried onion flakes), sliced olives, mushrooms, bacon bits, diced ham, or crumbled cooked sausage.

Serves 1

What You Need:

1–2 tablespoons butter, margarine, bacon fat, *or* vegetable oil

2–3 eggs
2–3 tablespoons milk (optional)

What You Do:

1. Melt fat over medium heat. (If using butter, don't let it turn dark brown. Reduce heat if necessary.)

2. Crack the eggs into a small mixing bowl. Add 1 tablespoon milk for each egg. Quickly stir with a fork to break the yolks and blend in the milk. Add any optional ingredients. Pour into frying pan.

3. As the eggs cook, stir so they heat evenly for about 5 to 6 minutes. When the eggs are still a bit runnier than you like, remove from heat and let sit for 1 or 2 minutes. (Eggs will continue to cook.) Fluff with a fork.

Apple Oatmeal

This is not your mother's oatmeal. With the fragrant aroma of apples and cinnamon, this oatmeal has the zing and spice of apple pie. Serve with milk. Enjoy.

 **Serves 4**

What You Need:

1 apple
1/3 cup oats (uncooked oatmeal; *not* instant)
1/4 cup raisins (optional)
1/4 teaspoon cinnamon
About 2 tablespoons brown sugar

What You Do:

1. Peel, core, and chop the apple. Place in a saucepan with the oats, raisins, and cinnamon. Stir and cook over medium heat until bubbly. Reduce heat to low. Simmer for 5 minutes, stirring occasionally.

2. Spoon into serving bowls. Sprinkle each with about 1 1/2 teaspoons brown sugar.

Pigs in a Blanket

Here's an easy, fun breakfast food you can eat alone or as a side with your favorite style of eggs. Add fruit juice and milk for a complete morning meal.

🍴 Yields 8 "pigs" 🍴

What You Need:
1 pound brown-and-serve *or* precooked sausage links
1 (8-ounce) can refrigerated crescent rolls

What You Do:
1. In a frying pan or microwave oven, cook the sausage links according to package directions. Drain on a few paper towels.
2. Preheat oven to 350°. Separate sections of dough and roll each section around 1 sausage link. Place seam-side down on an ungreased cookie sheet. Bake for 10 minutes, until golden brown.

Honey-Banana Bagel Spread 🥕

Make ahead—cover and refrigerate until ready to serve.

🍴 Yields enough for 4 bagel halves 🍴

What You Need:
3 ounces cream cheese
3 tablespoons butter *or* margarine

1 banana
3 tablespoons honey

What You Do:
1. Set out the cream cheese and butter to soften at room temperature for 10 to 15 minutes. Place in a small mixing bowl.
2. Peel the banana and slice crosswise. Add to the mixing bowl. Add the honey. Use a potato masher or electric mixer to stir together until smooth.

Peaches and Cream Bagel Spread 🥕

Add extra zip and flavor to your morning bagel and cream cheese. You can substitute your favorite flavor of jam.

🍴 Yields ½ cup 🍴

What You Need:
4 tablespoons cream cheese

2 tablespoons peach preserves

What You Do:
Set out the cream cheese for about 10 minutes. In a small bowl, mash cream cheese until smooth. Stir in jam until well blended.

Strawberry Bagel Spread

Strawberries and cream on a toasted bagel—yum!

Yields enough for 4 bagel halves

What You Need:

4 ounces cream cheese

½ cup fresh strawberries *or*
  3 tablespoons strawberry jam

⅓ cup white granulated sugar

1 tablespoon orange juice

What You Do:

Set out the cream cheese to soften for 10 to 15 minutes. Place in a small bowl. Clean the strawberries (see page 86), and cut into slices. Mash with a fork. Add the sugar and orange juice to the cream cheese. Use a spoon or electric mixer to blend until smooth.

Honey Butter

Try this melt-in-your-mouth spread on biscuits or dinner rolls.

Yields about ½ cup

What You Need:

½ cup butter *or* margarine

1 tablespoon honey

What You Do:

Set out butter for 10 to 15 minutes until soft. Place in a small mixing bowl. Use a fork or mixer to blend until smooth. Stir in the honey until well blended.

Home-Fried Potatoes

Here's a way to enjoy cottage fries without the trouble of peeling and deep-frying. Serve with Fried Egg (page 8).

M

🍴 Serves 2 🍴

What You Need:
1 tablespoon butter, margarine, *or* vegetable oil
1 (15-ounce) can sliced potatoes
¼ teaspoon garlic powder
¼ teaspoon onion powder
Salt and pepper, to taste

What You Do:
1. Melt the butter, margarine, or vegetable oil in a frying pan over medium heat.
2. Drain the potatoes. Add to the frying pan. Gently stir until potatoes are well coated with butter. Sprinkle with garlic powder, onion powder, salt, and pepper. Continue stirring until thoroughly heated and golden brown.

Potatoes in History

Potatoes are native to the Americas. When they were introduced to Europe about 500 years ago, people were afraid that they caused leprosy. However, 200 years later, the Irish recognized potatoes' food value. Potatoes are a good source of potassium and are high in vitamin C. If your potatoes sprout while you're storing them, you can still use them. Just break off the sprouts before you peel the potatoes.

French Toast

You can top this breakfast favorite with maple syrup, your favorite flavor of jam or jelly, honey, or confectioners' sugar. You can use slightly stale white or wheat bread that has become dry (but not moldy!) or 1"-thick slices of French bread left over from another meal.

Yields 6 slices

What You Need:

2 eggs
½ cup milk
2 tablespoons butter *or* margarine
6 slices bread

What You Do:

1. Crack the eggs into a medium-size mixing bowl. Add the milk and stir with a fork until well blended.

2. Melt the butter or margarine in a frying pan over medium heat. Dip each slice of bread into the egg mixture so it is coated on both sides. Place in the frying pan. Heat until bottom side is golden brown. Use a pancake turner to flip to the other side. Heat until golden brown. Serve immediately.

Vegan French Toast

Here's a tasty variation you might enjoy, even if you're not a vegetarian. Serve with warm maple syrup, confectioners' sugar, or fresh fruit.

Yields 8 slices

What You Need:
2 bananas
3/4 cup vanilla soymilk *or* rice milk
1 teaspoon cinnamon
1 teaspoon vegetable oil
8 slices bread

What You Do:
1. Peel the bananas and slice crosswise. Place in a medium-size mixing bowl. Mash with a potato masher or electric mixer. Stir in the soymilk and cinnamon. Mash or mix until smooth.
2. Pour the oil into a frying pan. Heat over medium heat.
3. Dip the bread slices one at a time in the banana mixture. Flip over once to coat both sides. Scrape off any excess mixture. Place the coated bread in the frying pan. Cook until lightly browned on the bottom. Use a pancake turner to flip to the other side. Cook until lightly browned. Serve immediately.

Nutty Banana Pancakes

If you like Baked Apple and Sausage Pancakes (page 24), you might also like this similar dish with a different fruit and without the sausage. Serve with maple syrup and butter.

Serves 2

What You Need:
2 eggs
1 cup all-purpose flour
1 cup milk
2 tablespoons vegetable oil
1 teaspoon cinnamon
1 teaspoon vanilla extract (*or* imitation)
2 tablespoons chopped pecans
1/8 teaspoon salt
1 banana

What You Do:
1. Preheat oven to 375°. In a large mixing bowl, combine the eggs, flour, milk, and vegetable oil. Stir until well blended, but still a bit lumpy. Stir in the cinnamon, vanilla extract, pecans, and salt.

2. Pour batter into a greased a 8" × 8" ovenproof baking pan. Slice the banana and place on top of the batter. Bake for 20 to 25 minutes, until puffy on the edges and golden brown on top.

Huevos Rancheros

Here's a *muy bien* dish to give your breakfast a spicy flavor. Serve with sour cream and your favorite picante sauce or salsa—chunky salsa works well.

Serves 4

What You Need:
½ cup vegetable oil
4 (6") corn tortillas
⅔ cup shredded Monterey jack cheese
⅔ cup shredded sharp Cheddar cheese
4 eggs

What You Do:
1. Pour the oil into a large frying pan to about ⅛" deep. Heat the oil on medium-high. One at a time, cook the tortillas in the oil until soft. Drain on paper towels or on a wire rack with a paper towel under it. Cover with paper towel to keep warm.

2. Mix the cheeses in a small mixing bowl and set aside.

3. Fry the eggs (see page 8). Place each tortilla on a serving plate. Place a cooked egg on top of each tortilla. Top with the cheese mixture.

Hash Brown Potatoes and Eggs

Combine these traditional favorites for a warm and tasty breakfast. For extra pizzazz, serve with salsa or picante sauce.

Serves 4 to 6

What You Need:
½ cup (1 stick) butter *or* margarine
½ (32-ounce) bag frozen uncooked hash brown potatoes
8 eggs

What You Do:
1. Preheat an electric skillet to 250°, or preheat a large frying pan over medium-low heat. Melt the butter (or margarine) in the pan. Sprinkle the potatoes into the pan. Pat down with a pancake turner. When golden brown on the bottom, use the pancake turner to flip the potatoes to the other side.

2. When the potatoes are golden brown on the second side, crack the eggs on top of potatoes, evenly spaced. Cover and cook until the eggs are cooked through.

Popovers

These warm crusty muffins puff up and brown, leaving a hollow center. Serve with butter or margarine and warm maple syrup. Bake popovers in ovenproof custard cups or in a deep muffin tin.

Yields 2–4 popovers

What You Need:
Shortening
1½ teaspoons butter *or* margarine
1 egg
½ cup milk
½ cup all-purpose flour
⅛ teaspoon salt

What You Do:
1. Preheat oven to 450°. Use solid shortening to grease oven proof custard cups or deep muffin tins. Melt the butter (or margarine) in a small saucepan over low heat.

2. In a medium-size mixing bowl, beat the egg. Stir in the milk and melted butter. Add the flour and salt. Beat just until smooth. *Do not overbeat.*

3. Fill the custard cups ⅓ full. If you're using a deep muffin tin, fill about ¾ full. Bake for 40 to 45 minutes, until golden brown. (Do not open the oven door to check on the muffins for the first 30 minutes.)

Pumpkin-Nut Bread

This tasty bread brings the pumpkin flavor of fall holidays to the breakfast table any time of year. You can omit the nuts if you prefer.

Yields 1 loaf

What You Need:

Shortening, as needed
2 cups all-purpose flour
2 teaspoons baking powder
½ teaspoon salt
½ teaspoon pumpkin pie spice
¼ teaspoon baking soda

1 firmly packed cup brown sugar
⅓ cup vegetable oil
2 eggs
1 cup canned pumpkin
¼ cup milk
½ cup chopped walnuts

What You Do:

1. Preheat oven to 350°. Use solid shortening to grease the bottom (not the sides) of a 9½" × 5¼" × 2¾" or 8½" × 4½" × 2½" loaf pan.

2. Combine the flour, baking powder, salt, pumpkin pie spice, and baking soda in a medium-size mixing bowl; stir until well mixed.

3. In a separate, large mixing bowl, use a portable hand mixer to beat together the brown sugar, vegetable oil, and eggs until well blended. With a spoon, stir in the pumpkin and milk.

4. Add the flour mixture about ¼ cup at a time, stirring until the batter is just smooth. Gently stir in the nuts. Pour the batter into the loaf pan. Bake for 1 hour. Let cool for 10 minutes; then remove from pan and place on a wire rack until cooled.

Sausage Soufflé

A soufflé is a fluffy baked egg dish with a wide variety of other ingredients. Prepare the night before. Some of the fat necessary in this recipe comes from the milk. So, if you use skim milk, add 1½ teaspoons of butter or margarine.

 **Serves 4**

What You Need:

1 pound ground medium *or* hot pork sausage
6 eggs
1¼ cups milk (2% *or* whole)
3 slices bread
¾ cup shredded Cheddar cheese
¾ teaspoon dry mustard
½ teaspoon salt

What You Do:

1. In a frying pan, cook the sausage until browned. Drain off grease and set aside the sausage.

2. In a medium-size mixing bowl, beat together the eggs and milk. Cut the bread (including crust) into 1" cubes. Stir into the egg mixture, along with cheese, dry mustard, and salt until well mixed. Pour into an ungreased 9" × 13" ovenproof baking pan. Cover and refrigerate overnight so the bread can absorb the flavors.

3. Preheat oven to 325°. Cover and bake for 45 minutes. Remove cover and bake for another 15 minutes.

Baked Apple and Sausage Pancakes

These special pancakes are easier to make than regular pancakes and tastier, too. You can substitute 3/4 cup blueberries for the apples. Serve with maple syrup and butter.

 **Serves 6**

What You Need:

Shortening, as needed
½ (12-ounce) package medium
   or spicy ground pork sausage
1 cup pancake mix
⅔ cup milk

2 eggs
2 tablespoons vegetable oil
1 apple
1½ teaspoons cinnamon
1½ teaspoons white granulated sugar

What You Do:

1. Preheat oven to 375°. Use the shortening to grease a 9" × 13" ovenproof baking pan.

2. Brown the sausage in a frying pan. Drain off fat and set aside the sausage.

3. In a large mixing bowl, combine the pancake mix, milk, eggs, and vegetable oil; stir until well blended but still a bit lumpy. Add drained sausage.

4. Pour the batter into the greased baking pan.

5. Peel the apples and remove the cores. Slice the apples lengthwise and layer them on top of the batter. Sprinkle lightly with the cinnamon and sugar. Bake for 25 to 30 minutes, until puffy on the edges and golden brown on top. Serve warm.

Breakfast Burrito

Buenos días! Start your morning with a flavor from south of the border. Serve with salsa and sour cream.

Yields 10 burritos

What You Need:

4 medium-size red russet potatoes
1 pound lean ground beef
8 eggs

¼ cup milk
10 (8") flour tortillas
2 cups shredded Cheddar cheese

What You Do:

1. Rinse the potatoes under cold, running water. Peel and cut into 1" cubes. Place the potatoes in a large frying pan with the ground beef. Brown the beef and potatoes (see "Browning Ground Beef," page 115). Drain off the fat.

2. Preheat oven to 350°. In a medium-size mixing bowl, beat together the eggs and milk with a fork, wire whisk, or electric mixer until well blended. Pour into the beef mixture. Stirring, cook until the eggs are done.

3. Place about ⅓ cup of the mixture onto the middle of a tortilla and sprinkle with cheese. Fold the bottom ¼ of the tortilla over the mixture. Fold one side over the mixture. Fold the other side over the first side. Gently roll the tortilla over and place seam-side down in a 9" × 13" ovenproof baking pan that has been sprayed with cooking spray. Continue until all the tortillas are filled.

4. Cover with aluminum foil and bake for 25 to 30 minutes, until heated through. Or, cover with a paper towel and microwave on high until hot. (Do *not* use aluminum foil in a microwave.)

Quiche Lorraine

Quiche is a pie that tastes like an omelet in a pie crust. Serve it as an appetizer or use it as an entrée.

 **Serves 6–8**

What You Need:

1 (9") frozen pie crust
1 large onion
¼ pound bacon
1 cup grated Swiss cheese
4 eggs

¼ teaspoon salt
¼ teaspoon nutmeg
Dash cayenne pepper
2 cups milk

What You Do:

1. Preheat oven to 375°. Bake the empty pie crust for 10 minutes, until lightly browned.

2. While the pie crust is baking, chop the onion; set aside. Fry the bacon (see Makin' Bacon, page 6). Remove the cooked bacon from the pan and drain the fat, leaving about 2 tablespoons in the frying pan. When the bacon has cooled, break the slices into crumbles; set aside.

3. Cook the onions in the bacon fat over medium-high heat, stirring constantly until tender.

4. Grate the cheese. Spread in an even layer in the bottom of the pie crust. Sprinkle the bacon and onions over the cheese.

5. In a medium-size mixing bowl, beat the eggs with a whisk or fork. Beat in the salt, nutmeg, and cayenne pepper until well mixed. Stir in the milk until well blended. Pour the egg mixture over the cheese, onions, and bacon in the pie crust. Bake for 30 minutes or until golden brown.

Mushroom Quiche

Here's an easy quiche for veggie lovers. You can use all one kind of mushroom or a combination of different varieties.

Serves 6–8

What You Need:

1 (9") frozen pie crust
1 pound fresh mushrooms (any type)
1 clove garlic *or* ⅛ teaspoon dried minced garlic
1 tablespoon butter *or* margarine
Salt and pepper, to taste

2 tablespoons chopped fresh parsley (*or* 2 teaspoons dried)
3 eggs
1½ cups whipping cream
½ cup grated Parmesan cheese

What You Do:

1. Preheat oven to 375°. Bake empty pie crust for 10 minutes, until lightly browned.

2. While the pie crust is baking, wipe the mushrooms with a slightly damp paper towel. Slice the mushrooms and chop the garlic (if using fresh).

3. Melt the butter (or margarine) in a large frying pan over medium-high heat. Stir in the mushrooms and garlic. Season with salt and pepper. Cook, stirring constantly, until all the liquid is cooked out of the mushrooms. Stir in the parsley.

4. In a medium-size mixing bowl, beat together the eggs, whipping cream, and Parmesan cheese. Gently stir in the mushrooms and garlic. Pour the mixture into the pie crust. Bake for 30 minutes or until golden brown.

Banana Bread

Moist and aromatic, this banana bread will become a family tradition. When serving, sprinkle with confectioners' sugar. If you're going to make 1 loaf, why not make 3 loaves at once? Purchase foil loaf pans you can give away. Leave loaves in the pans. Let cool. Cover with plastic wrap and tie with ribbons to give as gifts.

Yields 3 loaves

What You Need:
1 cup solid vegetable shortening, plus extra for greasing
2½ cups cake flour, plus 3 tablespoons for flouring
2 cups white granulated sugar
4 eggs
6 ripe bananas
1 teaspoon baking soda
1 teaspoon salt

What You Do:
1. Grease 3 loaf pans with shortening. Add about 1 tablespoon flour to each. Tilt in all directions, tapping gently until the pans are lightly coated. Preheat oven to 350°.
2. In a large mixing bowl, use a spoon or electric mixer to beat together the 1 cup shortening and sugar until soft and smooth; set aside.
3. In a separate medium-size mixing bowl, use a potato masher or electric mixer to mash together the eggs and bananas; set aside.

Banana Bread
(continued)

4. Measure the 2½ cups flour, baking soda, and salt into a sifter or strainer. Sift 3 times over waxed paper or into another large mixing bowl. If using a strainer, shake the dry ingredients through the strainer 9 times.

5. Add about ½ cup of the banana mixture to the sugar and shortening mixture; beat. Add about ½ cup of the flour mixture; beat. Continue alternating the banana and flour mixtures until well blended. Do not overbeat.

6. Pour into the greased and floured loaf pans. Bake for 45 minutes. Let cool in the pans. To freeze, wrap loaves in waxed paper, then wrap again in aluminum foil. Use directly from the freezer, slicing off ¾" slices as needed.

Bacon and Egg Casserole

Here's another casserole that you prepare the night before and pop into the oven in the morning. Some of the fat necessary in this recipe comes from the milk. So, if you use skim milk, add 1½ teaspoons of butter or margarine. You can also serve this dish for dinner as an inexpensive main course; make it in the morning and cook it at dinnertime.

Serves 6

What You Need:

8 slices bacon
8 eggs
1 quart milk (2% *or* whole)
1 cup shredded American cheese
1 teaspoon salt
1 (6-ounce) box herb-seasoned croutons

What You Do:

1. Fry the bacon (see Makin' Bacon, page 6). Remove the cooked bacon from the pan and drain on paper towels. When the bacon is cooked, crumble it with your hands. Place in a cup or small bowl. Cover and refrigerate overnight.

2. In a large mixing bowl, beat together the eggs and milk. Stir in the cheese, salt, and croutons. Pour into an ungreased 9" × 13" ovenproof baking pan. Cover and refrigerate overnight.

3. Preheat oven to 350°. Sprinkle the crumbled bacon over the egg mixture. Cover and bake for 45 minutes.

Chapter 2

Sandwiches

Grilled Cheese Sandwich

Golden brown bread and melted cheese is a well-known kid favorite. For variety, add a slice of lunchmeat and/or a slice of tomato before grilling. You can substitute margarine for the butter.

Serves 1

What You Need:
2 tablespoons butter

2 slices bread

1 slice American cheese

What You Do:
1. In a frying pan or on a griddle, melt 1 tablespoon of the butter over medium heat.

2. Butter one side of one piece of bread and place in the frying pan, buttered-side down. Place a slice of cheese on top. Butter one side of the remaining slice of bread and place on top of the cheese, buttered-side up.

3. Cook for 2 to 3 minutes, until the bottom is golden brown. Use a pancake turner to flip the sandwich. Cook another 1 to 2 minutes or until the second side is golden brown. Serve warm.

Grilled Cheese Variations
If you like grilled cheese but are ready for a more grown-up taste, try adding an extra slice of a different type of cheese. Or, add one of these ingredient combinations before grilling: dried Italian seasoning and grated Parmesan cheese; thinly sliced tomato and luncheon ham or bologna; cooked bacon slices, sun-dried tomatoes, and basil; sliced jalapeño peppers (from a jar) and bean dip; thinly sliced tomato, thinly sliced avocado, Dijon mustard, and mayonnaise.

BLT

Here's a traditional American favorite. You can use freshly cooked bacon or leftover bacon that you have covered and stored in the refrigerator. If you like, add a slice of your favorite cheese.

Yields 1 sandwich

What You Need:
2 slices bacon
1 leaf lettuce
1–2 slices fresh tomato
2 slices bread
1–2 tablespoons mayonnaise *or* mayonnaise-like salad dressing

What You Do:
1. Fry bacon (see Makin' Bacon, page 6). Drain on paper towels. When cool, break each slice in half crosswise to make 4 strips about the width of the bread.

2. Rinse the lettuce under cold, running water and pat dry with a paper towel. Slice the tomato.

3. Toast the bread. Spread mayonnaise on one side of each piece. On one slice, stack lettuce, bacon, and tomato. Top with second slice (mayonnaise-side down).

Grilled PB&J 🥕

Here's a new twist on an old favorite. Try it with other peanut butter sandwich variations, using pickles, raisins, bananas, or other ingredients. Serve with fresh fruit or raw, sliced carrots.

🍴 Yields 1 sandwich 🍴

What You Need:
2 tablespoons peanut butter
2 pieces bread
2 tablespoons jam *or* jelly (any flavor)
2 tablespoons butter *or* margarine, divided

What You Do:
1. Spread the peanut butter on a slice of bread. Spread jam or jelly on the other. Put the 2 slices together. Spread ½ tablespoon of the margarine on the top slice.

2. Melt 1 tablespoon of the margarine in a large frying pan or griddle. Place the sandwich in the margarine, margarine-side down. Spread the remaining ½ tablespoon of margarine on the outside of the bread slice that is now on top. Cook until the bottom slice is slightly browned and crusty. Use a pancake turner to flip once. Cook until the second side is slightly browned.

Bacon, Onion, and Cheese Sandwich

This sandwich is quite tasty, especially when the bacon is freshly fried. You can make this with toast, but also try it on untoasted bread, which soaks up the bacon fat and melted cheese. Yum!

 **Serves 1**

What You Need:
2 slices bacon
1 slice white onion
1 slice American cheese
Mayonnaise *or* mayonnaise-like salad dressing, as needed (about 1 tablespoon)
2 slices bread

What You Do:
1. Cut the bacon slices in half horizontally and fry (see Makin' Bacon, page 6). When you have turned the bacon the final time, arrange the 4 halves of bacon slices in row in the bottom of the frying pan. Reduce heat to low.

2. While the bacon continues to cook, place the onion slice on top. Place the cheese on top of the onion. Heat until the cheese melts.

3. Spread the mayonnaise on one side of each slice of bread. Use a pancake turner to remove the bacon, onion, and cheese from the pan as one unit. Place on bottom slice of bread. Top with the second slice.

Egg Sandwich

Egg sandwiches aren't just for breakfast. You can eat them for lunch—or even for dinner. Here are a couple of delicious versions.

⚷ Serves 1 ⚷

What You Need:
1 egg
2 tablespoons butter, margarine, *or* bacon fat plus 1 pat butter *or* margarine
1 slice American cheese (*or* your favorite cheese)
2 slices bread

What You Do:
1. Fry the egg (page 8) in the 2 tablespoons butter, margarine, or bacon fat. Break the yolk in the pan. Flip the egg once.

2. While the egg is cooking on the second side, place the cheese on top. Heat until the cheese melts.

3. Butter one side of each slice of bread. Use a pancake turner to remove the egg from the pan and place on buttered side of one piece of bread. Top with the second slice of bread (buttered side down).

Variation:
Open-Face Egg Sandwich

Soft-boil the egg (see Boiled Egg, page 9). Toast and butter a slice of bread. When the egg is done, gently crack the shell. Use a knife or spoon to scoop the egg onto the toast. Use a knife to cut up the egg and spread it in an even layer on the toast. Eat with a knife and fork.

Hot Ham and Turkey
Open-Face Sandwich

Here's a quick way to serve a hot lunch in the time it takes to make a sandwich. Hot and yummy.

 **Serves 1**

What You Need:
1 slice dark rye bread
1 slice luncheon turkey
1 slice luncheon ham
1 slice tomato
½ cup shredded mozzarella cheese

What You Do:
1. Toast the bread. Stack the turkey, ham, tomato, and cheese on top. Place on an ungreased baking sheet.
2. Broil until the cheese melts.

Tuna Salad Sandwich

Recipes for tuna salad abound. Eat the salad by itself, or serve on bread or toast with a leaf of lettuce. Because tuna salad contains mayonnaise, you should keep it cold until ready to eat. It's not a good choice for a trip to the beach on a hot day. For a slightly different flavor, you can substitute mayonnaise-like salad dressing for the mayonnaise.

Yields 2 cups

What You Need:

2 eggs (optional)

1 (12-ounce) can tuna

1 stalk fresh celery

$^2/_3$ cup mayonnaise *or* mayonnaise-like salad dressing

2 slices bread *or* 1 hamburger bun

What You Do:

1. Hard-boil the eggs (see Boiled Egg, page 9). Remove the shells. Chop the eggs and place them in medium-size mixing bowl.

2. Drain the tuna. Use a fork to flake it into the bowl.

3. Chop the celery and add it to the bowl.

4. Stir in the mayonnaise until well blended. Chill for at least 1 hour before serving.

5. Spread on bread or bun.

Variation: Chicken Salad Sandwich

Follow the directions for Tuna Salad Sandwich, but substitute 1½ cups of precooked chicken (see "Cooked Chicken for Casseroles and Salads," page 81) or a 10-ounce can drained chunk chicken for the tuna.

Egg Salad Sandwich

Serve egg salad by itself or as a sandwich filling. Keep cold until ready to eat.

Serves 2

What You Need:
4 eggs
1½ stalks fresh celery
2 tablespoons mayonnaise *or* mayonnaise-like salad dressing
½ teaspoon prepared mustard
1 teaspoon white granulated sugar
Salt and pepper, to taste
4 slices bread *or* 2 hamburger buns

What You Do:
1. Hard-boil the eggs (see Boiled Egg, page 9). Gently crack the shell and remove the shell from each egg. Chop the eggs and place them in a medium-size mixing bowl.

2. Chop the celery and add it to the bowl. Add the mayonnaise, mustard, sugar, salt, and pepper; stir until well blended. Cover and refrigerate until ready to serve.

3. Spread on bread or buns.

Hot Cheese Toast

You can serve this toast for lunch, as a snack, or as a side dish with Peachy Beef-Zucchini Stew (page 57) or The Best Chili Ever (page 54). You can make this in a toaster oven or under a broiler in a conventional oven. Do *not* substitute mayonnaise-like salad dressing.

Serves 4

What You Need:

½ green onion
¼ cup shredded sharp Cheddar cheese
¼ cup shredded Monterey jack cheese
¼ cup mayonnaise
Garlic powder, to taste (less than ⅛ teaspoon)
Cayenne pepper, to taste
¾ teaspoon dried parsley flakes
4 slices French bread, about 1½" thick
1 tablespoon grated Parmesan cheese

What You Do:

1. Chop the green onion, including part of the dark green top. Place in a medium-size mixing bowl. Stir in Cheddar cheese, Monterey jack cheese, mayonnaise, garlic powder, cayenne pepper, and parsley until well blended.

2. Spread the cheese mixture on one side of each slice of bread. Sprinkle the Parmesan cheese on top. Place face up on an ungreased baking sheet or on the rack of a toaster oven. Broil until the cheeses melt and bubble. Serve hot.

Sandwich in Your Pocket

Make your favorite sandwich in pita bread. Pita bread, which originated in the Middle East, has a convenient pocket to hold your choice of filling. Try this combination; then experiment with your choice of others.

Yields 4 pita sandwiches

What You Need:
2 pita bread rounds
Mayonnaise, as needed
Prepared mustard, as needed
4 slices luncheon ham

4 slices luncheon turkey
4 slices Swiss cheese
4 lettuce leaves

What You Do:
1. Cut the pita bread rounds in halves. Gently use your fingers to open the bread and expose the pocket. Spread mayonnaise and mustard inside the pockets.

2. Cut the ham, turkey, and cheese into bite-size pieces. Place in a medium-size mixing bowl. Gently stir until well mixed.

3. Rinse the lettuce leaves under cold, running water. Pat dry. Slide a lettuce leaf into each pita pocket and stuff with the ham and turkey mixture.

Variation:
Salad in Your Pocket
Fill the pita bread with ½ cup cauliflower florets, ½ cup broccoli florets, sliced yellow bell pepper, and 1 to 2 tablespoons bottled salad dressing.

Grilled Reuben Sandwich

This grilled sandwich is a favorite among lovers of German food. Use slices of corned beef left over from Boiled Corned Beef and Cabbage (page 125). Serve with a dill pickle and frozen French fries cooked according to package directions.

 **Serves 1**

What You Need:

2 tablespoons bottled Thousand Island salad dressing
2 slices pumpernickel rye bread
2–4 thin slices corned beef

1 slice Swiss cheese
¼ cup canned sauerkraut
1 tablespoon butter *or* margarine

What You Do:

1. Spread the salad dressing on one side of each slice of bread.

2. Stack the thinly sliced corned beef on the bread. Layer the Swiss cheese on top. Drain the sauerkraut and use a fork to scoop it on top of the cheese. Top with the other piece of bread.

3. Melt the butter or margarine in a frying pan over medium heat. Place the sandwich in the frying pan. Cook for about 1 minute, until the bottom side of the bread is browned. (It will be hard and crisp.) Use a pancake turner to flip the sandwich to the other side; cook until the second side is browned.

Variation:
Grilled Rachel Sandwich

Follow the directions for Grilled Reuben Sandwich, but substitute pastrami for the corned beef, and coleslaw for the sauerkraut.

Mini Pepperoni Pizza

Pizza flavor without the work. No long wait. And no need to tip for delivery. If you're a cheese lover, top with grated Parmesan cheese.

 **Serves 2**

What You Need:
1 English muffin
¼ cup canned spaghetti sauce
Sliced pepperoni, as needed
1 green onion
½ cup shredded mozzarella cheese

What You Do:
1. Preheat oven to 350°. Slice the English muffin in half. Spread ½ of the spaghetti sauce on each half. Arrange the pepperoni slices on top of the sauce.

2. Chop the onion, including the green top. Sprinkle half of the onion on each mini pizza. Top with cheese.

3. Place on a baking sheet. Bake for 10 to 12 minutes, until the cheese melts and bubbles.

Broiled Tuna Puffs

Bubbly and cheesy, this yummy open-face tuna sandwich with a slightly tangy flavor will satisfy your hunger. The ingredient list may seem long, but this tasty recipe is easy to prepare—and worth the effort. You can substitute hamburger buns for the English muffins.

 **Serves 4**

What You Need:
2 English muffins
1 fresh tomato
½ fresh green bell pepper (optional)
1 (6-ounce) can tuna
1½ teaspoons prepared mustard
¼ teaspoon Worcestershire sauce
½ teaspoon dried minced onion
¾ cup mayonnaise
½ cup shredded Cheddar cheese

What You Do:
1. Preheat oven broiler. Cut the English muffins in half horizontally.

2. Slice the tomato into 4 slices about ¼" thick. Set aside. Clean the green pepper and remove the seeds. Cut the pepper in half. Cover and store 1 half in the refrigerator for another use. Chop the remaining half and place in a medium-size mixing bowl. (Depending on your preference, you may want to limit the amount of this ingredient to about 2 tablespoons or less.)

Broiled Tuna Puffs
(continued)

3. Drain the tuna and add to the bowl. Add the mustard, Worcestershire sauce, onion, and just ¼ cup of the mayonnaise. (You'll use the rest in step 5.) Stir until well blended.

4. Toast the English muffins, and heap ¼ of the tuna mixture on each muffin slice. Spread the mixture all the way to the edges of the muffin to prevent burning. Place a tomato slice on each muffin.

5. In a separate bowl, mix the remaining ½ cup mayonnaise with the cheese. Top each muffin slice with ¼ of the cheese mixture. Place the muffins on a baking sheet and broil in the oven on the second rack from the top for 3 to 5 minutes until mixture "puffs" and the sandwich is heated through. To prepare ahead, loosely cover with aluminum foil or plastic wrap (toothpicks stuck in the muffins help keep the covering from touching the tuna mixture). Store in refrigerator until ready to broil.

Open-Face Crab Sandwiches

If you love crabmeat, this hot and tasty sandwich is for you. Serve with fresh fruit or Waldorf Salad (page 97).

 **Serves 4**

What You Need:
1 (8-ounce) package cream cheese
1 (6-ounce) can crabmeat (*or* flaked imitation crabmeat)
2 tablespoons dried parsley flakes
Garlic salt, to taste
Seasoned salt, to taste
4 (1½"-thick) slices French bread

What You Do:
1. Preheat oven to 400°. Let the cream cheese soften at room temperature for 10 or 15 minutes. Place in a medium-size mixing bowl. Add the crabmeat, parsley, garlic salt, and seasoned salt. Stir until well blended.

2. Spread on one side of each French bread slice. Place on an ungreased baking sheet. Bake for 5 to 10 minutes.

> **How to Grate Cheese**
> To grate hard cheese, start with a block of cheese rather than cheese slices. Place a cheese grater across the top of a small mixing bowl (or stand it on one end in the bottom of the bowl) with the sharp-edged bumps facing up. Unwrap the cheese and hold it by one end. Pull it across the grater so the sharp edges on the bumps "grab" the cheese and cut it into strings. Continue until you have the amount you need.

Hummus Pocket Sandwiches

Tired of ordinary sandwiches on ordinary white bread? Try this high-protein vegetarian sandwich instead. Serve with spicy pickles.

🍴 Serves 4 🍴

What You Need:
12 ripe cherry tomatoes
4 (7") pita bread rounds
2 cups Hummus (page 272)
1 (¾-ounce) package alfalfa sprouts
Olive oil, as needed

What You Do:

1. Rinse the cherry tomatoes under cold, running water and cut into halves.

2. Slice an opening at the top of each pita. Spread the hummus on the inside of each side. Stuff alfalfa sprouts and 6 cherry tomato halves into the opening of each pita.

3. Drizzle olive oil over the sandwich filling. Serve.

Saucy Hot Ham and Cheese Sandwiches

Here's hot ham and cheese with extra flair and flavor. For a spicy variation, substitute your favorite bottled barbecue sauce for the Mustard Sauce (below).

 **Serves 4**

What You Need:

½ pound precooked ham
½ pound block processed cheese

1 recipe Mustard Sauce (below)
4 hamburger buns

What You Do:

1. Preheat oven to 400°. Cut the ham and cheese into ¾" cubes and place in a medium-size mixing bowl. Add the Mustard Sauce and stir until well coated.

2. Spoon the mixture onto the hamburger bun bottoms. Replace the bun tops. Tightly wrap each sandwich in aluminum foil.

3. Bake for 10 to 15 minutes or until heated through.

Mustard Sauce

For mustard sauce that goes well with Saucy Hot Ham and Cheese Sandwiches or other ham recipes, chop ¼ cup fresh green bell pepper, 2 sweet pickles, and 3 hard-boiled eggs (see Boiled Egg, page 9). Stir together in a small mixing bowl. Add 1½ teaspoons dried minced onion, ¼ cup mayonnaise, and 2 tablespoons prepared mustard. Stir until well blended. For extra zip, substitute prepared horseradish mustard for the prepared mustard. You can omit the green bell pepper from the sauce, if you prefer.

Sloppy Joes

Here's an easy make-ahead dinner for a crowd. To serve, spoon about ⅓ cup of the beef mixture onto hamburger buns. Or, for an open-face version, spoon onto buttered English muffin halves. Top with some shredded Cheddar and broil until the cheese bubbles.

Yields 4 cups (enough for 12 sandwiches)

What You Need:

¼ medium-size white *or* yellow onion
1 tablespoon vegetable oil
2 pounds ground beef
2 stalks celery
⅔ cup ketchup
½ cup water

2 tablespoons lemon juice
1 tablespoon brown sugar
1½ teaspoons Worcestershire sauce
1½ teaspoons salt
1 teaspoon vinegar
¼ teaspoon dry mustard

What You Do:

1. Chop the onion. Heat the vegetable oil in a large frying pan over medium-high heat. Add the onion. Stir until the onion is tender. Crumble in the ground beef and brown (see "Browning Ground Beef," page 115). Drain off fat.

2. Rinse the celery under cold, running water. Chop the celery and add it to the beef mixture. Reduce heat to low. Stir in the ketchup, water, lemon juice, brown sugar, Worcestershire sauce, salt, vinegar, and dry mustard until well mixed. Cover. Cook for 30 minutes, stirring occasionally. Serve hot.

Variation: Vegetarian Sloppy Joe Sandwich

Follow the directions for Sloppy Joes, except substitute 2 pounds of veggie burgers for the beef.

Artichoke-Feta (Never Had Bettah) Tortilla Wraps

To serve, garnish with plain yogurt and cilantro leaves. This prize-winning original recipe was created by Judith Bader Jones after her son asked, "Why don't you ever make anything with feta cheese?" It is reprinted here with her permission.

 **Serves 8**

What You Need:
1 (14-ounce) can artichoke hearts
3 green onions
3 tablespoons prepared pesto sauce (or homemade Pesto, page 228)
¼ cup crumbled feta cheese
2 tablespoons grated Parmesan cheese
2 tablespoons Romano cheese
8 (8") flour tortillas

What You Do:
1. Preheat oven to 350°. Rinse the artichoke hearts. Drain. Chop into small pieces. Place in a medium-size mixing bowl. Slice the green onions. Add to the bowl.
2. Stir in the pesto sauce, feta, Parmesan, and Romano.
3. Spoon ¼ cup of the mixture onto the center of each tortilla. Fold one side of the tortilla to cover the mixture. Fold the second side to overlap. Secure with toothpicks. Arrange in a rectangular, ovenproof baking dish that has been sprayed with nonstick cooking spray. Bake uncovered for 25 minutes.

Chapter 3

Soups and Stews

Chicken Noodle Soup

The chicken bites and wide egg noodles in this soup make it a hearty alternative to canned soup. Freeze some to save for the next time you're under the weather with a cold or the flu. Serve with chilled canned or fresh fruit and saltine crackers.

 **Serves 4**

What You Need:

2 (10.5-ounce) cans chicken broth (*or* 2½ cups chicken broth made from bouillon cubes or granules)

1 stalk celery

¾ cup cooked, cut-up precooked chicken (see "Cooked Chicken for Casseroles and Salads," page 81) *or* leftover carryout chicken

⅛ teaspoon pepper

½ cup uncooked wide egg noodles

1 teaspoon dried parsley flakes

What You Do:

1. Pour the chicken broth into a 2-quart saucepan. Cut the celery, crosswise, into slices and add to the broth. Stir in the chicken and pepper. Bring to a boil over medium heat.

2. Stir in the noodles. Continue cooking for 10 to 15 minutes until noodles are tender. Reduce heat to low. Sprinkle with parsley flakes.

Tomato Soup

You can make tomato soup out of a can, but if you're in the mood to try an easy soup recipe, give this a try. Serve with Grilled Cheese Sandwich (page 32) or Cheese Biscuits (page 249).

Yields 6 cups

What You Need:

1 slice onion
1 (46-ounce) can tomato juice
1 (10¾-ounce) can tomato purée
2 cups water
1 beef *or* vegetable bouillon cube
1 bay leaf
4 whole cloves
2 teaspoons white granulated sugar
1 teaspoon salt

What You Do:

Separate the rings of the onion slice. Combine all the ingredients in a Dutch oven and stir to mix. Bring to a boil. Reduce heat to low and simmer for 5 minutes. Remove and discard the bay leaf. Serve warm.

The Best Chili Ever

If you like spicy chili, this recipe is for you! Serve with saltine crackers, shredded Cheddar cheese, and sour cream if you can't take the "heat."

🍴 Yields about 2 quarts 🍴

What You Need:
2 pounds ground beef
1 (1.25-ounce) package chili seasoning mix
¼ teaspoon garlic salt
Salt and pepper, to taste
Chili powder, to taste (about 1–3 teaspoons)
1 (15.5-ounce) can kidney beans
2 (15.75-ounce) cans hot chili beans
1 (15-ounce) can tomato sauce for chili
1 (12-ounce) can tomato paste

What You Do:
1. In a large frying pan, brown the ground beef (see "Browning Ground Beef," page 115) along with chili seasoning mix, garlic salt, salt, pepper, and chili powder. Drain off the fat. Place the mixture in a Dutch oven, stew pot, or 2-quart slow cooker.

2. Drain the kidney beans and chili beans. Stir into the ground beef mixture. Stir in the tomato sauce and tomato paste. Cover and cook over low heat on the stovetop or high heat in a slow cooker until warmed through. For best flavor, cook at least 1 hour—longer to let seasonings mingle.

Matzo Ball Soup

When the ancient Hebrews fled Egypt, they made bread to take with them. They didn't have time to let the dough rise before they baked it. Today, matzo, an unleavened bread, is a traditional Passover food.

 Yields about 2 quarts

What You Need:
2 eggs
2 tablespoons vegetable oil
½ cup matzo meal
1 teaspoon salt
1½ quarts (6 cups) canned chicken broth *or* vegetable broth (*or* prepared using
    bouillon cubes)

What You Do:

1. Break the eggs into a medium-size mixing bowl and slightly beat with a fork or wire whisk. Stir in the vegetable oil, matzo meal, salt, and 2 tablespoons of the broth. Cover and refrigerate the dough for 15 minutes.

2. In a saucepan, bring the remaining broth to a boil. Reduce heat to low. Remove the dough from refrigerator. Use your hands to form balls about 1" in diameter. Gently drop into the broth. Cover and cook over low heat for 30 to 40 minutes.

French Onion Soup

If you like, place a slice of toasted French bread into each serving bowl. Top with shredded mozzarella or grated Parmesan cheese. Let the cheese melt before serving.

 **Serves 4**

What You Need:
3 yellow onions
2 tablespoons butter *or* margarine
2 (10½-ounce) cans condensed beef broth (do not dilute)
½ cup water
1 teaspoon Worcestershire sauce
Dash pepper

What You Do:
1. Remove and discard the outer skin of the onions. Cut the onions into thin slices. Melt the butter (or margarine) in a large frying pan over medium heat. Stir in the onions. Cook for about 20 minutes, until tender. Scoop the onions and butter into a slow cooker or Dutch oven.

2. Stir in the beef broth, water, Worcestershire sauce, and pepper. Cover. In a slow cooker, cook on low for 4 to 6 hours (or 2 to 3 hours on high). In a Dutch oven, cook over low heat for 30 minutes until heated through.

Peachy Beef-Zucchini Stew

This hearty stew brings a splash of orange color to your dinner table. Serve with Cheese Biscuits (page 249) or Easy Dinner Rolls (page 280). If your meat market doesn't offer cubed stewing beef, use round steak cut into 1" cubes.

 **Serves 6**

What You Need:

1 pound beef stew meat

1 (8-ounce) can tomato sauce

1 cup water

1 teaspoon salt

3 carrots

2 medium-size potatoes

1 zucchini

1 small white or yellow onion

1 (15-ounce) can sliced peaches, with liquid

What You Do:

1. Place the meat, tomato sauce, water, and salt in a Dutch oven. Stir. Bring to a boil over medium-high heat. Cover and reduce heat to low. Simmer for 1½ hours, stirring occasionally.

2. While the meat mixture is cooking, rinse the carrots, potatoes, and zucchini under cold, running water. Peel and cut into bite-size pieces. Slice the zucchini about ½" thick. Chop the onion. Place all the vegetables in a small mixing bowl. Cover and refrigerate until the meat is done.

3. Add the vegetables to the Dutch oven; stir. Cover and continue to simmer for 30 minutes. Add the peaches. Cook for 10 minutes more.

Fiesta Bean Soup

Here's another easy soup using different vegetables and full-of-fiber beans. Serve with saltine crackers.

Serves 4

What You Need:

1/4 red bell pepper

1/2 cup canned red kidney beans

1/2 cup canned chickpeas (also called garbanzo beans)

1/2 (8-ounce) can cut green beans (or 1/2 cup frozen cut green beans)

1/2 cup frozen chopped broccoli

1/2 cup frozen cut carrots

1 (14.5-ounce) can stewed tomatoes, with juice

2 vegetable bouillon cubes (or substitute chicken bouillon cubes for nonvegetarian)

1/4 teaspoon celery salt

1/4 teaspoon garlic salt

2 teaspoons dried parsley flakes

1/4 teaspoon salt

1/8 teaspoon pepper

Water, as needed (about 1 quart)

What You Do:

1. Chop the red bell pepper. Place in a slow cooker, Dutch oven, or stew pot. Drain the kidney beans, chickpeas, and green beans. Add to the pot, along with the broccoli, carrots, and tomatoes.

2. Unwrap the bouillon cubes and add to the pot. Sprinkle with celery salt, garlic salt, parsley flakes, salt, and pepper. Add water to the Dutch oven to just cover all the ingredients; stir. In a slow cooker, cover and cook on low for 10 to 12 hours or on high for 5 to 6 hours. In a Dutch oven or stew pot, cover and simmer over low heat for 1 to 2 hours.

Gazpacho

When it's hot outside, you can still enjoy this nutritious soup served cold. Gazpacho is most often served as an appetizer in place of salad.

✦ Serves 4 ✦

What You Need:

½ cucumber
¼ green bell pepper
1 fresh tomato
¼ small white *or* yellow onion
¼ cup beef broth
¼ cup tomato juice

1 tablespoon vegetable oil
2 tablespoons red wine vinegar
½ teaspoon salt
Hot pepper sauce, to taste
Worcestershire sauce, to taste

What You Do:

1. Rinse the cucumber, bell pepper, and tomato in cold, running water. Peel the cucumber. Remove the seeds from the bell pepper. Chop the cucumber, green pepper, tomato, and onion, and place in large mixing bowl.

2. Gently stir in the beef broth, tomato juice, vegetable oil, wine vinegar, and salt. Add the hot pepper sauce and Worcestershire sauce a few drops at a time, to taste. Cover and chill for at least 1 hour in the refrigerator before serving.

Cold Avocado Soup

Spices and pepper blend with the mild flavor of avocado to add some zip to this soup, which you can serve by itself or as an appetizer. Garnish with fresh chopped parsley and a lemon slice or sour cream with crumbled bacon. A ripe avocado is soft to the touch regardless of color. The Haas variety turns black when ripe, but most varieties remain green.

Serves 4

What You Need:
1 ripe avocado
2 (10.5-ounce) cans chicken broth
1 cup heavy cream
½ teaspoon salt
½ teaspoon pepper
¼–½ teaspoon (to taste) curry powder
Hot pepper sauce, to taste

What You Do:
1. Peel the avocado and remove the seed. Cut into fourths and place in an electric blender. Add the chicken broth, cream, salt, pepper, curry powder, and hot pepper sauce. Blend until smooth. Cover and refrigerate for several hours (overnight is okay).

2. When ready to serve, blend again. Serve cold.

> **How to Remove Avocado Seeds**
> Here's an easy way to remove the seed from an avocado. First, slice through the avocado lengthwise, deep enough to touch the seed. Cut all the way around the fruit. With one hand on each half, gently twist to separate. Plunge a knife into the seed with a quick thrust. Twist the seed and lift out.

Veggie Lovers' Chili

Each serving of this tasty vegetarian chili provides approximately 19 grams of protein and 18 grams of fiber. Serve with saltine crackers.

Serves 2

What You Need:

½ large white *or* yellow onion

2 tablespoons vegetable oil

1 (15-ounce) can red kidney beans

1 (8.5-ounce) can corn

1 medium-size zucchini (about 8" long)

1 (14.5-ounce) can stewed tomatoes, with juice

¼ teaspoon dried minced garlic

1 tablespoon chili powder

2 teaspoons oregano

What You Do:

1. Chop the onion. In a frying pan, cook the onion in the vegetable oil over medium-high heat, stirring constantly until tender. Transfer the onion and oil to a Dutch oven, stew pot, or 2-quart slow cooker.

2. Drain the beans and corn. Add to the pot.

3. Rinse the zucchini under cold, running water. Chop the zucchini and add to the pot.

4. Stir in the tomatoes, with the juice. Add the garlic, chili powder, and oregano. In a Dutch oven or stew pot, cover and bring to a boil over medium-high heat. Reduce heat to low. Cook for about 15 minutes, until the zucchini is tender. Uncover for the last 5 minutes. In a slow cooker, cover and cook for 1 hour on high. Reduce heat to low until ready to serve. Uncover for the last 5 minutes.

Curried Vegetable Stew

You don't have to be a vegetarian to enjoy this spicy and colorful stew. Serve with saltine crackers or Easy Dinner Rolls (see page 280). You can use the other half of the sweet potato for another meal in Stir-Fry Parsnip Medley (page 234).

Serves 4

What You Need:
1 (10-ounce) package frozen lima beans *or* 1¼ cups canned lima beans
1 (8-ounce) can cut green beans
½ fresh sweet potato
3 zucchini (6" to 8" long)
1 large white *or* yellow onion
1 red bell pepper
2 tablespoons olive oil
1 teaspoon curry powder
Salt and pepper, to taste
2 cups water

What You Do:
1. Thaw the lima beans if using frozen or drain canned lima beans. Let the green beans thaw. Place the lima beans and green beans in a Dutch oven, stew pot, or 2-quart slow cooker. Set aside.
2. Cut the sweet potato in half lengthwise. Wrap ½ and store in the refrigerator for another use. Peel the remaining half. Cut in half lengthwise again. Slice crosswise. Place in a large mixing bowl. Cut the zucchini in half lengthwise; then slice crosswise. Chop the onion and red bell pepper. Add to the mixing bowl.

Curried Vegetable Stew
(continued)

3. Heat the olive oil in a large frying pan over medium-high heat. Fry the sweet potato, zucchini, onion, and red bell pepper, stirring constantly until tender but still firm. Sprinkle with curry powder, salt, and pepper. Add the mixture to the slow cooker or other pot. Add the water. (If 2 cups is not enough to cover the ingredients, add more.)

4. In a slow cooker, cover and cook on high for 1 hour. Reduce heat to low and cook until the sweet potatoes are tender. In a Dutch oven or stew pot, cover and bring to a boil. Reduce heat to low. Keep covered. Simmer for 30 minutes. Keep warm until ready to serve.

Perfect Pea Soup

If you like peas, you'll love this soup. If you're watching your waistline, you can omit the cream. If you're in a hurry, you can use canned peas and omit the first 10 minutes of cooking time.

Serves 4

What You Need:

1 small white *or* yellow onion
1 teaspoon butter *or* margarine
3 cups thawed frozen peas

2 cups water
Salt and pepper, to taste
3–4 tablespoons whipping cream (optional)

What You Do:

1. Chop the onion. Heat the butter (or margarine) in a Dutch oven. Add the onion and cook over medium heat for 3 to 4 minutes, until the onion is transparent. Reduce heat to low. Add the peas, water, salt, and pepper. Cover and cook for 10 minutes, stirring occasionally until the peas are tender.

2. Use a slotted spoon to remove the peas and onion from the pot. (Leave the liquid in the pot.) Place the peas into an electric blender. Add 1 tablespoon of the cooking liquid. Blend until smooth. Return the pea mixture to the pot. Stir in the whipping cream and cook until heated through.

Cooking Term: Purée

Sauces and soups sometimes call for a smooth, thick mixture made from cooked fruits or vegetables. *Purée* means to create this mixture. The easiest way to purée cooked foods is with an electric blender. Or, you can rub the fruit or vegetables through a strainer.

Beef Barley Soup

This soup is flavorful, and it's good for you, too. It's loaded with vitamins A and C, but you don't have to tell! The bouillon cubes have lots of salt, so add extra salt sparingly to taste, rather than all at once.

 **Serves 4**

What You Need:

1 small white *or* yellow onion
2 tablespoons vegetable oil
1 pound ground beef
2 raw carrots
2 stalks celery
1 (8-ounce) can tomatoes, with juice
⅓ cup barley

1 tablespoon dried parsley flakes
2 beef bouillon cubes
½–1 (to taste) teaspoon salt
¼ teaspoon pepper
¼ teaspoon basil
2½ cups water

What You Do:

1. Thinly slice the onion. Pour the vegetable oil into a large frying pan over medium-high heat. Stir in the onion. Crumble the ground beef into the pan. Stir often until the beef browns. Drain off the fat. Transfer the mixture to a slow cooker or Dutch oven.

2. Rinse the carrots and celery under cold, running water. Peel the carrots. Thinly slice the carrots and celery crosswise. Add to the pot. Stir in the tomatoes, barley, parsley, bouillon cubes, salt, pepper, basil, and water. Cover. In a slow cooker, cook on high for 5 to 6 hours (or on low for 10 to 12 hours). In a Dutch oven, bring the mixture to a boil over medium-high heat. Reduce heat to low. Cook, covered, for 1 hour, stirring occasionally.

Southwestern Ham Stew

You can make this stew in a slow cooker or in a Dutch oven. Avoid touching your face or eyes after handling chilies. Serve in bowls or spoon over warm corn bread.

 **Serves 6**

What You Need:
1 pound precooked ham slice *or* leftover baked ham
1 (4-ounce) can green chilies
Onion, as needed to yield ¼ cup finely chopped
2 cups shredded Monterey jack cheese
1 (8-ounce) can tomato sauce
3 drops hot pepper sauce

What You Do:
1. Cut the ham into 1″ cubes. Place in a slow cooker or Dutch oven. Drain the chilies. Remove the seeds and chop the chilies. Chop enough onion into very small pieces to yield ¼ cup. Add the chilies and onion to the pot.

2. Stir in the cheese, tomato sauce, and hot pepper sauce. Cover. In a slow cooker, cook on low for 2 hours. In a Dutch oven, cook over low heat for 30 minutes or until the cheese melts and the stew is heated through.

Chicken Veggie Stew

This stew is quick, easy, and nutritious. Okra is known for thickening and flavoring soups and stews. It is highly perishable, so buy only what you need. Instead of fresh, you can use frozen or canned chopped okra in this recipe.

Serves 4

What You Need:

1½ cups precooked chicken (see "Cooked Chicken for Casseroles and Salads," page 81)
1 large potato
½ cup fresh *or* frozen cut okra
½ cup frozen lima beans
½ cup frozen corn
2 cups chicken broth

1 (8-ounce) can crushed tomatoes, with juice
1½ teaspoons white granulated sugar
½ teaspoon salt
¼ teaspoon rosemary
⅛ teaspoon pepper
Dash ground cloves
1 bay leaf

What You Do:

1. Cut the chicken into bite-size cubes. Place in a slow cooker or Dutch oven. Rinse the potato under cold, running water. Peel and cut into ½" cubes. Add to the pot.

2. Rinse the fresh okra under cold, running water. Slice crosswise into circles. (If using canned okra, drain.) Add the okra to the pot, along with the lima beans and corn. Stir in the chicken broth, tomatoes, sugar, salt, rosemary, pepper, cloves, and bay leaf. Cover.

3. In a slow cooker, cook on high for 4 to 5 hours. In a Dutch oven, bring to a boil over high heat. Reduce heat to low. Cook for 1 hour. Remove the bay leaf before serving.

Carrot Soup

You can serve this festive soup warm or cold. For a slightly different flavor, substitute ½ teaspoon ground ginger for the dill.

Serves 6

What You Need:

¾ cup chopped white *or* yellow onion
1½ pounds fresh carrots
2 tablespoons butter *or* margarine
4 cups canned vegetable broth
2 cups water

Salt and pepper, to taste
½ cup ricotta cheese
1 tablespoon chopped fresh dill
 (*or* 2 teaspoons dried)

What You Do:

1. Chop the onion. Peel the carrots and slice crosswise into circles. Melt the butter (or margarine) in the bottom of a Dutch oven over medium heat. Stir in the onions and carrots.

2. Add the vegetable broth, water, salt, and pepper; stir. Bring the mixture to a boil. Reduce heat to low, and cook for 30 minutes. If foam forms on the surface, use a large spoon or ladle to skim it off. Discard the foam.

3. Remove from heat. Leave the liquid in the cooking pot, and use a slotted spoon to transfer the carrots and onions to a food processor. (A food processor makes this step easier. Or, you can use an electric blender, electric mixer, or manual potato masher.) Add 1 cup of the cooking liquid and the ricotta cheese. Blend until liquefied.

4. Pour the carrot mixture back into the pot with the cooking liquid. Stir until well blended. Bring to a boil over medium heat. Stir in the dill.

Potato Soup

Rich and creamy, this potato soup is a winter favorite. To prevent scorching, be sure to add the milk just before serving.

Yields 6 cups

What You Need:
3 medium potatoes
½ small white *or* yellow onion
2 tablespoons butter
1 teaspoon salt
⅛ teaspoon pepper
1 teaspoon caraway seed
3–4 cups water
2 cups milk

What You Do:
1. Peel and chop the potatoes. Chop the onion. Add the potatoes and onion to a Dutch oven or soup kettle. Add the butter, salt, pepper, and caraway seed. Cover with water. Stir. Cook over medium-high heat for about 10 minutes, until the potatoes are tender.

2. Reduce heat to low. Stir in the milk. Cook until heated through. (Do not boil.)

Taco Soup

Here's a new way to enjoy a Mexican food favorite. Serve with tortilla chips and shredded cheese. If you have leftover cooked chicken, you can substitute it for the beef.

 **Serves 4**

What You Need:
1 small white *or* yellow onion
1 clove garlic (*or* ⅛ teaspoon dried minced garlic)
1 pound ground beef
1 (4-ounce) can diced green chilies
1 (16-ounce) can Mexican-flavored stewed tomatoes, with liquid
1 (15-ounce) can tomato sauce
2 cups water
1 cup bottled or fresh salsa
1 (15-ounce) can pinto beans, with liquid
1 (15-ounce) can kidney beans, with liquid
1 (2.25-ounce) envelope taco seasoning *or* 2 tablespoons chili powder

What You Do:
1. Chop the onion and garlic. Place the ground beef in a large frying pan. Add the onion and garlic. Brown the beef (see "Browning Ground Beef," page 115). Drain off the fat. Place the beef mixture in a Dutch oven or stew pot.

2. Drain the chilies. Add to the pot. Stir in the stewed tomatoes, tomato sauce, water, salsa, pinto beans, kidney beans, and taco seasoning (or chili powder). Bring to a boil over medium-high heat, stirring occasionally. Reduce heat to low. Cover and cook for 30 minutes.

Pepperoni with Bean Soup

For ease of preparation, use a slow cooker for this spicy soup. If you prefer, you can cook it in a Dutch oven or stew pot. Bring to a boil, then reduce heat to low and cook for 1 hour, stirring occasionally.

 **Serves 6**

What You Need:

½ green bell pepper
½ medium onion
1 clove garlic (*or* ⅛ teaspoon dried minced garlic)
1 (4-ounce) package sliced pepperoni
2 (15.8-ounce) cans great northern beans, with liquid
1 (14.5-ounce) can crushed tomatoes, with liquid
½ teaspoon salt
2 cups water

What You Do:

1. Rinse the green pepper under cold, running water. Slice in half lengthwise. Remove and discard the seeds and inner ribs. Cover half and refrigerate for another use. Chop the remaining half. Chop the onion. Chop the garlic into very small pieces. Place the green bell pepper, onion, and garlic in a slow cooker. Cut the pepperoni slices into fourths. Add to the pot.

2. Stir in the great northern beans, tomatoes, salt, and water. Cover. Cook for 3 to 4 hours on high or for 1 hour on high plus 5 to 6 hours on low.

Veggie Beef Soup

This aromatic blend of spices makes a delicious homemade soup to warm a cold winter night. Serve with Hot Cheese Toast (page 40) or dinner rolls with Honey Butter (page 14). This soup is easy to make in a slow cooker.

 **Serves 4**

What You Need:

1 pound cubed beef for stew (*or* ask your butcher to cube round steak for you)
½ (10-ounce) package frozen mixed vegetables (carrots, peas, potatoes, and greenbeans)
1 (14.5-ounce) can crushed *or* stewed tomatoes, with juice
1 baking potato (*or* 2–3 russet potatoes smaller than baseballs)
1½ large stalks celery
½ small white *or* yellow onion (*or* substitute 1 tablespoon dried minced onion)
½ teaspoon salt
⅛ teaspoon pepper
1 bay leaf
⅛ teaspoon garlic powder
⅛ teaspoon basil
⅛ teaspoon rosemary
Pinch of thyme
¼ teaspoon dried parsley flakes
2 beef bouillon cubes
Water, as needed (about 1 quart)

Veggie Beef Soup (continued)

What You Do:

1. Place the beef, mixed vegetables, and tomatoes with juice in a Dutch oven, stew pot, or slow cooker. Rinse the potato and celery under cold, running water. Peel the potato. Cut in half lengthwise; then cut crosswise to make 1½" cubes. Add to the pot.

2. Chop the onion and celery. Add to the pot. Sprinkle with salt, pepper, bay leaf, garlic powder, basil, rosemary, thyme, and parsley. Unwrap the bouillon cubes and add to the pot.

3. Add enough water to cover all the ingredients; stir. In a slow cooker, cover and cook on low for 10 to 12 hours or on high for 5 to 6 hours. In a stew pot, cover and simmer over low heat for 3 or 4 hours, until the meat is tender and cooked through. Remove the bay leaf before serving.

Variation: Vegan Veggie Soup

For a vegetarian variation, substitute 1 eggplant for the beef. Rinse the eggplant under cold, running water. Peel and remove the seeds. Cut the eggplant into ½" cubes. Substitute vegetable bouillon cubes or granules for the beef bouillon.

Using Frozen Vegetables

When a recipe calls for a portion of a 10-ounce package of frozen vegetables, all you do is place the package on a cutting board and cut it crosswise with a sharp knife. Wrap the part you won't use in aluminum foil and replace in the freezer for later use. Or, purchase the vegetables in a 16-ounce bag and simply pour out the amount you need.

Black Bean Soup

You'll need to start this soup the night before you plan to serve it, but it is worth the effort. Serve with Mexican Corn Bread (page 252).

Yields 8 cups

What You Need:

2 cups dried black beans
6 cups, plus 2 quarts water
½ small white or yellow onion
2 stalks celery
2 teaspoons salt

⅛ teaspoon pepper
1 tablespoon butter
2 tablespoons all-purpose flour
1 lemon
2 hard-boiled eggs (see Boiled Egg, page 9)

What You Do:

1. Place the beans and the 6 cups water in a Dutch oven or soup kettle. Bring to a boil over high heat. Cover and reduce heat to low. Simmer for 1½ hours. Remove from heat and let cool. Refrigerate overnight.

2. Drain the beans in a colander. Rinse in cold, running water. Drain. Return to the Dutch oven.

3. Chop the onion and celery. Add to the pot. Stir in the 2 quarts water, salt, and pepper. Cook over low heat for 3 to 4 hours.

4. In a saucepan, melt the butter over low heat. Stir in the flour until well blended. Gradually add in a few tablespoons of the soup liquid from the Dutch oven, stirring until thickened. Pour the thickened liquid back into the Dutch oven with the beans.

5. Rinse the lemon in cold running water and thinly slice (do not peel). Remove the shell from the hard-boiled eggs and slice (an egg slicer makes this step easy). When ready to serve, place egg and lemon slices on top of each serving.

Chili Blue

Here's an old favorite from Girl Scout camp. The chili has a sweet flavor that tastes almost as good cooked indoors as it does over an open fire in the woods. You'll find chili sauce in the ketchup aisle. Serve with French bread (see "Preparing French Bread," page 117) or Mexican Corn Bread (page 252).

 **Serves 4**

What You Need:
3 slices bacon
1 pound ground beef
³/₄ cup bottled chili sauce
¼ cup brown sugar
2 teaspoons prepared mustard
2 (15-ounce) cans pork and beans

What You Do:
1. Preheat oven to 350°. Fry the bacon (see Makin' Bacon, page 6) until crisp. Remove the bacon from the pan and set it aside on paper towels to absorb excess fat. Brown the ground beef in the bacon drippings (see "Browning Ground Beef," page 115). Use a slotted spoon to remove the meat from the frying pan and place into an ungreased 9" × 13" ovenproof baking pan.

2. Stir in the chili sauce, brown sugar, mustard, and pork and beans until well mixed. Cover with aluminum foil and bake for 30 to 45 minutes, until thoroughly heated. Or, place all the ingredients in a slow cooker. Cover and cook on high for 1 to 3 hours or on low for 2 to 6 hours until heated through.

Black-Eyed Peas

Eating black-eyed peas on New Year's Day is thought to bring good luck in the coming year. Serve with corn muffins made from a mix. To prepare in a slow cooker, perform step 1 the day before. If you like, you can substitute cut-up turkey ham for the ham hocks.

 **Serves 6**

What You Need:
4–6 cups water
1¼ cups dry black-eyed peas
½ medium-size white *or* yellow onion
1½ stalks celery
1½ pounds smoked ham hocks
2 bay leaves
⅛ teaspoon cayenne pepper

What You Do:

Method 1: On a Stovetop
1. In a covered Dutch oven, bring 4 cups water and the black-eyed peas to a boil over high heat. Boil for 2 minutes. Keeping the cover in place, remove from heat. Let sit for 1 hour.
2. Chop the onion and celery. Add to the pot along with the ham hocks, bay leaves, and cayenne pepper. Stir until well mixed. Bring to a boil. Cover and reduce heat to low. Simmer for 1 hour, stirring occasionally.

Black-Eyed Peas
(continued)

3. Uncover and cook for 1 more hour. Remove ham hocks and cut the meat from the bone. Discard the bones, and add the meat to the pot and stir. Remove bay leaves before serving.

Method 2: In a Slow Cooker

1. In a covered Dutch oven over high heat, bring 6 cups water and the black-eyed peas to a boil. Cover. Reduce heat to low. Cook for 1½ hours. Remove from heat. Uncover and cool at room temperature. Cover and refrigerate overnight. (The peas will absorb most of the water.)

2. In the morning, chop the onion and celery. Add to slow cooker along with the peas, ham hocks, bay leaves, and cayenne pepper. Stir until well mixed. Cover, and cook on low for 10 to 12 hours or on high for 5 to 6 hours. Stir occasionally. Remove bay leaves before serving.

Italian Sausage Soup

A taste of Italy in a bowl. The aroma of this soup cooking will make you imagine yourself in a villa in Venice.

Serves 4 to 6

What You Need:

¾ pound Italian sausage
½ medium-size white *or* yellow onion
3 stalks celery
1 clove garlic
2 tablespoons olive oil
1 (8-ounce) can tomatoes, with liquid
½ cup tomato purée
2 (10.5-ounce) cans chicken broth

¼ cup water
¼ teaspoon oregano
¼ teaspoon basil
¼ teaspoon thyme
1 tablespoon dried parsley flakes
½–¾ cup uncooked macaroni noodles
Grated Parmesan cheese, as needed

What You Do:

1. Remove the sausage casing with a sharp knife and place the meat in a skillet. Use a wooden spoon to break up the meat. Brown the sausage as you would ground beef (see page 115). Drain off the fat. Set the meat aside.

2. Chop the onion and celery. Mince the garlic. Pour the oil into a Dutch oven over medium-high heat. Stir in the onion, and celery; cook, stirring constantly until tender.

3. Stir in the sausage, tomatoes, tomato purée, chicken broth, water, oregano, basil, thyme, and parsley. Reduce heat to low. Cover and cook for 1 hour, stirring occasionally.

4. Add the macaroni noodles. Cook for another 30 minutes, stirring occasionally. To serve, top each bowlful with grated Parmesan cheese.

Moroccan Vegetable Stew

An exotic blend of spices adds a distinctive flavor to this dish that's heavy on garlic. Although the ingredient list may be daunting, all you do is chop a few vegetables and stir everything together. (The hardest part is lining up the ingredients.) Serve over rice or couscous.

 **Serves 6**

What You Need:

1 medium zucchini

1 carrot

1 medium-size white *or* yellow onion

1 tablespoon vegetable oil

1/8–1/4 teaspoon dried minced garlic

1 cup vegetable broth

1 1/2 teaspoons ground ginger

1 (15-ounce) can stewed tomatoes, with juice

1 1/2 teaspoons cumin

3/4 teaspoon ground coriander

1/2 teaspoon salt

1/4 teaspoon cinnamon

1/4 teaspoon pepper

2 (15-ounce) cans chickpeas, with liquid (also called garbanzo beans)

What You Do:

1. Rinse the zucchini and carrot in cold, running water. Peel the carrot. Chop the zucchini, carrot, and onion. Heat the vegetable oil in a large frying pan over medium-high heat. Add the vegetables and stir constantly for about 5 minutes, until tender but still firm.

2. Stir in the garlic, vegetable broth, tomatoes, ginger, cumin, coriander, salt, cinnamon, pepper, and chickpeas. Bring to a boil. Cover and reduce heat to low. Cook for 10 minutes.

Mulligatawny Soup

Curry gives this heavily spiced, flavorful soup an East Indian flavor. You can cook this soup on a stovetop or in a slow cooker. (If using a slow cooker, melt the butter in a small frying pan and cook the onion, stirring constantly until tender. Then add it to the slow cooker along with the remaining ingredients.)

Serves 6

What You Need:

1 carrot
1 stalk celery
1 green bell pepper
1 apple
1 medium-size white *or* yellow onion
¼ cup butter
1 cup precooked chicken (see "Cooked Chicken for Casseroles and Salads," page 81)
2 (10.5-ounce) cans chicken broth
⅓ cup all-purpose flour
1 teaspoon curry powder
1 teaspoon lemon juice
½ teaspoon white granulated sugar
2 whole cloves
1 teaspoon dried parsley flakes
1 (8-ounce) can crushed tomatoes
Salt and pepper, to taste

Mulligatawny Soup (continued)

What You Do:

1. Rinse the carrot, celery, green pepper, and apple under cold, running water. Peel the carrot. Chop the carrot, celery, and green bell pepper. Peel and core the apple. Slice vertically. Slice the onion.

2. Melt the butter in the bottom of a Dutch oven over medium heat. Add the onion, stirring constantly until the onion is tender. Reduce heat to low. Stir in the carrot, celery, green bell pepper, apple, chicken, and chicken broth.

3. Transfer some of the liquid to a small mixing bowl and stir in flour a little at a time until well blended. Return to the pot. Stir in the curry powder, lemon juice, sugar, cloves, parsley, tomatoes, salt, and pepper. Cover and cook for 30 minutes. (In a slow cooker, cook on low for 8 to 10 hours.) Remove the cloves before serving.

Cooked Chicken for Casseroles and Salads

To cook chicken to use later in casseroles or salads, rinse the chicken under cold running water (about 3 pounds of chicken breasts and/or thighs yields 4 to 5 cups). Place in an ovenproof baking pan that has been sprayed with nonstick cooking spray. (*Always* wash your hands with soap after handling raw chicken.) Sprinkle with salt and pepper. Put a pat of butter on each piece of chicken. Cover with baking pan lid or aluminum foil. Bake at 350° for 1 hour or until the chicken is tender and the juices run clear. Remove from oven and let cool. Remove skin. Cut away the meat from bones into bite-size pieces. Separate into 1- or 2-cup servings. Cover and refrigerate or freeze until needed.

Minestrone

If you like Italian food, this soup is for you. If you don't have time to cook the dried beans, you can substitute one 15.5-ounce can of beans (drained) and reduce the cooking time to 45 minutes total.

Serves 4

What You Need:

½ cup dried kidney beans
  or great northern beans
1 cup beef stock
3 cups water
1 carrot
1 stalk celery
1 medium-size potato

½ large white *or* yellow onion
1 tablespoon olive oil
⅛ teaspoon dried minced garlic
¼ cup uncooked macaroni noodles
½ (8-ounce) can crushed tomatoes
1½ teaspoons salt
⅛ teaspoon pepper

What You Do:

1. In a Dutch oven, bring the beans, beef stock, and water to a boil. Cover and reduce heat to low. Cook for 3 to 4 hours. Stir once or twice per hour.

2. During the last half-hour of cooking time, prepare the vegetables. Rinse the carrot, celery, and potato under cold, running water. Peel the carrot and potato. Chop the carrot, celery, potato, and onion. Place the olive oil in a large skillet over medium-high heat. Cook the chopped vegetables in the olive oil, stirring constantly until tender but still firm.

3. Stir the vegetables and garlic into the beans. Cover and continue cooking for 30 minutes. Stir often.

4. Stir in the macaroni noodles, tomatoes, salt, and pepper. Cook for 15 minutes.

Chapter 4

Salads

Orange-Banana Salad

Fresh bananas and sweet mandarin oranges blend for a mellow flavor you can use as a snack, salad, or light dessert. Bananas are tropical fruits, so do not refrigerate until after they are cut. You can substitute chopped walnuts for the chopped pecans.

Serves 4

What You Need:
2 bananas
Lemon juice, as needed (a few drops)
1 (8-ounce) can mandarin orange slices
¼ cup chopped pecans

What You Do:
1. Peel the bananas. Slice crosswise into circles about ¼" thick and place in a medium-size mixing bowl.
2. Sprinkle the bananas with a few drops of lemon juice to help prevent browning. Drain off the liquid from the oranges and add the orange slices to the bowl.
3. Add the pecans, stirring gently until well mixed. Chill in the refrigerator until ready to serve.

Fruit and Coconut Salad

You can eat this salad right away if you like, but if you make it the day before and chill it in the refrigerator overnight, the flavors will blend for an even more delicious result.

E

Serves 4

What You Need:
1 cup mandarin orange slices
1 cup pineapple tidbits
1 cup flaked coconut
1 cup sour cream

What You Do:
1. Prechill the mandarin oranges and pineapple tidbits in the cans. Drain the oranges and pineapple. Place in a large mixing bowl.

2. Add the coconut and sour cream. Gently stir together until all the ingredients are coated with sour cream and well mixed. Cover and refrigerate for at least 1 hour before serving.

Nutty Banana-Strawberries

You can substitute sliced almonds for the chopped pecans. You can also substitute mandarin oranges (drained) for the strawberries. For a lower-calorie, vegan variation, substitute frozen nondairy whipped topping for the whipped cream.

Serves 2

What You Need:

½ cup strawberries
½ teaspoon white granulated sugar
1 banana
A few drops of lemon juice
¼ cup chopped pecans
Pressurized, canned whipped cream, as needed

What You Do:

1. Clean and slice the strawberries (see "How to Clean Strawberries"). Sprinkle with sugar.

2. Peel and slice the banana. Sprinkle the slices with a few drops of lemon juice to help prevent browning.

How to Clean Strawberries

Strawberries grow low to the ground, so rinse well to remove field dirt. Place strawberries in a large mixing bowl and fill with cold water. Pour into a colander. Repeat at least 3 times. With the strawberries still in the colander, rinse again under cold, running water. Drain. Remove the stem and green part (the large green calyx called the *hull*) by cutting it out with a knife or using a huller, a small utensil that resembles tweezers with large flat prongs.

3. Gently stir together the banana, strawberries, and pecans. Place in serving dishes. Top each serving with whipped cream.

Grape Salad

If you'd like to add color and flavor, use ½ bunch of each color of seedless grapes for this cool fruit salad. For a vegan variation, substitute tofu sour cream (see "How to Make Tofu Sour Cream," page 207).

Serves 4

What You Need:
½ cup slivered almonds
1½ pounds red *and/or* green seedless grapes
½ cup sour cream
1 teaspoon brown sugar

What You Do:
1. Preheat oven to 400°. Place the almonds on a baking sheet that has been sprayed with nonstick cooking spray. Bake for about 4 to 5 minutes until brown. (Watch carefully so they don't burn!) Remove from oven. Set aside.

2. Rinse the grapes under cold, running water. Drain. Remove from stem.

3. In a large mixing bowl, stir together the sour cream and brown sugar. Add the grapes and stir until coated. When ready to serve, spoon into serving dishes and top with toasted almonds.

Quick Cottage Cheese Salad

E Low in fat and chock-full of vegetables, this satisfying salad is a great midday pick-me-up. Keep covered in the refrigerator until ready to eat.

Serves 4

What You Need:
2 green onions
1 green bell pepper
2 carrots
½ bunch radishes
1 (24-ounce) carton small-curd cottage cheese

What You Do:
1. Rinse the green onions, green bell pepper, carrots, and radishes under cold, running water. Chop the green onions (including the dark green tops) and the green bell pepper. Place in a medium-size mixing bowl. Use a potato peeler to remove the outer skin of the carrots. Use the large holes on the grater to grate the carrots into the bowl with the onions and green pepper. Slice the radishes and add to the bowl.

2. Gently stir in the cottage cheese until all the ingredients are well mixed. Cover and chill in the refrigerator for at least 1 hour before serving.

Avocado and Shrimp Salad

The avocado peel creates a decorative serving bowl for this salad. To eat, spoon the avcado and shrimp from the peeling. The shrimp in this recipe is also called baby shrimp or cocktail shrimp. You can serve this dish for lunch or as an appetizer.

 **Serves 2**

What You Need:

1 ripe avocado	⅛ teaspoon garlic powder
¾ cup frozen salad shrimp	¼ teaspoon pepper
2 teaspoons minced red onion	¼ teaspoon celery salt
½ cup sour cream	Lemon juice, as needed (a few drops)

What You Do:

1. Prechill the avocado. Set out the shrimp to thaw. Mince the onion (chop into very small pieces) and place in a medium-size mixing bowl. Add the sour cream, shrimp, garlic powder, pepper, and celery salt. Stir together until well blended. Cover and chill in refrigerator.

2. Cut the avocado in half lengthwise and remove the seed. Place halves on serving plates. Sprinkle lemon juice on the avocado to help prevent browning. Spoon chilled shrimp mixture on top of the avocado halves.

Variation: Sliced Avocado and Shrimp Salad

Prepare Avocado and Shrimp Salad as directed, except peel and slice the avocado. Sprinkle with a few drops of lemon juice to help prevent browning. Arrange the slices on top of a bed of salad greens. Top with the shrimp mixture.

Cucumber Salad

This cool, crisp salad makes a refreshing contrast to main courses with heavy sauce. If the dressing is too tart for your taste, add sugar. If it's too sweet, add a little vinegar.

Serves 4

What You Need:

2 cucumbers
2 green onions
Water, as needed (about 1 quart)
1 teaspoon salt

¼ cup white vinegar
5 teaspoons white granulated sugar
⅛ teaspoon pepper

What You Do:

1. Rinse the cucumbers under cold, running water. Peel and thinly slice the cucumbers crosswise. Place in a medium-size mixing bowl. Slice the green onions, including the dark green tops. Add to the cucumbers. Add enough water to the bowl to cover the cucumbers and onions. Stir in the salt until it dissolves. Soak in the refrigerator for 2 to 3 hours. The cucumber slices will soften.

2. In a small mixing bowl, stir together the vinegar and sugar until the sugar dissolves. Set aside.

3. Drain the cucumbers and green onions. Gently squeeze the cucumbers with your hands to remove excess salt water (do not rinse). Place in a serving bowl and sprinkle with pepper. Stir in the vinegar and sugar mixture. (There will be extra liquid in the serving bowl.) Serve with a slotted spoon.

Broccoli-Cauliflower Salad

Black olives accent the bright red, deep green, and white vegetables that make this salad colorful as well as delicious. A clear glass serving bowl makes an attractive presentation. You can substitute grape tomatoes for the cherry tomatoes.

E

Serves 4

What You Need:
1 pint cherry tomatoes
½ head cauliflower
½ bunch broccoli
1 (8-ounce) can pitted black olives
Bottled Italian salad dressing

What You Do:
Prepare ahead:

1. Rinse the cherry tomatoes, cauliflower, and broccoli in cold, running water. Drain.

2. Remove the stems from the cauliflower and broccoli, and cut the crowns into bite-size pieces.

Uses for Broccoli Stems
After cutting broccoli florets (the "treetops") from a bunch of broccoli, save the stems. Cover and store in the refrigerator for another use. You can eat them raw with veggie dip, or cut them into bite-size pieces and add to soup or tossed salad. You can also steam them for a side dish, or place the cooked stems on a piece of toast and cover with melted cheese for an easy hot lunch.

3. In a serving bowl, gently stir together the cherry tomatoes, cauliflower, and broccoli. Drain the olives and add to the serving bowl. Gently stir to mix the ingredients. Cover with plastic wrap and chill in the refrigerator.

4. When ready to serve, sprinkle with Italian salad dressing. Gently stir until all the ingredients are lightly coated.

Blue Cheese Wedge Salad

If you like blue cheese, you'll love this salad, which also has a dramatic presentation to wow your date. You can vary the recipe by substituting 2 crumbled, hard-boiled eggs (see Boiled Egg, page 9 for the blue cheese and substituting bottled Thousand Island dressing for the vinaigrette.

Serves 2

What You Need:
½ head iceberg lettuce
1 cup crumbled blue cheese
Bottled vinaigrette *or* Italian salad dressing, to taste (about ¼ cup)

What You Do:
Prepare ahead:
1. Remove the loose outer leaves from the head of lettuce and rinse in cold, running water. Drain. Cut the ½ head in half (each piece is a wedge that is ¼ of the original whole head of lettuce). Cut away the core.
2. Place each wedge on a salad plate with the rounded side down. (The wedges will have 2 sloping sides that come to a peak.) Sprinkle ½ of the blue cheese over each wedge. Chill for at least 1 hour.
3. When ready to serve, drizzle the salad dressing over each wedge.

Cold Mixed Veggies Salad

This crisp, cold salad is a nice accompaniment to creamy casserole dishes. Try it with Beef Gumbo Casserole (page 122) or Mac 'n' Cheese (page 195).

Serves 4

What You Need:

1 green bell pepper
1 carrot
2 stalks celery
1 cucumber
1 medium-size red onion

1 teaspoon lemon juice
3 tablespoons vegetable oil
½ teaspoon water
¼ teaspoon basil
¼ teaspoon salt

What You Do:

1. Rinse the green bell pepper, carrot, celery, and cucumber in cold, running water. Peel the carrot and cucumber. Chop all the vegetables and place in a large mixing bowl. Chop the onion and add it to the bowl.

2. In a small mixing bowl, stir together the lemon juice, vegetable oil, water, basil, and salt until well mixed. Pour the mixture over the chopped vegetables. Stir until the vegetables are well coated. Cover and refrigerate at least 1 hour until ready to serve.

Tarragon-Mustard Vinaigrette

You can make this salad dressing in a cruet or jar with a lid. Place all the ingredients in it. Cover and shake well.

Yields ¼ cup

What You Need:

3 tablespoons olive *or* vegetable oil
2 tablespoons vinegar
⅛ teaspoon dried minced garlic
1 teaspoon Dijon mustard

¾ teaspoon dried tarragon
⅛ teaspoon pepper
1 teaspoon salt

What You Do:

Stir together all ingredients until well blended.

Types of Vinegar

Vinegar is an acidic liquid with a sharp, tangy taste that enhances the flavor of salad dressings, soups, and other foods. It has also been used as a beverage, a food preservative, a solvent, a home-cleaning product, and to heal wounds. Vinegar was first discovered about 10,000 years ago as good wine gone bad—wine that had fermented beyond the alcohol stage. In fact, the word derives from the French *vinaigre*, or "sour wine." Vinegar can be distilled from almost any food that contains sugar. Popular vinegars include cider vinegar, which comes from apples; white vinegar, from grains; red wine vinegar, from *(duh!)* red wine; and rice vinegar, from *(duh again!)* rice. In addition, gourmet vinegars are flavored with such herbs as garlic, basil, and tarragon, as well as fruits or fruit juices. Unless you're adventurous (and willing to risk disaster), it's best not to substitute one type of vinegar for another in a recipe.

Creamy Caesar Salad Dressing

Dressing makes the salad, and that's especially true with the popular Caesar Salad (see page 98). You can use bottled dressing, but it's so easy to make your own. Give it a try!

E

Yields 1 ⅓ cup

What You Need:
2 large cloves garlic
1 cup extra-virgin olive oil
½ teaspoon Worcestershire sauce
1½ teaspoons lemon juice
1 tablespoon red wine vinegar
⅓ cup heavy cream
¼ teaspoon salt
¼ teaspoon pepper

What You Do:
1. Mince the garlic by chopping it into very small pieces. Place in a small mixing bowl.

2. Stir in the olive oil, Worcestershire sauce, lemon juice, vinegar, cream, salt, and pepper until well blended. When ready to serve, spoon 1 or 2 tablespoons at a time onto the salad. Toss until lightly coated.

Garlic Salad Dressing

Fresh garlic is a must for this one. This dressing separates easily, so stir well just before serving.

Yields ½ cup

What You Need:

½ clove fresh garlic
¼ cup olive oil
¼ cup vegetable oil
2 tablespoons vinegar
2 tablespoons lemon juice

½ teaspoon salt
¼ teaspoon dry mustard
¼ teaspoon paprika
⅛ teaspoon black pepper

What You Do:

1. Mince the garlic by chopping it into very small pieces. Place in a small mixing bowl.

2. Stir in the olive oil, vegetable oil, vinegar, lemon juice, salt, dry mustard, and paprika. Chill for 1 hour. Stir well before serving.

Preparing Head Lettuce for Salad

To prepare head lettuce for salad, find the bottom of the core (a round, white circle about 1" in diameter). Face the core toward your (clean) counter. Hold the head of lettuce like a basketball and whack it down on the counter. Turn over the head and use your fingers to twist out the core; discard it. Hold the lettuce under cold running water, letting it run into the hole where the core was. Turn the lettuce several times under the water. Place hole-side-down in a colander set in the sink. Drain. Pat dry with paper towels. Tear off a section of lettuce leaves about the size of your palm and about ¼" thick. Tear the leaves into bite-size pieces and place them in a salad bowl.

Waldorf Salad

This cold salad has been a favorite for generations. The lemon juice helps keep the apples from turning brown. Serve in a bowl or on a lettuce leaf on a salad plate.

M

Serves 3–4

What You Need:

3 medium-size apples (about ¾ pound total)
4 stalks celery
½ cup chopped walnuts
¼ cup mayonnaise
1 tablespoon white granulated sugar
½ teaspoon lemon juice
⅛ teaspoon salt
½ cup frozen nondairy whipped topping
   (*or* canned whipped cream)

> ### Storing Celery
> Save the sleeve packaging and use it to cover celery when you store it in the refrigerator. If left uncovered, it will become dehydrated. If that happens, don't throw it out. Place it in a large container of ice water. The celery will absorb the moisture. Celery is a good source of vitamin C, and 2 stalks contain only 25 calories.

What You Do:

1. Rinse the apples and celery under cold, running water. (Do not peel the apples.) Remove the core with a knife or apple corer. Cut the apples into 1" cubes. Chop the celery. Place in a medium-size mixing bowl. Stir in the walnuts.

2. In a large mixing bowl, stir together the mayonnaise, sugar, lemon juice, and salt until well blended. Stir in the frozen nondairy whipped topping or whipped cream.

3. Add about ⅓ of the apple mixture to the mayonnaise mixture and stir to coat the fruit. Continue adding about ⅓ of the mixture at a time until the ingredients are well coated.

Caesar Salad

A popular favorite, this salad calls for a special type of dark lettuce called romaine. The original recipe called for anchovies, a small saltwater fish. However, many people don't care for them, so they are seldom used today. Use purchased croutons, or make your own (see page 101).

Serves 2

What You Need:
2–3 cups romaine lettuce
2–3 tablespoons bottled *or* homemade Creamy Caesar Salad Dressing (see page 95)
¼ cup croutons
Freshly grated Parmesan cheese, to taste

What You Do:
1. Tear off any limp or discolored leaves from the head of romaine lettuce. Pull off 4 to 6 leaves. Place in a colander and rinse under cold, running water. Turn the leaves to rinse both sides. Drain. Pat dry with paper towels, so the dressing will stick to the leaves. Wrap the lettuce in dry paper towels and chill in the refrigerator for at least 30 minutes.

2. Tear the lettuce into bite-size pieces. Place in a salad bowl or large mixing bowl. Add the salad dressing 1 tablespoon at a time. Toss with salad utensils or 2 large spoons. Continue adding dressing and tossing salad until the lettuce is lightly coated.

3. Add the croutons. Sprinkle with Parmesan cheese. Toss again until well mixed. Serve immediately.

Feta and Spinach Salad

This unusual combination of ingredients adds texture and interest to any meal. You can substitute green or black seedless grapes for red seedless ones. Or, use all 3 varieties for added color.

 **Serves 2**

What You Need:
2 cups fresh spinach
½ small red onion
1 cup red grapes
½ (8-ounce) jar julienne-style sun-dried tomatoes
½ cup crumbled feta cheese
Bottled sweet-and-sour salad dressing
Croutons

What You Do:
Prepare ahead:

1. Rinse the spinach. Drain and pat dry with paper towel. Remove and discard the stems. Place the spinach in a serving bowl.

2. Chop the onion. Slice the grapes in halves. Add the onion and grapes to the salad bowl. Drain and rinse the tomatoes in cool water. Add to the salad bowl, along with the cheese. Gently toss together using salad utensils. Cover and chill in the refrigerator for at least 1 hour.

3. When ready to serve, add the dressing 1 tablespoon at a time. Gently toss using salad utensils, or 2 spoons, until all the ingredients are lightly coated. Top with croutons.

Cold Veggie Pasta Salad

 Here's a colorful cold salad you can serve for lunch or as a delightful side dish with roasted or grilled meats. You can substitute penne pasta or fettuccine for the spiral pasta if you prefer. Use remaining olives for Mini Pepperoni Pizza (page 43).

Serves 4

What You Need:
1 cup frozen corn
1 cup fresh *or* frozen sliced carrots
1 cup fresh *or* frozen green beans
6 ounces uncooked spiral pasta
½ red bell pepper
½ (2.25-ounce) can sliced black olives
½ cup bottled Italian salad dressing

What You Do:
1. Set out the corn, carrots, and green beans to thaw.

2. Cook the pasta according to package directions. Drain in a colander. Rinse under cold, running water. Drain again. Place in a medium-size mixing bowl.

3. Chop the red bell pepper and add to the mixing bowl. Add the thawed corn, carrots, and green beans. Drain the black olives and add to bowl. Add salad dressing 1 tablespoon at a time. Gently toss the ingredients. Repeat until all the ingredients are lightly coated with dressing and well mixed. Cover and chill in the refrigerator for at least 1 hour.

Chilled Pea Salad

Bright green and red ingredients give this salad a festive look. You can use canned peas (drained), but frozen peas look and taste much better. For a vegan variation, omit the egg and substitute your choice of nondairy bottled salad dressing for the mayonnaise.

Serves 2

What You Need:

1 egg
1 cup frozen peas
1 tomato

½ stalk celery
2 tablespoons mayonnaise

What You Do:

1. Hard-boil the egg (see Boiled Egg, page 9).
2. Rinse the peas in cold water, drain, and let thaw.
3. Chop the tomato, celery, and egg, and place in a bowl.
4. Gently stir in the peas. Stir in the mayonnaise until all the ingredients are lightly coated. Chill in the refrigerator for at least 1 hour before serving.

How to Make Your Own Croutons

Preheat the oven to 375°. In a clean paper or plastic bag (or a plastic container with a lid), mix together 1 teaspoon salt, 1 teaspoon paprika, and 3 tablespoons grated Parmesan cheese. Set aside. Remove the crust from a slice of bread. Lightly butter both sides. Cut to make ½" cubes. Place the cubes on an ungreased baking sheet. Bake for 10 minutes or until golden brown. Remove the cubes from the oven and immediately put into the bag with the seasonings. Shake until well coated. Spread on a plate to cool. Makes enough for 2 salads.

Three-Color Pasta Salad

For best results, you'll need to start early (or the day before) to give the flavors a chance to mingle in this popular cold salad.

Serves 6

What You Need:

½ bunch raw broccoli
½ head raw cauliflower
2 raw carrots
2 scallions or green onions
¼ cup sliced black olives
8 ounces uncooked tri-color spiral pasta

1–1½ cups bottled *or* homemade Italian salad dressing
½ cup cubed Cheddar cheese
⅓ cup shredded Gouda
⅓ cup grated Parmesan cheese
Salt and pepper, to taste

What You Do:

1. Rinse the broccoli, cauliflower and carrots under cold, running water. Peel the carrots. Chop and place together in a medium-size mixing bowl. Remove outer skin of scallions and slice them crosswise into circles. Add to the bowl. Drain the black olives. Add to the bowl. Stir in ½ cup of the salad dressing until the veggies are well coated. Set aside for 30 minutes at room temperature, stirring occasionally.

2. Cook the pasta according to package directions. Drain. Transfer to a large mixing bowl and add ¼ cup of the salad dressing. Cool to room temperature, stirring occasionally. Cover both bowls and refrigerate for at least 6 hours (or overnight).

3. When almost ready to serve, cut the Cheddar into cubes. Shred the Gouda using the large holes on a cheese grater. Grate the Parmesan using the small holes on the grater. Add the vegetables to the bowl of pasta. Toss. Sprinkle with salt and pepper.

Old-Fashioned Coleslaw

Coleslaw is a favorite summertime side dish. You can also spoon it onto a sandwich to add flavor and crunch. Use it on a Grilled Rachel Sandwich (page 42) or on a turkey or bologna and cheese sandwich.

 **Serves 4**

What You Need:

½ head cabbage
4 carrots
3 tablespoons vinegar
½ teaspoon salt

¼ teaspoon paprika
3 tablespoons white granulated sugar
½ cup sour cream

What You Do:

1. Remove the outer leaves of the cabbage. Cut in half lengthwise. Store ½ in the refrigerator for another use. Cut the remaining half crosswise into 2 pieces. Use the large holes on a grater to grate the cabbage into a colander. (Grate only the amount you need. Do *not* store grated or shredded cabbage for future use.)

2. Peel the carrots and rinse under cold, running water. Grate the carrots, using the large holes on the grater into the bowl with the shredded cabbage. Use 2 forks to toss together. Cover and refrigerate for at least 2 hours.

3. In a small mixing bowl, stir together the vinegar, salt, paprika, sugar, and sour cream until well blended.

4. Remove the cabbage mixture from the refrigerator. Add the slaw dressing 1 tablespoon at a time, using 2 table forks to toss until the cabbage and carrots are lightly coated. Chill and serve.

Exotic (Yet Simple) Couscous Salad

If you'd like to try something a bit different, consider this flavorful cold salad. Couscous is a North African dish made from a ricelike steamed, crushed grain. You'll find instant couscous in the rice aisle of your supermarket

Serves 6

What You Need:

1 (10-ounce) box instant couscous

1 cucumber

3 fresh tomatoes

2 green onions

3 roasted red bell peppers (from a jar)

1 (4¼-ounce) can chopped black olives

2 cloves fresh garlic *or* ¼ teaspoon dried minced garlic

¼ cup olive oil

¼ cup lemon juice

1 teaspoon ground cumin

¼ teaspoon salt

⅛ teaspoon black pepper

⅛ teaspoon cayenne pepper (optional)

What You Do:

1. Cook the couscous according to package directions.

2. Peel and chop the cucumber. Chop the tomatoes, green onions, and roasted red bell peppers. Stir together in a medium-size mixing bowl. When the couscous is done, fluff with a fork. Stir in the cucumber, green onion, tomatoes, and peppers. Drain the chopped olives. Add to the salad and stir. Set aside.

3. Finely chop the garlic and place in a small mixing bowl. Stir in the olive oil, lemon juice, cumin, salt, black pepper, and cayenne pepper. Pour over the salad. Toss with 2 forks until well mixed. Chill for about 1 hour, until cool.

Tabbouleh Salad

You can make this lemony salad with either bulgar wheat or couscous. And you can use either flat leaf or curly parsley.

Serves 6

What You Need:
1 small cucumber
2 medium-size tomatoes
Fresh chives (enough to yield 2 tablespoons chopped)
1 cup fresh parsley
3 scallions
1 cup uncooked cracked instant bulgar wheat (*or* instant couscous)
½ cup olive oil
½ cup lemon juice
Salt and pepper, to taste

What You Do:
1. Rinse the cucumber, tomatoes, chives, and parsley under cold, running water. Drain. Chop and place in a large mixing bowl. Remove the outer layer of the scallions. Chop and add to the bowl.

2. Cook the wheat or couscous according to package directions. While it's cooking, stir together the olive oil, lemon juice, salt, and pepper until well mixed. When the wheat is done, add it to the vegetables in the large mixing bowl.

3. Pour the dressing over the ingredients in the mixing bowl. Gently toss until well coated. Cover and refrigerate for 2 to 3 hours to allow the flavors to mingle.

Artichoke-Lettuce Salad

Make this salad a day early to give the flavors time to blend.

Serves 4

What You Need:
½ (14-ounce) can artichoke hearts
1 (15-ounce) can sliced carrots
1 (3.8-ounce) can sliced black olives
6 tablespoons Italian dressing
4 cups lettuce chunks
¼ pound fresh spinach
Blue cheese crumbles, as needed
Croutons, as needed

What You Do:
1. Drain the artichoke hearts. Slice into halves. Place in a small mixing bowl. Drain the carrots and olives. Add to the bowl. Stir in the Italian dressing. Cover and marinate in the refrigerator overnight (or for at least 3 hours).

2. Prepare the lettuce as for tossed salad (see page 96) and place in a large salad bowl. Tear the spinach into bite-size pieces. Add the marinated artichoke hearts, carrots, and olives. Gently toss using salad utensils. Sprinkle with blue cheese crumbles and croutons.

Blue Cheese and
Roast Beef Salad

Here's a salad you can serve as an entrée. Serve with French bread (see "Preparing French Bread," page 117) or Hot Cheese Toast (page 40). It's a great way to use leftover Beef Roast, too (page 112).

 **Serves 1**

What You Need:
½ pound precooked roast beef
2 cups romaine lettuce
4 cherry tomatoes *or* grape tomatoes
¼ cup crumbled blue cheese
2–3 tablespoons bottled Italian salad dressing

What You Do:

1. Slice the roast beef crosswise into strips about 1" wide, 2" long, and ¼" thick.

2. Rinse the lettuce under cold, running water. Pat dry with a paper towel. Tear into bite-size pieces and place on a serving plate. Arrange the strips of beef in a row across the middle of the bed of lettuce.

3. Rinse the tomatoes under cold, running water. Cut the tomatoes in half and arrange them in a circle around the meat. Crumble the blue cheese over the top of the salad. Sprinkle with salad dressing.

Bacon-Avocado Salad

Don't let the long list of ingredients scare you away from this easy-to-prepare salad. You can substitute juice of ½ lime for the lemon juice.

Serves 4

What You Need:

2 slices bacon
½ orange bell pepper
1 green onion
¼ cup butter
3 tablespoons white granulated sugar
3 tablespoons ketchup

3 tablespoons red wine vinegar
1 tablespoon soy sauce
1 small head Bibb lettuce
4 avocados
Lemon juice, as needed (about
  1 teaspoon)

What You Do:

1. Fry the bacon (see Makin' Bacon, page 6). Drain on paper towels. When cool, crumble. Set aside.

2. Chop the bell pepper and green onion, including the dark green top.

3. In a saucepan over low heat, stir together the bell pepper, onion, butter, sugar, ketchup, vinegar, and soy sauce until the sugar dissolves. Keep warm.

4. Cut the lettuce head into fourths. Rinse in cold, running water. Drain. Pat dry with paper towels. Separate the leaves to make a bed of lettuce on each serving plate.

5. Peel, seed, and slice the avocados. Arrange the slices on top of the bed of lettuce. Sprinkle a few drops of lemon juice over the avocado slices to keep fruit from turning brown. Top with the warm dressing and crumbled bacon. Serve immediately.

Potato Salad

There's no single "right" way to make potato salad. It's likely that almost every family in America has its own recipe. Here's a basic recipe to get you started. You can substitute 2 to 3 small red russet potatoes (about 1 handful total) for each baking potato.

 Serves 4–6

What You Need:

4 medium-size white potatoes

2 eggs

¼ medium white onion

1 stalk celery

¾ cup mayonnaise *or* mayonnaise-
   like salad dressing

1 teaspoon prepared mustard

½ teaspoon celery seed

½ teaspoon salt

½ teaspoon pepper

1 teaspoon white granulated
   sugar (optional)

What You Do:

1. Rinse potatoes under cool, running water and place in a Dutch oven. Cover with water. Boil for 30 to 35 minutes, until tender when pierced with a fork. Drain and let cool. Peel and cut into ¾" cubes. Place in a large mixing bowl.

2. While the potatoes are cooking, hard-boil the eggs (see Boiled Egg, page 9). Peel and chop the eggs. Add to the potatoes. Chop the onion and celery. Add to the potatoes.

3. In a separate small mixing bowl, stir together the mayonnaise, mustard, celery seed, salt, and pepper until well blended. (Taste the mixture. Add 1 teaspoon sugar if you like.) Pour over the potato mixture. Gently stir until the potatoes are well coated. Refrigerate for at least 1 hour before serving.

Hot German Potato Salad

This potato salad is traditionally served warm. If the dressing is too tangy for your taste, use 1 additional teaspoon of sugar.

Serves 4

What You Need:

4 medium-size potatoes

6 slices bacon

½ small white onion

2 tablespoons all-purpose flour

4 teaspoons white granulated sugar

1½ teaspoons salt

½ teaspoon celery seeds

⅛ teaspoon pepper

⅔ cup water

6 tablespoons vinegar

What You Do:

1. Place rinsed potatoes in a 2-quart saucepan. Cover with water. Bring to a boil over high heat. Boil for 8 to 10 minutes, until the potatoes are soft when pierced with a fork. Drain and let cool. Peel and slice crosswise about ¼" thick.

2. Fry the bacon (see Makin' Bacon, page 6) in a large frying pan. Leave the fat in the pan. Drain the bacon on paper towels. When the bacon is cool, break it into crumbles. Set aside.

3. Chop the onion. Heat the bacon fat over medium-high heat. Cook the onion until tender. Reduce heat to low. Stir in the flour, sugar, salt, celery seeds, and pepper until well blended and the mixture bubbles. Remove the frying pan from the heat.

4. Stir in the water and vinegar. Return the frying pan to the stovetop. Stir constantly until the mixture boils. Continue boiling for 1 minute. Remove from heat.

5. Gently stir in the potatoes and bacon until well coated. Cover to keep warm until ready to serve.

Main Dishes for Carnivores— Beef and Pork

Chapter 5

Beef

Beef Roast

When people talk about "meat and potatoes," they're talking about beef. Because roast beef is simple and unadorned, when it is served as an entrée, it opens up a wide variety of interesting salads and side dishes with or without sauces. Serve with Garlic Mashed Potatoes (page 218), Green Bean Casserole (page 219), or Broccoli-Cauliflower Salad (page 91)

Yields 2 servings per pound

What You Need:
Rump or round roast (any size cut)
Garlic salt, to taste
Salt and pepper, to taste

What You Do:

1. Preheat oven to 325°. Be sure to set the dial to "bake" before cooking food. Rinse the meat under cold, running water. Place fat-side-up in a roasting pan or ovenproof baking pan. Insert a meat thermometer into the thickest part of the meat (optional). Sprinkle with garlic salt, salt, and pepper.

> ### Cooking Times for Bone-in Roasts
> If you had 2 roasts that weighed the same, but one had a bone and the other didn't, you'd have to cook the one without the bone a bit longer. Leaving the bone in the meat helps it cook faster, because the bone conducts heat and helps cook the meat.

Beef Roast
(continued)

2. For rare meat, roast for 22 to 26 minutes per pound, or until the meat thermometer reads 140°. For medium, roast for 26 to 30 minutes per pound, or until the meat thermometer reads 160°. For well done, roast for 33 to 35 minutes per pound, or until the meat thermometer reads 170°.

3. Remove from oven. Slice as needed. (As the roast sits outside the oven, it will continue to cook. So if you like rare or medium-rare meat, cook it for the shorter amount of time listed.) Note: for best results, you should always let roasts sit for about 5 minutes before slicing to give juices time to settle. Serve warm. Save leftovers for Blue Cheese and Roast Beef Salad (page 107).

Baking Potatoes

One of America's favorite side dishes is a simple baked potato, served with a variety of toppings: butter, sour cream, chopped chives, or cottage cheese. Or, try sour cream mixed with ranch or French onion dried soup or dip mix. To bake a potato, rinse the potato under cold, running water. Cut 2 slits in an X shape on the top of the potato to let heat escape during baking. Place directly on a baking rack in the oven. (Or, for a softer potato skin and mushy flesh, rub butter or margarine on the skin and wrap the potato in aluminum foil before placing it in oven.) Bake at 350° for 1 hour. Test for doneness by piercing with a fork or gently squeezing the potato (while holding a potholder). When done, the potato will feel soft.

Tacos

Here's an easy favorite you're probably used to buying at fast-food drive-up windows. Instead, make your own. You can substitute reheated precooked chicken (see "Cooked Chicken for Casseroles and Salads," page 81) or pork (see Pork Roast, page 139) cut into bite-size pieces for the beef.

🍴 Yields 6–8 tacos 🍴

What You Need:
1 pound ground beef
2 tablespoons chili powder *or* 1 (1.25-ounce) packet dry taco seasoning mix
1 tablespoon dried minced onion (optional)
¼ head iceberg lettuce
1 large tomato
6–8 prepared taco shells *or* 6" flour tortillas (for soft tacos)
1 cup shredded Cheddar cheese
½ cup salsa *or* picante sauce
2 tablespoons sour cream

What You Do:
1. In a frying pan, brown the ground beef (page 115) along with chili powder (or taco seasoning mix) and the onion. Drain off the fat. Cover to keep warm.

2. While the meat is browning, shred the lettuce using the large holes on a grater. (Or slice into narrow strips with a knife.) Place in a serving bowl. Chop the tomato and place in a small serving bowl.

Tacos
(continued)

3. Heat the taco shells according to package directions. (If you're using flour tortillas for soft tacos, omit this step. Instead, wrap the tortillas together in aluminum foil. Set the oven to the lowest temperature, and place the tortillas in the oven before you begin browning the meat. Remove the tortillas from the oven when you are ready to serve. Or, you can wrap the tortillas individually in damp paper towels and heat them for 40 seconds on high in the microwave. (Heated flour tortillas taste better, and they are easier to roll up.)

4. To serve, spoon about ¼ cup of the beef mixture into each taco shell. Top each with some lettuce, tomato, cheese, salsa, and sour cream.

Browning Ground Beef

Ground beef is a versatile meat for casseroles and other dishes. Use in Baked Spaghetti (page 116), Chili Blue (page 75), or Stuffed Green Bell Peppers (page 134). You can brown ground pork sausage using the same method. Use your hands to crumble the meat into a frying pan over medium-high heat. Stir occasionally as the meat cooks. Heat until the juices run clear and there is no tinge of pink in the meat. Drain. Do not pour fat down the kitchen sink drain. Discard by pouring into an empty can with a lid, such as a coffee can. Cover and store in the refrigerator until the fat turns solid. Throw away. (You can add used fat from other sources to the can until it is full, and then throw it away.)

Baked Spaghetti

This mild but hearty casserole makes a fine Italian-style main course for a crowd, without the need for last-minute preparation. You won't have to rattle around in the kitchen boiling noodles after your guests arrive. Prepare ahead and store in the refrigerator until ready to bake. Serve with grated Parmesan cheese, a salad (see page 96), and French bread (see "Preparing French Bread," page 117). Cover and store leftovers in the refrigerator for up to 3 to 4 days.

Serves 8

What You Need:

1 (10-ounce) package thin spaghetti
1 pound ground beef
¼ cup milk
1 egg
1 (28-ounce) jar spaghetti sauce (any kind)
2 cups shredded mozzarella cheese

What You Do:

1. Break the uncooked spaghetti into thirds and cook according to package directions (boil for about 8 minutes, until the noodles are tender but still firm).

2. While the noodles are cooking, brown the ground beef (see "Browning Ground Beef" on page 115) in a large frying pan. Drain off the fat.

3. Preheat the oven to 350°. Spray a 9" × 13" ovenproof baking pan with nonstick cooking spray. When the noodles are done, drain. Pour the noodles into the baking pan.

4. In a small mixing bowl, quickly stir together the milk and egg with a fork until well blended. Pour the mixture onto the noodles and stir until the noodles are well coated.

Baked Spaghetti
(continued)

5. Stir the beef into the noodles. Add the spaghetti sauce and gently stir until well blended. Cover the surface with shredded mozzarella. Bake uncovered for 30 minutes.

Variation:
Vegetarian Baked Spaghetti

For a vegetarian version of Baked Spaghetti, omit the beef. For more substance, add a 7-ounce can of drained sliced mushrooms (or mushroom stems and pieces), and/or use a jar of spaghetti sauce with vegetable chunks. Or, substitute 1 diced eggplant for the meat.

Preparing French Bread

Preheat the oven to 400°. Slice the French bread loaf into 1" thick pieces. Leave the slices standing in a loaf shape. Take 1 of the heel pieces and spread butter or margarine on the interior side. Replace the heel on the end of the loaf. Take out the next slice, spread butter or garlic butter on both sides, and replace it in the loaf, continuing until all the slices are buttered. When finished, wrap the entire loaf in aluminum foil. Bake for 10 minutes. Plan for 2 to 3 slices per person. If you don't need an entire loaf, cut the amount you need from the whole loaf. Tightly wrap the portion you won't use in aluminum foil and freeze. Use for another meal or for Hot Cheese Toast (page 40).

Slow-Cooked Swiss Steak

Round steak is the tastiest choice for this recipe. However, because this dish cooks slowly, you can use arm steak or chuck roast, which are less expensive cuts. Serve with baked potatoes (see "Baking Potatoes," page 113) and a green vegetable.

 **Serves 4**

What You Need:

1 pound round steak, about 1" thick

½ medium white *or* yellow onion

1 (28-ounce) can stewed tomatoes, with juice

¼ teaspoon garlic salt

Salt and pepper, to taste

What You Do:

1. Rinse the meat under cold, running water. Cut into serving-size pieces. Place into a slow cooker or a 9" × 13" ovenproof baking pan that has been sprayed with nonstick cooking spray.

2. Slice the onion and place on top of the meat. Pour the tomatoes and juice over the top. Sprinkle with garlic salt, salt, and pepper.

3. Cover the slow cooker or baking pan. In a slow cooker, cook on high for 1 hour. Reduce heat to low and cook for another 8 or 9 hours until the meat is tender. In the oven, bake at 350° for 1½ to 2 hours, until the meat is tender. To serve, place the meat on a serving plate. Spoon onions, tomatoes, and drippings over the meat.

Variation: Creamy Swiss Steak

Substitute one 10.5-ounce can condensed mushroom soup for the tomatoes. When meat is done, use the drippings as gravy.

Hamburger Pizza Casserole

This dinner entreé tastes like pizza, but you don't have to spin dough over your head. Serve with a salad (see page 96) and bottled Italian dressing.

E

 **Serves 4**

What You Need:
2 pounds ground beef
1 (7-ounce) can mushroom stems and pieces (optional)
1 (15-ounce) can pizza sauce
1 (7.5-ounce) can refrigerator biscuits
1 cup grated Parmesan cheese

What You Do:
1. Brown the ground beef in a frying pan (see page 115). Drain off the fat. Reduce heat to low. Drain the mushrooms, and add to the beef along with the pizza sauce. Stir.

2. Lay the uncooked biscuits on top of the meat. Sprinkle with cheese. Cover and simmer for 20 to 25 minutes, until the biscuits are cooked.

A Preheating Reminder
When preheating an oven, pay particular attention to your oven dials. When a recipe calls for baking or roasting, be sure to set the dial to "bake" before placing the food in the oven. If you leave the dial on preheat, the top of your food will be overcooked or even burned, and the rest of it won't heat evenly. If cooking time is longer than 1 hour, you don't need to preheat the oven.

Tomato Rice with Beef Casserole

This casserole is a meaty variation of a Mexican side dish. You can substitute cooked pork from a leftover roast or pork chops for the beef. You also can substitute 2 servings of instant rice.

E

🍴 Serves 4–6 🍴

What You Need:

2 cups water

1 cup uncooked rice

1 teaspoon salt

1 pound ground beef

1 medium onion

1 (14.5-ounce) can stewed tomatoes, with juice

Salt and pepper, to taste

What You Do:

1. In a saucepan over high heat, bring the water, rice, and salt to a boil. Reduce heat to low and cover. Simmer for about 15 minutes until all the water is absorbed.

2. While the rice is cooking, crumble the ground beef into the frying pan. Chop the onion and add it to the frying pan. Brown the beef and onion (see page 115). Drain off the fat.

3. Stir in the stewed tomatoes with juice until well blended. Sprinkle with salt and pepper. Stir in the rice. Cook uncovered for 5 to 10 minutes, until heated through.

Don't Cry for Me

Some people are quite sensitive to the tear-producing quality in onions. If your eyes water when you slice or chop onions, try refrigerating them first. To cut down on onion odors in the kitchen, store leftover cut onions in a sealed container and refrigerate immediately. Discard unused pieces of onion in your outside garbage. Wash your hands with soap after handling.

Ground Beef and Cabbage

This dish may not sound good to picky eaters, but it is delicious. Serve it with Easy Dinner Rolls (see page 280).

 **Serves 4**

What You Need:
1 pound ground beef
1 small head cabbage (about the size of a softball)
¼ (½ stick) cup butter *or* margarine
1 teaspoon garlic salt
Salt and pepper, to taste

What You Do:
1. Brown the beef (see "Browning Ground Beef," page 115) in a large frying pan. Drain off the fat. Set aside.
2. Slice the cabbage and place it in a Dutch oven. Cover with water and boil for about 10 minutes. The cabbage will look very green and a little transparent and its texture will be tender, but still firm. (Don't overcook.) Drain in a colander and return the cabbage to the pot.
3. Stir in the butter, garlic salt, salt, and pepper. Stir in the browned beef. Serve warm.

Beef Gumbo Casserole

E

Add a Cajun flair to your dining experience. It's not too spicy, so if you like, sprinkle a few drops of hot cayenne pepper sauce on top when serving.

 **Serves 4**

What You Need:
1 pound ground beef
½ small onion
1 (10¾-ounce) can condensed chicken gumbo soup
1 (14.5-ounce) can Spanish rice
1 (8.5-ounce) can cream-style corn
½ cup uncooked macaroni noodles

What You Do:
1. Preheat oven to 350°. Crumble the ground beef into a frying pan. Chop the onion and add to the meat. Brown the ground beef mixture (see "Browning Ground Beef," page 115). Drain off the fat.

2. Stir in the soup, rice, corn, and noodles until well mixed. Pour the mixture into a 2-quart ovenproof baking pan that has been sprayed with nonstick cooking spray. Bake for 35 minutes, until the macaroni is done. Or, microwave for about 5 minutes until the macaroni is done.

Spaghetti and Meatballs

Tired of spaghetti sauce that comes in a jar? Make your own and add tasty meatballs for an authentic Italian dinner. Serve over spaghetti cooked according to package (10-ounce package) directions.

 **Serves 4**

What You Need:

For the meatballs:
1 pound ground beef
2 eggs
1/8 teaspoon dried minced garlic
1/4 cup grated Parmesan cheese
1 teaspoon salt
3 tablespoons vegetable oil

For the sauce:
1 1/2 cups water
2 (6-ounce) cans tomato paste
1 teaspoon dried sweet basil
1 teaspoon salt
1/8 teaspoon pepper
1/2 teaspoon white granulated sugar

What You Do:

1. To make the meatballs, crumble the ground beef into a large mixing bowl. In a separate small mixing bowl or cup, beat the eggs with a table fork until well blended. Add to the beef, along with the garlic, cheese, and salt. Use your hands to squish the ingredients together until well blended. Pour the vegetable oil into a large frying pan over medium heat. With wet hands, form the beef mixture into about 16 meatballs. Fry in the oil until well browned. Drain off the fat. Reduce the heat to low.

2. Heat the water in a saucepan until small bubbles form. Pour into a bowl. Stir in the tomato paste, basil, salt, pepper, and sugar until well blended. Pour the sauce over the meatballs. Cover and cook for at least 1 hour, stirring occasionally.

The Easiest Lasagna in the World

This popular layered pasta dish is a favorite at potluck dinners. You can use cottage cheese in place of the ricotta.

 **Serves 6**

What You Need:

1 pound ground beef
1 (32-ounce) jar spaghetti sauce
1 egg
12 ounces ricotta cheese
1 cup shredded mozzarella cheese
1 teaspoon dried basil

1 teaspoon dried oregano
Salt and pepper, to taste
Dash chili powder (optional)
9 uncooked lasagna noodles
¼ cup grated Parmesan cheese

What You Do:

1. Brown the ground beef (page 115). Drain off the fat. Stir in the spaghetti sauce.

2. In a large mixing bowl, beat the egg with a fork until well blended. Stir in the ricotta and mozzarella, along with basil, oregano, salt, pepper, and chili powder.

3. Preheat oven to 350°. Use just enough of the sauce mixture to cover the bottom of an ovenproof 7" × 11" × 3" baking dish. Place 3 of the uncooked noodles on top of the sauce in a row to form a bottom layer. Spread about ⅓ of the cheese mixture on the noodles; then spread about ⅓ of the sauce mixture on top of the cheese. Repeat the process twice: 3 noodles, cheese mixture, sauce mixture; 3 noodles, cheese mixture, sauce mixture.

4. Sprinkle with Parmesan cheese. Cover with aluminum foil. Bake for 1 hour. Uncover and bake 15 minutes more, until the noodles are soft. Let stand 10 to 15 minutes before cutting.

Boiled Corned Beef and Cabbage

Nothing is more traditional for St. Patrick's Day than boiled corned beef and cabbage. Use leftover corned beef for Reuben Sandwiches (page 42).

 **Serves 6–8**

What You Need:

3–4 pounds packaged corned beef
brisket with spice packet
Water, as needed (about 1 quart)
2 small heads green cabbage

What You Do:

1. Unwrap the meat and rinse under cold, running water. Place in a Dutch oven. Cover with water. Stir in the contents of the spice packet. On the stovetop, cover and bring to a boil over medium-high heat. Reduce heat to low. Simmer for 2½ hours or until the meat is tender when pierced with a fork.

2. Remove and discard the outer leaves from the cabbages. Rinse the cabbage under cold, running water. Cut in half from top to bottom. Cut each half from top to bottom in half again to make wedges. Place the cabbage in the pot surrounding the meat. Cover and cook another 30 minutes. (In a slow cooker, place the cabbage in the pot first. Place the meat on top of the cabbage. Cover with water. Cook on low for 8 to 10 hours.)

> ### Choosing and Storing Cabbage
>
> Cabbage is high in vitamin C and very low in sodium. Use it in Old-Fashioned Coleslaw (page 103) or in place of lettuce in Miniature Taco Salads (page 276) to add flavor and nutrition. When purchasing cabbage, avoid heads with outer leaves that have separated from the stem. Do not rinse cabbage before storing. (Moisture favors decay.) Shred the cabbage only when ready to use. Do not store shredded cabbage for future use.

Cowboy Hash

M

How easy is *this*? It makes you feel right at home on the range. Serve with Hot Cheese Toast (page 40) and ketchup, barbecue sauce, or chunky salsa.

 **Serves 4**

What You Need:
4 small white *or* red russet potatoes
1 small white *or* yellow onion
1 green bell pepper (optional)
¼ cup vegetable oil
1 pound ground beef
1 teaspoon chili powder
1 teaspoon salt
¼ teaspoon pepper

What You Do:
1. Peel and slice the potatoes. Set aside. Chop the onion and green bell pepper. Pour the vegetable oil into a large frying pan over medium-high heat. Add the onions and green bell pepper. Cook until tender but still firm, stirring frequently.

2. Crumble the ground beef into the pan and brown it (see page 115). Gently stir in the potatoes. Add the chili powder, salt, and pepper; mix well. Continue frying for about 30 minutes, stirring often. Cook until the potatoes are tender and golden brown. Drain off excess fat before serving.

Asian Rice with Beef

You can use leftover Beef Roast (page 112), steak, or even browned ground beef (see "Browning Ground Beef," page 115) in this recipe. If the water has not been absorbed at the end of the cooking time, uncover and cook a few minutes longer.

Serves 2

What You Need:

2 stalks celery	⅔ cup uncooked rice
1 green bell pepper	1½ teaspoons salt
1 medium-size white *or* yellow onion	1 beef bouillon cube
1½ cups water	2 teaspoons soy sauce
2 tablespoons vegetable oil	¾ pound cooked beef

What You Do:

1. Rinse the celery and green bell pepper under cold, running water. Remove the seeds and inner ribs from the green pepper. Chop the celery, green bell pepper, and onion. Place in a small mixing bowl. Set aside. Boil the water in a small saucepan.

2. Pour the vegetable oil into a large frying pan over medium-high heat. Place the rice in the hot oil. Stir constantly until golden brown. Pour in the boiling water. Add the salt, bouillon cube, and soy sauce. Stir until well mixed. Reduce heat to low. Cover and cook for 20 minutes. (Keep covered; no need to stir.)

3. While the rice is cooking, cut the cooked beef into bite-size pieces. At the end of the cooking time, stir in the beef, onion, celery, and green bell pepper. If the dish looks too dry, add 1 or 2 tablespoons water. Cover and cook 10 minutes more.

Beef and Noodles

In the grocery store, look for stew beef that has already been cut into approximately 1½" cubes. Or, ask the meat cutter to cube round steak for you. Plan ahead to use the leftover onion soup mix, mushroom soup, and canned mushrooms for Cranberry Chicken (page 155) and Green Bean Casserole (page 219) in the next day or so.

Serves 4

What You Need:
1 pound cubed stew beef
½ (1.25-ounce) envelope dry onion soup mix
½ (10¾-ounce) can condensed cream of mushroom soup
½ (7-ounce) can sliced mushrooms
½ (12-ounce) package uncooked wide egg noodles

What You Do:
1. Place the beef into an ovenproof baking pan that has been sprayed with nonstick cooking spray.
2. In a small mixing bowl, stir together the onion soup mix and undiluted mushroom soup until well blended. Gently stir in the mushrooms. Pour over the meat. Cover and bake at 300° for 3 hours. You don't have to preheat if cooking time exceeds 1 hour.
3. During the last 15 minutes of cooking time, cook the egg noodles according to package directions. Drain. Place the noodles on serving plates. Spoon the beef mixture on top. Serve immediately.

Hungarian Goulash

This tasty blend of seasonings brings a unique flavor to this popular traditional stew. Serve over rice or noodles.

 **Serves 4**

What You Need:

2 small onions

1 pound cubed stew beef *or* round steak

2 tablespoons vegetable oil

¼ teaspoon dry mustard

1¼ teaspoons paprika

2 tablespoons brown sugar

1 teaspoon salt

3 tablespoons Worcestershire sauce

¾ teaspoon white vinegar

2 cups water

½ cup ketchup

What You Do:

1. Chop the onion. Cook the onion and meat in vegetable oil in large frying pan over medium-high until the meat has browned and the onion is tender.

2. Reduce heat to low. Stir in the remaining ingredients. Cover and cook for 2½ hours, stirring occasionally.

Pot Roast

This is best when prepared with rump or eye of round roast. But because this cooks slowly, you can cook it with a less expensive cut of beef, such as chuck roast or arm roast. Serve with Garlic Mashed Potatoes (page 218).

 **Serves 4**

What You Need:

4 carrots
3 stalks celery
1 medium-size white *or* yellow onion
2 tablespoons vegetable oil
2-pound beef round, chuck, or arm roast
Salt and pepper, to taste
½ cup water

Optional gravy:
3 tablespoons all-purpose flour
⅓ cup cold water

What You Do:

1. Rinse the carrots and celery under cold running water. Peel the carrots. Cut the carrots and celery diagonally into 1"-to 1½"-long sections. Chop the onion. Place the carrots, celery, and onion in a slow cooker.

2. Heat the vegetable oil over medium-high heat. Place the roast in the hot oil and brown on one side. Turn the roast. Generously sprinkle salt and pepper over the browned side. When the second side is browned, sprinkle with salt and pepper. Place in a slow cooker.

Pot Roast
(continued)

3. Pour ½ cup water over the beef. Cover. Cook on low for 8 to 10 hours (or on high for 4 to 5 hours).

4. To make the gravy: At the end of the cooking time, pour the cooking liquid from the slow cooker into a saucepan over medium-high heat. (Leave the beef and vegetables in the cooker to keep warm.) In a small mixing bowl, stir together the flour and ⅓ cup water until well blended. Pour into the cooking liquid. Stir constantly until the mixture bubbles and thickens.

5. When ready to serve, place the meat on a serving dish. Use a slotted spoon to remove the vegetables. Spoon around the beef to form a border along the edge of the serving dish. Serve the gravy on the side.

Roasting Meat and Poultry

Roasting is the easiest way to prepare meat. All you do is rinse the meat under cold, running water. Place it in a roasting pan, sprinkle with seasonings, and put it in the oven. All you need to know is the time and temperature for each type of meat. A meat thermometer inserted into the meat before cooking takes the guesswork out of roasting, but you can roast meat without one. If you use a meat thermometer, insert it into the center of the thickest portion of the meat, and be sure the tip does not touch bone. If it does, it will give an inaccurate reading. At the end of the cooking time, remove from oven and let sit for about 5 minutes to give juices a chance to settle before slicing. To serve, slice across the grain.

They'll Think You're a Genius Beef Brisket

M

Prepare this recipe the day before you plan to serve it.

✴ Yields 2–3 servings per pound ✴

What You Need:

3- to 6-pound beef brisket

½ (3.5-ounce) bottle liquid smoke

1 cup lemon juice

1 tablespoon celery seed

½ teaspoon garlic salt

¼ teaspoon pepper

½ cup water

About ¾ cup bottled barbecue sauce

What You Do:

1. Rinse the brisket in cold, running water. Place in a shallow roasting pan, fat side up. Pour the liquid smoke and lemon juice over the top. Sprinkle with celery seed, garlic salt, and pepper. Bake uncovered at 275° for 1½ hours.

2. Remove from oven. Pour water into the side of the roasting pan (not on top of the meat). Tightly cover with aluminum foil. Return to the oven. Cook for another 2½ hours.

3. Uncover. Pour the barbecue sauce over the top. Reseal the foil. Cook for another 30 minutes. Remove from oven. Remove the foil until the meat has cooled. Cover and refrigerate in the juices overnight. (Don't cut the meat before it's chilled!)

4. Preheat oven to 350°. Remove brisket from the juices and place on cutting board. (Discard juices.) Thinly slice the cold brisket crosswise. Place in an ovenproof baking pan that has been sprayed with nonstick cooking spray. Cover and heat in the oven for 20 to 30 minutes, until warmed through.

Enchiladas

Don a sombrero and invite some friends over for a fiesta!

Yields 10 enchiladas

What You Need:

1¼ cups canned red enchilada sauce

1 (10.5-ounce) can condensed cream of mushroom soup

1 (10¾-ounce) can condensed tomato soup

1 small white *or* yellow onion

2 pounds ground beef

1½ cups shredded Cheddar cheese

10 (6") flour tortillas

What You Do:

1. Spray a 9" × 13" ovenproof baking pan with nonstick cooking spray. Set aside. In a saucepan, stir together the enchilada sauce, undiluted mushroom soup, and undiluted tomato soup. Heat over medium heat until well blended. Remove from heat.

2. Chop the onion. Place in a frying pan. Crumble the ground beef into the pan. Brown the beef and onion together (see "Browning Ground Beef," page 115). Drain off fat. Stir in ½ cup of the enchilada sauce mixture and ½ cup of the shredded cheese.

3. Preheat oven to 350°. Scoop ⅓ cup to ½ cup of the beef mixture and spoon it in a 2"-wide line down the middle of a flour tortilla. Fold the bottom ¼ of the tortilla over the beef mixture. Wrap the right side of the tortilla halfway over the beef mixture (and the already folded bottom section). Wrap the left side of the tortilla over the right side. Carefully turn over the enchilada and place seam-side down in the baking pan. Repeat until all the enchiladas are prepared and placed in the baking pan.

4. Pour the remaining sauce mixture over the enchiladas. Top with the remaining cheese. Bake uncovered for 30 minutes.

Stuffed Green Bell Peppers

The green peppers in this recipe double as serving bowls. You can use instant rice to make ½ cup cooked rice if you like.

 **Serves 2**

What You Need:

¼ cup uncooked rice
2 large green bell peppers
Water, as needed (about 2 quarts)
½ small white *or* yellow onion

¾ pound lean ground beef
1 (8-ounce) can tomato sauce
Salt and pepper, to taste
2 slices American cheese

What You Do:

1. Cook the rice according to package directions. Set aside.

2. Rinse the green bell peppers under cold, running water. Cut off the tops of the green peppers. Remove the seeds and carefully cut out the ribs from the inside of the pepper. Fill a 2-quart saucepan with water. Bring to a boil. Place the green peppers in the boiling water. Cover and cook for 5 minutes to soften. Drain.

3. While the peppers are cooking, chop the onion. Brown the ground beef along with the onion (see "Browning Ground Beef," page 115) in a frying pan. Drain off the fat. Stir in the tomato sauce, cooked rice, salt, and pepper.

4. Preheat oven to 325°. Place the green peppers open-side up in a 1-quart ovenproof baking pan that has been sprayed with nonstick cooking spray. Spoon ¼ of the beef mixture into each pepper. Top with 1 slice of cheese. Use a knife or your fingers to tear off any cheese that hangs over the edge of the pepper.

5. Add ¼ cup water to the bottom of the baking pan. Bake uncovered for 1 hour, or until the peppers are tender.

Meat Loaf

Meat loaf makes an inexpensive entrée, and you can use left-overs for cold meat loaf sandwiches the next day. Serve with baked potatoes (see "Baking Potatoes," page 113) and Green Bean Casserole (page 219).

 **Serves 4**

What You Need:

³/₄ pound ground beef	¹/₈ teaspoon celery salt
3 slices white bread	¹/₈ teaspoon garlic salt
2 tablespoons dried minced onion	1¹/₂ teaspoons Worcestershire sauce
¹/₂ teaspoon salt	¹/₂ cup milk
¹/₈ teaspoon pepper	1 egg
¹/₈ teaspoon dry mustard	¹/₂ cup bottled barbecue sauce

What You Do:

1. Preheat oven to 350°. Use your hands to crumble the ground beef into a large mixing bowl. Tear the bread and the crusts into small pieces about ¹/₂" to 1" squares. Add to the beef in the bowl. Sprinkle with onion, salt, pepper, dry mustard, celery salt, garlic salt, and Worcestershire sauce.

2. In a small mixing bowl, beat together the milk and egg until well blended. Pour over the beef mixture.

3. With your hands, squish together all ingredients until well blended. Form into a loaf shape. (*Always* wash your hands with soap and water after handling raw meat, especially raw ground meat.) Place in a shallow roasting pan that has been sprayed with nonstick cooking spray. Pour the barbecue sauce over the loaf. Bake for 1 hour. To serve, cut crosswise into slices about 1" thick.

Shepherd's Pie

Although this recipe calls for beef, traditional Shepherd's Pie is made with lamb. You can substitute cooked chopped lamb if you prefer. Serve with Cold Mixed Veggies Salad (page 93) or cold sliced peaches.

 **Serves 6**

What You Need:

2½ pounds baking potatoes
Water, as needed
4 tablespoons butter, divided
1 cup milk
1 medium-size white *or* yellow onion
2 cloves fresh garlic *or* ¼ teaspoon
   dried minced garlic
1 tablespoon vegetable oil

1½ pounds ground beef
1 tablespoon all-purpose flour
½ cup beef broth
1 teaspoon dried thyme
1 teaspoon dried rosemary
Dash of nutmeg
Salt and pepper, to taste

What You Do:

1. Boil and mash potatoes (see Mashed Potatoes, page 218) with 2 tablespoons of the butter, the milk, and salt and pepper. Set aside.

2. Chop the onion and mince the garlic. Pour the vegetable oil into a large frying pan over medium heat. Stir in the onion and garlic. Crumble the ground beef into the pan. Brown the meat (see "Browning Ground Beef," page 115). Drain off the fat.

Shepherd's Pie
(continued)

3. Stir in the flour. Continue stirring for 2 to 3 minutes to thicken. Stir in the beef broth, thyme, rosemary, and nutmeg. Season with salt and pepper, to taste. Reduce heat to low. Cook, uncovered, 15 minutes, stirring occasionally. Remove from heat.

4. Pour the mixture into a deep-dish pie pan or ovenproof baking dish that has been sprayed with nonstick cooking spray. Spread the mashed potatoes in an even layer over the mixture, covering it completely (as though you are frosting a cake). Cut the remaining 2 tablespoons butter into small pieces and place a few inches apart on top of the mashed potatoes. Bake for 35 minutes, until the mashed potatoes are lightly browned.

Choosing Ground Beef

The type of ground beef depends on which cut of meat is used. The more expensive the cut, the higher the price (unless it is on sale). For the best value, choose ground beef or ground chuck. Ground round and ground sirloin taste great, but may not be worth the extra expense. In addition, lower-fat ground beef choices cost more per pound, but have greater value because less fat cooks out, leaving more meat. To kill bacteria that can cause illness, always cook ground meat until there is no tinge of pink inside. (Cut a small slit in the middle to check for color.) And always wash your hands with soap and warm water after handling raw ground beef.

Beef Stroganoff

Sour cream makes this creamy dish fit for a king—or a Russian baron. Serve over fluffy cooked rice or egg noodles. You can substitute ground beef for the round steak if you like.

 **Serves 4**

What You Need:

1 pound round steak *or* cubed stew beef
¼ medium-size white *or* yellow onion
¼ cup butter *or* margarine
⅛ teaspoon dried minced garlic
2 tablespoons all-purpose flour
¼–½ teaspoon salt, or to taste
¼ teaspoon pepper
1 pound fresh sliced mushrooms
1 (10.5-ounce) can condensed cream of chicken soup
1 cup sour cream
1 tablespoon parsley flakes

What You Do:

1. Cut the beef into 1" to 2" cubes. Set aside. Chop the onion. Melt the butter (or margarine) over medium heat. Stir in the onion. Cook until tender. Stir in the beef and garlic. Cook until the meat is browned, stirring often.

2. Stir in the flour, salt, pepper until thickened. Reduce heat to low. Add the mushrooms and soup. Cook for 15 minutes, stirring often.

3. Stir in the sour cream. Remove from heat. Sprinkle with parsley flakes. Serve hot.

Pork Roast

E

Applesauce is a traditional side dish with pork. For different apple flavors, serve with Baked Apples (page 292) or Waldorf Salad (page 97).

Yields 2 servings per pound

What You Need:
1 pork roast
Salt and pepper, to taste
Garlic salt, to taste (*or* seasoned salt)

What You Do:
1. Preheat oven to 350°. Rinse the meat under cold, running water. Place fat-side up in a roasting pan or ovenproof baking pan. (*Always* wash your hands with soap after handling raw meat.) Insert a meat thermometer into the thickest portion of the meat (optional). Sprinkle with salt, pepper, and garlic salt.

2. Roast according to the following times: loin or center cut roast, 35 to 40 minutes per pound; leg roast, 25 to 40 minutes per pound; shoulder roast, 35 to 40 minutes per pound; butt roast, 45 to 50 minutes per pound.

3. Check for doneness. The meat thermometer should read 185°. If you don't use a meat thermometer, cut into the center of the roast and check color. Pork is done when there is no tinge of pink.

Easy Pork Tenderloin

E Sweet and tender, pork tenderloin makes a romantic entrée for your dinner date. Serve with peas and applesauce. Do *not* substitute white vinegar in this recipe.

 **Serves 2**

What You Need:
2 tablespoons cider vinegar
¼ cup honey
2 tablespoons brown sugar
1 tablespoon prepared spicy whole-grain mustard
1-pound pork tenderloin

What You Do:
1. Preheat oven to 425°. In a large mixing bowl, stir together the vinegar, honey, brown sugar, and mustard until well blended.
2. Rinse the pork under cold, running water and place in a roasting pan. Pat dry with a paper towel. (*Always* wash your hands with soap after handling raw meat.) Pour the honey mixture over the pork. Roast for 25 minutes or until the juices run clear and the pork has no tinge of pink. If using a meat thermometer, it should read 185°.

Pork Chop Dinner in a Dish

The sauce created by the pork drippings and mushroom soup makes tasty gravy. To serve, place the pork chops on serving plates and serve the beans and potatoes on the side. Spoon the rest of the gravy over the pork, beans, and potatoes.

Serves 2

What You Need:
4 small red russet potatoes
1 (8-ounce) can cut green beans
2 bone-in pork chops, about ¾" thick
1 (10¾-ounce) can condensed cream of mushroom soup
Salt and pepper, to taste

What You Do:
1. Spray an 8" × 8" ovenproof baking pan with nonstick cooking spray. Rinse the potatoes under cold, running water. (Do not peel.) Cut the potatoes in half lengthwise and in half again crosswise. (Each potato is cut into 4 pieces.) Place skin-side down in the baking pan.

2. Drain the green beans and sprinkle in a layer over the potatoes. Rinse the pork chops in cold, running water and place on top of the green beans. Dump the condensed soup into a small mixing bowl and stir until the consistency is smoother and easier to pour. (Do *not* add milk or water.) Pour over the meat and vegetables. Sprinkle with salt and pepper.

3. Cover and bake 350° for 2 hours or until the meat is tender and there is no tinge of pink on the inside.

Slow-Cooked Pork Chops in Cherry Sauce

For easy preparation, make this dish in a slow cooker. Because you are using a slow cooking method, you can substitute a less expensive cut of pork, like shoulder steak, with equally delicious results. To serve, pour the remaining sauce into a serving bowl. Spoon the sauce over the meat.

 **Serves 4**

What You Need:
1 tablespoon vegetable oil
4 pork chops
Salt and pepper to taste
$2/3$ cup canned cherry pie filling
$1\frac{1}{4}$ teaspoons lemon juice
$\frac{1}{4}$ teaspoon instant chicken bouillon granules
$\frac{1}{16}$ teaspoon ground mace
1 teaspoon dried parsley flakes

What You Do:
1. Place the vegetable oil in a large frying pan over medium-high heat. Brown the pork chops on each side, but don't cook through. Remove from heat. Sprinkle with salt and pepper.

2. Place the cherry pie filling in a slow cooker. Stir in the lemon juice, bouillon granules, and mace until well mixed. Place the browned pork chops on top of the sauce. Cover and cook on low for 4 to 5 hours. To serve, place the pork chops on a serving plate. Spoon the sauce over. Sprinkle with parsley.

Slow-Cooked Polish Sausage and Kraut

Here's a dinner entrée version of a football concession stand favorite. Start cooking early and turn on the game! Serve with sliced raw veggies.

 **Serves 2**

What You Need:
1 pound Polish sausage
1 (14-ounce) can sauerkraut, with liquid
¼ teaspoon caraway seed
1½ tablespoons white granulated sugar
1 tablespoon dried minced onion (*or* ¼ cup chopped fresh onion)
2 cups water

What You Do:
1. Slice each sausage into 4 pieces of equal length. Place in a slow cooker or a large saucepan.
2. In a medium-size mixing bowl, stir together the sauerkraut, caraway seed, sugar, and onion. Place on top of the sausage. Add the water and cover.
3. In a slow cooker, cook on low for 3 to 4 hours. On the stovetop, cook over low heat for 1 hour.

Ham Fettuccine Casserole

E

Romano cheese and garlic add Italian flavor to this plentiful pasta dish. You can use precooked ham steak, turkey ham, or ham lunchmeat in this recipe.

Serves 4

What You Need:

1 (12-ounce) package uncooked fettuccine
½ pound ham
3 tablespoons butter *or* margarine
2 tablespoons olive oil
¼ teaspoon dried minced garlic
1½ cups frozen broccoli florets

1 (14-ounce) can diced tomatoes, with juice
¼ teaspoon black pepper
Salt, to taste
¼ cup grated Romano cheese

What You Do:

1. Cook the fettuccine according to package instructions.

2. While the noodles are cooking, slice the ham into 2"- to 3"-long flat strips about the width of cooked fettuccine noodles.

3. Place the butter and olive oil in a large frying pan and heat over medium-high heat until the butter melts. Add the ham, garlic, and broccoli; sauté, stirring constantly, for about 5 minutes. Stir in the tomatoes and juice. Season with salt and pepper. Cook until the broccoli is tender but still firm.

4. Drain noodles when done. Add to the frying pan. Gently stir until all the ingredients are well mixed and heated through. Sprinkle with grated Romano cheese.

Ham and Asparagus Roll-Ups

This makes a nice lunch or a light supper. Serve with Fruit and Coconut Salad (page 85) or sliced tomatoes.

 **Serves 2**

What You Need:

1 (15-ounce) can whole asparagus spears
4 slices packaged ham lunchmeat
½ (10¾-ounce) can condensed
   Cheddar cheese soup
2 tablespoons milk
1 teaspoon prepared mustard
⅛ teaspoon paprika

What You Do:

1. Preheat oven to 350°. Drain the asparagus. Divide the asparagus spears evenly among the ham slices. Place 3 or 4 spears near one edge on top of each slice of ham. Roll the ham over the asparagus. Place seam-side down in an ovenproof baking pan that has been sprayed with nonstick cooking spray.

2. In a medium-size mixing bowl, stir together the soup, milk, and mustard. Pour the mixture over the ham. Sprinkle with paprika. Bake uncovered for 30 minutes, until heated through.

> **Fun Facts about Asparagus**
>
> First known in the Mediterranean area more than 2,000 years ago, asparagus was enjoyed by the ancient Greeks, who gathered wild asparagus, and Romans, who cultivated it. In the 1600s in France, royal gardeners grew it in greenhouses so King Louis XIV could eat it year-round. About the same time, asparagus made its way to the New World from England and northern Europe.

Ham Slice with Pineapple

If you have leftover cooked ham, you can use it in this recipe by reducing the cooking time to 30 minutes. You can also substitute 2 peeled and sliced tart apples (McIntosh, Granny Smith, or Jonathan varieties) and ¼ cup water or apple juice for the pineapple and juice in this recipe.

 **Serves 2**

What You Need:
1-pound uncooked ham slice
4 cloves
½ cup canned crushed pineapple, with juice
3 tablespoons brown sugar

What You Do:
1. Place the ham in an oven-proof baking pan that has been sprayed with nonstick cooking spray. Stick the cloves into the ham several inches apart.
2. Spoon the pineapple and juice over the ham. Sprinkle with brown sugar.
3. Cover with aluminum foil (or a baking dish lid). Bake at 325° for 1 hour and 15 minutes. Uncover and bake for 15 minutes more.

> ### Horseradish Go-Togethers
> Horseradish is the grated or shredded root of a plant that originated in Europe and western Asia. It is sold in a jar in the grocery store's refrigerated section. Horseradish has a pungent flavor that can rival hot chili peppers in its ability to make your eyes water! So, you will use only a small amount at a time. Horseradish is often used as a condiment with ham, roast beef, and steak. It is also used to make cocktail sauce (see "Make Your Own Easy Seafood Sauce," page 177).

Ham Slice with Raisin Sauce

Here's a sweet topping that adds fruity flavor to ham. You can use leftover ham or purchase a precooked ham slice.

 **Serves 2**

What You Need:
1-pound cooked ham slice
1 tablespoon butter *or* margarine
1 tablespoon all-purpose flour
1 cup apple juice (*or* cider)
¼ cup seedless raisins

What You Do:
1. Preheat oven to 325°. Place the ham in an ovenproof baking pan that has been sprayed with nonstick cooking spray.

2. In a saucepan or small frying pan, melt the butter over low heat. Stir in the flour until well blended. Remove from heat. Stir in the apple juice and raisins. Continue stirring until the mixture boils; boil for 1 minute. (The mixture will thicken.) Remove from heat.

3. Pour the mixture over the ham. Cover with aluminum foil (or a baking dish lid). Bake for 30 to 35 minutes, until warmed through. Uncover and cook 5 minutes more.

Pork Chops with Rice

To serve, carefully remove the chops from the pan, maintaining the layered ingredients for a nice visual effect. Top each pork chop with a sprig of parsley.

 **Serves 4**

What You Need:

4 pork chops
Salt and pepper, to taste
1 tablespoon vegetable oil
4 thin (about ⅛" thick) slices white *or* yellow onion
4 thin (about ⅛" thick) slices green bell pepper
¼ cup uncooked rice
1 (28-ounce) can whole peeled tomatoes
4 sprigs fresh parsley (a sprig is a little "branch")

What You Do:

1. Sprinkle the pork chops with salt and pepper. In a frying pan, brown both sides in the vegetable oil over medium-high heat. Spray a 9" × 13" ovenproof baking pan or a roasting pan (large enough for all the pork chops to lie flat) with nonstick cooking spray. Place the pork chops in the bottom of the pan.

2. Place 1 slice of onion and 1 slice of green pepper on top of each pork chop. Spoon 1 tablespoon uncooked rice inside of each pepper ring, and place 1 whole tomato on top of the rice. Pour the juice from the tomatoes, along with any leftover tomatoes, around the sides of the pork chops.

3. Cover with baking pan lid or aluminum foil. Bake at 350° for 1½ hours, until the meat is tender and has no tinge of pink.

Slow-Cooked Pork
in Mushroom Sauce

Cook this dish in a slow cooker. Serve with rice or Mashed Potatoes (page 218), a steamed green vegetable (see Appendix C), and Baked Apples (page 292). To serve, remove the pork chops from the cooker. Stir together the remaining liquid and use as gravy.

 **Serves 4**

What You Need:

4 pork chops *or* 2 pounds pork shoulder
1 medium-size white *or* yellow onion
½ cup canned sliced mushrooms (*or* stems and pieces)
1 can cream of mushroom soup
½ cup milk
Salt and pepper, to taste

What You Do:

1. Place the pork chops in a slow cooker.
2. Slice the onion. Separate the rings. Add to the pot.
3. In a small mixing bowl, stir together the mushrooms, soup, and milk. Pour over the onions. Season with salt and pepper. Cover and cook for 4 to 5 hours on high or for 1 hour on high plus 6 to 8 hours on low.

> ### Easy Gravy
> Our grandmothers learned to make gravy from their mothers. With years of practice, they made pretty good gravy. But, believe me, gravy is *really* difficult to make. It turns out too runny or too lumpy. It's easy to burn. And, it's not worth the trouble. So, take my advice. Buy jars of prepared gravy. Place in saucepan over medium heat until warm. Hide the empty jars.

Red Beans and Rice

You'll have to start the night before serving for this traditional dish from the Big Easy. Choose your favorite sausage. Serve with cooked rice, either on the side or mixed together with the beans. You can substitute two 16-ounce cans of red beans (drained), omit the overnight soaking, and reduce the cooking time until the onion and green bell pepper are just tender.

Serves 6

What You Need:

1 (16-ounce) package dried small red beans
Water, as needed
1 medium-size white *or* yellow onion
½ green bell pepper

2 cloves garlic
½ pound sausage
Cayenne pepper, to taste
Salt and pepper, to taste

What You Do:

1. Place the dried beans in a colander and rinse with cool, running water. Place the beans in a large mixing bowl or Dutch oven. Fill with enough cold water to cover the beans. Set aside for 8 hours or overnight (but not longer than 24 hours).

2. Drain the beans and rinse with cold water. Drain again. Place the beans in a Dutch oven or large pot.

3. Chop the onion, green bell pepper, and garlic. Add to the beans. Slice the sausage and add it to the beans. (If using ground sausage, crumble into the beans.) Cover the ingredients with water. Season with cayenne, salt, and pepper. Cover and cook over medium heat, stirring occasionally, until the beans are tender, about 1 to 1½ hours. During the cooking, add water as needed to keep all the ingredients simmering in thick gravy.

Apple-Pineapple Pork Chop Bake

Preparation for this delicious dish takes only minutes. The pork bakes slowly, simmering in apple and pineapple flavors. The result is tender, sweet meat you'll want to make again and again.

Serves 4

What You Need:

2 tablespoons vegetable oil
4 pork chops
2 tablespoons all-purpose flour
1 apple
1 small onion

1 (8-ounce) can pineapple slices in juice
³/₄ cup water
1 chicken bouillon cube
Salt and pepper, to taste

What You Do:

1. Heat the vegetable oil in a large frying pan over medium-high heat. Dust the pork chops with the flour. Cook in the hot oil for 3 minutes per side. Place the pork chops in an ovenproof baking pan that has been sprayed with nonstick cooking spray. Set aside.

2. Preheat oven to 350°. Peel, core, and chop the apple. Chop the onion. Spoon the apple and onion over the pork chops. Arrange the pineapple slices in a layer on top. Reserve the pineapple juice.

3. In a small saucepan, stir together the juice from the canned pineapple, the water, and bouillon cube. Heat on low until the cube dissolves. Pour over the pork chops. Sprinkle with salt and pepper. Cover with aluminum foil or baking dish lid. Bake for 45 minutes.

Pork Chow Mein

Serve over chow mein noodles. Or, if you prefer, you can turn this recipe into chop suey simply by serving it over cooked white rice. For a slightly different flavor, you can substitute chicken for the pork.

 **Serves 4**

What You Need:

1 cup canned water chestnuts
1 (16-ounce) can bean sprouts
3 stalks celery
2 green onions, with tops
1 pound raw pork

⅓ cup vegetable oil
2 tablespoons soy sauce, divided
2 tablespoons cornstarch
½ cup water

What You Do:

1. Drain the water chestnuts and bean sprouts. Slice the water chestnuts and celery into thin strips. Slice green onions and tops crosswise. Place together in a small mixing bowl. Set aside. Slice the pork into thin strips about 1½" long. (*Always wash your hands after handling raw meat.*) Place in a separate bowl. Set aside.

2. Pour the vegetable oil into a large skillet. Cook the pork strips in the oil over medium-high heat for 20 minutes, stirring occasionally.

3. Stir in the bean sprouts, water chestnuts, and celery. Add 1 tablespoon soy sauce; stir. Cover and cook over low heat for 20 minutes, stirring occasionally.

4. In a small mixing bowl, stir together the cornstarch, water, and remaining tablespoon of soy sauce. Pour over the vegetables and stir until heated through.

Chapter 6

Main Dishes for Carnivores— Poultry

Roast Chicken

Whole fryers often cost less than packaged chicken parts. Cut left-overs into bite-size pieces and refrigerate or freeze for later use in salads or casseroles.

 **Serves 4**

What You Need:
1 whole fryer chicken
Salt, as needed (about ½ teaspoon)
Vegetable oil *or* solid vegetable shortening, as needed (about 1 teaspoon)

What You Do:
1. Rinse the chicken under cold, running water. Pat dry with a paper towel. Use your fingers to rub salt on the inside of the neck and body cavities. Place in roasting pan or ovenproof baking pan, breast-side up. Fold the wings back and under the chicken for support.

2. With your fingers, a paper towel, or cooking brush, spread vegetable oil over the entire chicken. Insert a meat thermometer, if desired. (To prevent illness, *always* wash hands with soap and water after handling raw chicken. Also wash any utensils and surfaces that came in contact with raw chicken.) Roast the chicken in the oven at 375°. For a 4-pound chicken, roast for about 1½ hours. Reduce or increase cooking time according to weight.

3. Test for doneness. When done, the juices should run clear and the drumstick should easily move in the joint. Protect your fingers with a paper towel or cloth and gently squeeze the large end of the drumstick. The meat should feel very soft. If using a meat thermometer, it should read 190°.

Cranberry Chicken

Here's your chance to use that potato masher in your kitchen drawer. If you don't have a potato masher, use a table fork.

 **Serves 4**

What You Need:
1 prepackaged cut-up fryer chicken
1 (8-ounce) can whole-berry cranberry sauce
1 (1.25-ounce) package dry onion soup mix

What You Do:
1. Preheat oven to 350°. Rinse the chicken in cold, running water. Pat dry with a paper towel. Place the chicken in a roasting pan or a 9" × 13" ovenproof baking pan that has been sprayed with nonstick cooking spray. (*Always* wash hands with soap after handling raw chicken.)

2. In a small mixing bowl, mash the cranberry sauce. Stir in the onion soup mix until well blended. Spoon over the chicken pieces. Cover with aluminum foil and bake for 2 hours.

> **Food Safety Tip**
> To avoid salmonella poisoning, always wash your hands with soap and warm water after handling raw chicken. Also wash all dishes, utensils, and surfaces that touched raw chicken. Take along sanitary hand wipes to picnics or tailgate parties. Use before and after touching the chicken.

Roast Turkey

Don't worry about stuffing the turkey before roasting. Instead, use stuffing mix, cooked on a stovetop according to package directions. Serve with Mashed Potatoes (page 218), canned gravy, and canned cranberry sauce. Use leftover turkey as a substitute for cooked chicken in casserole recipes.

✯ Yields about 2 servings per pound ✯

What You Need:
1 turkey (any size)
1 tablespoon vegetable oil
1 teaspoon salt

What You Do:
1. If you buy a frozen turkey, thaw it in the refrigerator for 24 to 48 hours before cooking. (Thawing at room temperature encourages growth of harmful bacteria.) Rinse under cold, running water. Remove the neck and package of turkey innards from both cavities. (You can discard these pieces or place them in a saucepan and simmer until tender and cooked through. Some people like to chop them and add them to stuffing mix or gravy. Others feed them to their cat or dog.)

2. Pat the turkey dry with a paper towel. Place breast-side up in a large roasting pan (you can buy a disposable foil pan if you don't have a pan big enough). If you have a meat thermometer, insert it into the center of a thigh or breast. Be sure it doesn't touch bone, or it will register an inaccurate temperature.

Roast Turkey
(continued)

3. Use your hands to spread vegetable oil all over the outside of the turkey. Sprinkle salt on your hand and rub it inside the neck and body cavities. Bend the wings up and under the turkey for support.

4. Roast the turkey at 325° (see "Turkey Roasting Times"), checking it after 2 hours or so and every 30 minutes after that. When the turkey is as brown as you like, make a tent with aluminum foil and place it loosely on top of the turkey so it won't brown further. The turkey is done when the meat thermometer reads 190°, or when the drumstick easily twists out of the joint. If you buy a turkey with a built-in timer, roast until the timer pops up. Let the cooked turkey sit about 20 minutes before carving.

Turkey Roasting Times

Approximate turkey-roasting times vary according to weight. Here are roasting times at 325°:

Weight	Roasting Time
8 to 12 pounds	4 to 4½ hours
12 to 16 pounds	4½ to 5½ hours
16 to 20 pounds	5½ to 7 hours
20 to 24 pounds	7 to 8½ hours

Baked Lemon Chicken

Citrus brings out the flavor of this baked chicken dish that's easy and delicious. Serve with warm rice, if you like.

 **Serves 4**

What You Need:
4 boneless, skinless chicken breast halves
½ cup butter *or* margarine
¼ cup, plus 2 tablespoons lemon juice
1 teaspoon garlic powder
1 teaspoon poultry seasoning
½ teaspoon salt
½ teaspoon pepper

What You Do:
1. Rinse the chicken in cold, running water. Place in an oven-proof baking pan that has been lightly greased with solid shortening or sprayed with nonstick cooking spray.

2. Preheat oven to 350°. Melt the butter (or margarine) in a small saucepan or frying pan. Pour into a medium-size mixing bowl. Stir in the lemon juice, garlic powder, poultry seasoning, salt, and pepper until well blended. Pour over the chicken. Cover the pan with aluminum foil or a baking pan lid. Bake for 1 hour. While the chicken is cooking, frequently spoon sauce from the bottom of the pan over the chicken.

Salsa Chicken

Olé! Here's an easy, spicy chicken dish. Parmesan cheese adds extra zing, even though it's usually used in Italian-style dishes.

 **Serves 2**

What You Need:
2 skinless, boneless chicken breasts
1 cup salsa
¼ cup grated Parmesan cheese

What You Do:
1. Preheat oven to 350°. Spray a 2-quart ovenproof baking pan with nonstick cooking spray. Cut the chicken breasts in half lengthwise. Place side-by-side in the baking pan.

2. Pour the salsa over the chicken. Top with Parmesan cheese.

3. Cover and bake for 30 minutes. Uncover and bake for another 10 minutes.

Money Saver
You can purchase packaged chicken according to your preferred pieces. Or, you can purchase a whole fryer and cut it yourself at a lower price per pound. Cut into 2 wings, 2 breasts, 2 thighs, and 2 drumsticks or leave wings attached to breasts and legs attached to thighs, depending on your preferences and cooking method. Use kitchen scissors to cut pieces apart at the joints. Wash hands, surfaces, and scissors with soap and warm water after handling raw chicken.

Chicken Breasts and Broccoli

E

This makes an elegant entrée when prepared with whole chicken breasts and whole broccoli spears (the floret with the stalk intact). You can also make it as a casserole with frozen chopped broccoli and cooked chicken or turkey cut into bite-size pieces. Serve with chilled canned whole spiced peaches placed on a piece of leaf lettuce.

 **Serves 4**

What You Need:
1 (16-ounce) package frozen broccoli spears
4 skinless chicken breasts
2 (10.5-ounce) cans condensed cream of chicken soup
½ teaspoon curry powder
¼ teaspoon paprika

What You Do:
1. Spray a 9″ × 13″ ovenproof baking pan with nonstick cooking spray. Boil the broccoli for 5 minutes only. Drain.

2. Line the bottom of the prepared pan with the broccoli spears, alternating floret-side up and stem-side up, so the broccoli fits closely together. Arrange the chicken breasts on top of the broccoli.

3. Preheat oven to 350°. In a small mixing bowl, stir together undiluted soup and curry powder. Pour over the chicken and broccoli. Lightly sprinkle with paprika. Bake uncovered for 40 to 45 minutes. Or, microwave on high for about 6 to 8 minutes until the chicken is tender and the juices run clear.

Apricot Chicken

This unusual combination of flavors livens up ordinary roast chicken. Your dinner date will think you've been to chef school. You can substitute peach jam for the apricot jam. Or, substitute bottled Russian salad dressing for the French flavor.

Serves 4

What You Need:
4 skinless, boneless chicken breasts
½ jar apricot jam
½ package dry onion soup mix
1 cup bottled French salad dressing

What You Do:
1. Grease a 9" × 13" ovenproof baking pan. Preheat oven to 350°. Rinse the chicken in cold, running water and place in the baking pan. Pat dry with paper towels. (*Always* wash your hands with soap after handling raw chicken.)

2. In a small mixing bowl, stir together the jam, dry soup mix, and salad dressing until well blended. Pour over the chicken. Bake uncovered for 30 minutes. Cover and cook for another 30 to 35 minutes.

Chicken and Pork Sausage Casserole

Spicy pork sausage gives this dish its flavor. Choose your own adventure from mild to super hot! Serve with Broiled Tomatoes (page 227) and steamed fresh green beans (see Appendix C).

 **Serves 6**

What You Need:
1½ cups uncooked rice
3 stalks celery
3 green onions
2 tablespoons butter *or* margarine
¼ pound ground pork sausage
3 cups precooked chicken (see "Cooked Chicken for Casseroles and Salads," page 81)
1½ cups whole-kernel corn
2 teaspoons lemon juice
Salt and pepper, to taste

What You Do:
1. Cook the rice according to package directions. While the rice is cooking, slice the celery and green onions. Heat the butter (or margarine) over medium-high heat in a large frying pan. Stir in the celery and green onions. Crumble in the pork sausage. Cook until the sausage is browned. Drain off the fat.
2. Stir in the cooked rice, chicken, corn, and lemon juice until well mixed. Sprinkle with salt and pepper. Cover and cook for 5 to 10 minutes, until heated through.

Chicken and Stuffing Casserole

This meal-in-a-dish provides meat, bread, and dairy products. All you need is a green vegetable or chilled canned fruit to complete the meal.

 **Serves 4**

What You Need:
4 boneless, skinless chicken breast halves
4 slices Swiss cheese
1⅓ cups herb-seasoned stuffing mix
1 (10.5-ounce) can cream of chicken soup
1 soup can water

What You Do:
1. Preheat oven to 350°. Rinse the chicken under cold, running water. Pat dry with a paper towel. Place in an ovenproof baking pan that has been sprayed with nonstick cooking spray. (*Always* wash your hands with soap after handling raw chicken.)
2. Place a slice of cheese on each piece of chicken. Sprinkle the dry stuffing mix on top of the cheese.
3. In a small mixing bowl, stir together the soup and water until well blended. Pour over the stuffing mix. Bake uncovered for 45 to 50 minutes.

Chicken Noodle Casserole

If you can operate a can opener, you can make this dish that mixes soft and crunchy noodles for interesting texture and flavor. You'll find evaporated milk in the baking aisle. (Do *not* substitute sweetened condensed milk.) You can substitute ¾ cup cut-up cooked chicken (see "Cooked Chicken for Casseroles and Salads," page 81) for the canned chicken.

 **Serves 4**

What You Need:

1 (10.5-ounce) can condensed cream of chicken soup
1 (10¾-ounce) can condensed chicken noodle soup
1 (5-ounce) can chow mein noodles
1 (5-ounce) can evaporated milk
1 (5-ounce) can chicken
1 (7-ounce) can sliced mushrooms (*or* mushroom bits and pieces)

What You Do:

1. Preheat oven to 375°. Spray a 2½-quart ovenproof baking pan with nonstick cooking spray. Pour the undiluted soups into the pan. Add ½ of the chow mein noodles and the evaporated milk. Stir together until well mixed.

2. Drain the chicken and mushrooms. Stir into the mixture. Top with the remaining chow mein noodles.

3. Bake uncovered for 45 minutes.

Chicken and Rice Casserole

Serve with chilled canned spiced peaches and frozen peas cooked according to package directions. If you have leftover mushrooms from another recipe, toss them in before heating.

 **Serves 4**

What You Need:
2 cups uncooked rice
1 stalk celery
2 cups cooked chicken (see "Cooked Chicken for Casseroles and Salads," page 81)
1 (10.5-ounce) can cream of mushroom soup
½ soup can milk

What You Do:
1. Cook the rice according to package directions. While the rice is cooking, chop the celery and cut the cooked chicken into bite-size pieces.
2. Preheat oven to 350°. Place the rice, chicken, and celery in a 2-quart ovenproof or microwave-safe baking pan. Stir in the mushroom soup and milk. Cover and bake for 30 minutes, or cover and microwave on high for 5 minutes, until heated through.

Italian-Style Chicken Spaghetti

This is not your mama's Italian spaghetti. But it's sure to become a new favorite. For quicker preparation, use precooked chicken (see "Cooked Chicken for Casseroles and Salads," page 81).

 **Serves 4**

What You Need:

¾ pound uncooked chicken
¾ cup bottled Italian salad dressing, divided
½ cup fresh *or* frozen cauliflower florets
½ cup fresh *or* frozen cut carrots
Water, as needed (about 2 quarts)

½ cup fresh *or* frozen cut asparagus (not whole spears)
½ (10-ounce) package thin spaghetti *or* angel hair pasta

What You Do:

1. Cut the chicken into thin strips about ½" wide and 2" long. Place in a large frying pan with ¼ cup of the salad dressing. (To prevent illness, *always* your hands with soap after handling raw chicken. Also wash all utensils and surfaces that touched the raw chicken.) Cook over medium-high heat, stirring constantly until the chicken slightly browns.

2. Reduce heat to low. Stir in the cauliflower, carrots, and asparagus. Pour in the remaining ½ cup salad dressing. Cover and cook over low heat for 7 to 9 minutes. Stir often until the vegetables are tender but still firm.

3. While the vegetables are cooking, bring about 2 quarts water to a boil in a Dutch oven or stew pot. Break the pasta into thirds and cook according to package directions (about 10 minutes) until tender but still firm. Drain. Stir into chicken and vegetable mixture.

Asian Fried Rice

Here's an entrée with a touch of the exotic. For fun, purchase prebaked fortune cookies. Use clean tweezers to remove fortunes and insert ones you write yourself.

⚒ Serves 4 ⚒

What You Need:
1½ cups uncooked rice
½ pound raw chicken, pork, *or* beef
1 large white *or* yellow onion
¼ cup vegetable oil
³⁄₈ teaspoon dried minced garlic
1 tablespoon soy sauce
1 teaspoon salt
½ teaspoon pepper
1 teaspoon white granulated sugar
1 cup frozen *or* leftover vegetables (type of your choice)
2 eggs

What You Do:
1. Cook rice according to package directions. Set aside.
2. Cut the meat into 1" cubes. Chop the onion.
3. Heat the oil in large frying pan over medium heat. Add the meat, onion, minced garlic, soy sauce, salt, pepper, and sugar. Cook, stirring frequently, until the meat is done.
4. Reduce heat to low. Stir in the rice and vegetables. Heat until warm. Just before serving, beat eggs in a small mixing bowl. Stir into mixture until the eggs are cooked.

Chicken Pot Pie

Thick and creamy, this pot pie will stick to your ribs. Fix the left-over potato soup for lunch the next day.

 **Serves 6 to 8**

What You Need:

2 (9") frozen pie shells (*not* deep dish)
½ cup frozen peas
½ cup frozen cut carrots
½ small onion (smaller than a baseball)
1 baking potato (*or* 2–3 red russet potatoes)
1 chicken bouillon cube

1 cup cooked, cut-up chicken
½ (10¾-ounce) can condensed
  cream of potato soup
3 tablespoons milk
¼ teaspoon poultry seasoning
Salt and pepper, to taste

What You Do:

1. Set out the pie shells to thaw. Place the peas and carrots in a large mixing bowl. Chop the onion. Add to the bowl. Set aside to thaw.

2. In a saucepan, cover the whole potatoes with water. Drop in the bouillon cube. Bring to a boil over high heat for about 15 minutes, or until tender when pierced with a fork. Drain.

3. While the potato is cooking, add the chicken, potato soup, milk, and poultry seasoning, and salt and pepper to the peas and carrots mixture; mix well.

4. Preheat oven to 375°. Peel the boiled potato(es). Cut into 1" cubes. Gently stir the potato cubes into mixture.

5. Pour the mixture into 1 pie shell. Remove the second pie shell from the pan it came in and place it on top. Use your fingers to crimp the edges of the top pie shell. Bake for 55 minutes, until the crust is golden brown.

Crisp Baked Chicken

You get all the crunch and flavor of fried chicken, but this dish is baked—not fried. Serve with Mashed Potatoes (see page 218) and sliced fresh tomatoes.

M

🍴 Serves 4 🍴

What You Need:
Shortening *or* vegetable oil, as needed
1½ cups crispy rice cereal
2 tablespoons all-purpose flour
½ teaspoon salt

¼ teaspoon poultry seasoning
¼ cup butter *or* margarine
4 boneless, skinless chicken breast halves

What You Do:
1. Grease an ovenproof baking pan with solid shortening. Set aside. Place the cereal on a cutting board. Cover with waxed paper. Use a rolling pin to coarsely crush the cereal. Scrape it into a medium-size mixing bowl. Stir in the flour, salt, and poultry seasoning.

2. Melt the butter (or margarine) in a small saucepan or frying pan. Preheat oven to 400°. Rinse the chicken in cold, running water. (*Always* wash your hands with soap and warm water after touching raw chicken.) Pat dry with paper towels. Dip the chicken in the melted butter. Turn the chicken to coat the other side, too.

3. Dip the chicken into flour mixture. Flip over to coat the other side. Place the chicken in the prepared baking pan. Bake uncovered for 20 to 25 minutes, until the juices run clear.

Bayou Chicken

Traditional Cajun spices perk up ordinary chicken and transport you to New Orleans's French Quarter. This is a fun dish for Mardi Gras, or anytime.

M

🍴 Serves 3 🍴

What You Need:

2 teaspoons paprika

2 teaspoons cayenne pepper
  or chili powder

1 teaspoon onion powder

³/₄ teaspoon garlic powder

¼ teaspoon ground cumin

Salt and pepper, to taste

½ cup milk

3 tablespoons butter

3 skinless, boneless chicken breasts

What You Do:

1. In a medium-size mixing bowl, stir together the paprika, cayenne pepper (or chili powder), onion powder, garlic powder, cumin, salt, and pepper.

2. Pour the milk into a small mixing bowl.

3. Melt the butter in a large frying pan over medium heat. Rinse the chicken under cold, running water. Dip the chicken into the milk to coat. Place in the melted butter. Sprinkle the chicken with the ½ of the spice mixture.

4. Cover and cook for 10 minutes. Uncover and sprinkle with the remaining spice mixture. Cook uncovered for 20 to 25 minutes more, until the juices run clear.

Chicken Flautas

Here's a Mexican restaurant favorite you can make at home. For a fiesta platter, serve with Black Bean Burritos (page 210), Tacos (page 114), and Rice Casserole (page 237).

M

Yields about 20 flautas

What You Need:

1 pound precooked chicken (see "Cooked Chicken for Casseroles and Salads," page 81)
$^3/_4$ cup picante sauce
2 cups shredded Cheddar cheese
1 package 6" flour tortillas

What You Do:

1. Cut the chicken into bite-size pieces. Place in a large mixing bowl. Stir in the picante sauce and ½ of the cheese.

2. Preheat oven to 375°. Spoon about 2 tablespoons of the chicken mixture onto the middle of each flour tortilla. Roll one side over the mixture. Continue rolling the tortilla in the same direction, leaving the ends open. Line the rolled-up tortillas seam-side down in an ovenproof baking dish that has been sprayed with nonstick cooking spray.

3. Spoon any leftover chicken mixture over the tops of the rolled tortillas. Sprinkle with the remaining cheese. Bake for 10 to 15 minutes, until the cheese melts and the tortillas are browned.

Mediterranean Chicken

You can substitute 4 lamb chops for the chicken in this recipe.

 **Serves 2**

What You Need:

1 small white *or* yellow onion
1 red bell pepper
2 skinless, boneless chicken breasts
1 tablespoon olive oil
1 (14.5-ounce) can whole peeled tomatoes
$\frac{1}{8}$ teaspoon dried minced garlic
3 tablespoons fresh chopped basil
2 tablespoons chopped black olives

What You Do:

1. Thinly slice the onion and red bell pepper. Set aside.

2. In a large frying pan, cook the chicken in olive oil over medium-high heat until golden brown on each side. Reduce heat to low.

3. Add the onion and peppers. Cook for about 3 minutes, until tender. Add the tomatoes, garlic, and basil. Cook uncovered for 20 minutes until the chicken is tender and the juices run clear. Stir in the olives and serve.

Main Dishes for Carnivores— Seafood

Tuna Noodle Casserole

Quick, cheap, easy, and yummy. What more can you ask for? How about a variation that adds extra substance and flavor? Serve with cooked frozen peas and Fruit and Coconut Salad (page 85).

 **Serves 4**

What You Need:
2 eggs
1 stalk celery
2 cups egg noodles
1 (6-ounce) can tuna
1 (10.5-ounce) can condensed cream of mushroom soup
½ soup can milk
4 slices American *or* Cheddar cheese

What You Do:
1. Hard-boil the eggs (see Boiled Egg, page 9). Let cool. Peel and chop. Rinse the celery under cold, running water. Chop. Set aside.

2. Cook the noodles according to package directions. Drain. Place in a 2-quart ovenproof or microwave-safe baking pan that has been sprayed with nonstick cooking spray. Preheat oven to 350°. Drain the tuna. Flake with a fork and add to the noodles. Gently stir in the mushroom soup and milk until well blended. Stir in the celery and eggs. Top with the cheese. Cover and bake for 30 minutes. Or, cover and microwave on high for 5 minutes.

Breaded Oven-Baked Fish

Fish is easier to cook than people think. You can use your favorite fish. Sole, catfish, and halibut work well in this recipe.

 **Serves 4**

What You Need:
2 cups milk
1 tablespoon, plus 1 teaspoon salt
1½ pounds fish fillets (sole, catfish, halibut, *or* other)
1 cup bread crumbs *or* cornmeal
½ cup butter (1 stick)
1 tablespoon lemon juice

What You Do:
1. In a large mixing bowl, stir together the milk and 1 table-spoon salt. Soak the fish in the salted milk for 10 minutes.
2. Preheat oven to 350°. Place the bread crumbs (or corn-meal) in a medium-size mixing bowl. Drag both sides of the milk-soaked fillets through the bread crumbs so they stick to the fillet. Place the fish in a greased 9" × 13" baking pan.
3. Melt the butter and use a spoon to drizzle a few drops at a time over the fish. Sprinkle with lemon juice and about 1 tea-spoon salt. Bake uncovered for 20 minutes or until the fish flakes easily with a fork.

Orange Roughy Picante

This tasty fish with a Southwestern flair makes an attractive, easy-to-prepare main course. You can substitute any other white fish fillet. You can also substitute bottled salsa for the picante sauce. For a nice color contrast, serve with steamed green beans or steamed broccoli (see Appendix C).

 **Serves 2**

What You Need:
2 orange roughy fillets (about ½ pound each)
½ cup bottled picante sauce
1 cup shredded Cheddar cheese

What You Do:
1. Preheat oven to 350°. Spray an ovenproof baking pan with nonstick cooking spray. Place the fillets on the bottom of the pan. Cover each fillet with ½ of the picante sauce. Top with shredded cheese.

2. Bake uncovered for 20 minutes or microwave on high for 3 to 4 minutes until the cheese melts and the fish flakes easily.

Hot Boiled Shrimp

Shrimp is expensive, but it's quick and easy to fix. Serve with baked potatoes (see "Baking Potatoes," page 113), a salad, French bread (see "Preparing French Bread," page 117), and bottled cocktail sauce (or homemade—see below). Cut a whole fresh lemon into wedges and place on serving plates.

 **Serves 2–4**

What You Need:
1 quart water

½ (3-ounce) package shrimp and crab boil spices (1 bag)

1 tablespoon salt

¼ cup lemon juice

2 pounds uncooked shrimp in the shell

What You Do:

1. Pour the water into a Dutch oven. Add the boil spices, salt, and lemon juice. Bring to a boil over high heat.

2. Place the shrimp in a colander and rinse under cold, running water. Add to the boiling water. Bring back to a boil. Cook for 3 to 5 minutes. Test 1 shrimp for tenderness after the first 3 minutes. Continue to test 1 shrimp every minute until pink and tender. Drain. Serve hot in the shell, or let cool and chill in the refrigerator for about 1 hour to serve cold.

Make Your Own Easy Seafood Sauce
If bottled cocktail sauce is too spicy or too mild, make your own. Pour 1 bottle chili sauce into a small mixing bowl. Stir in 1 teaspoon lemon juice. Stir in horseradish (from a jar) ½ teaspoon at a time, to taste. Chill for at least 1 hour to let the flavors blend.

Steamed Clams

If you're lucky enough to live where you can get fresh clams, here's how to cook them. Serve with a salad (see page 96) and Mexican Corn Bread (page 252) or saltine crackers.

 **Serves 4**

What You Need:
4 quarts fresh clams
Water, as needed
¼ cup butter (½ stick)
2 tablespoons lemon juice

What You Do:
1. Rinse the clams in cold, running water. Scrub if necessary to remove dirt. Inspect for any that are open. Keep only those that are tightly closed.
2. Place the clams in a Dutch oven or other large kettle. Pour water about 1" deep in the bottom of the pot. Cover. Bring to a boil over high heat. Cook for about 10 minutes, until the shells open.
3. While the clams are steaming, melt the butter in a saucepan or small frying pan over low heat. Stir in the lemon juice. Keep warm until ready to serve.
4. To serve, place the clams, in the shells, onto serving plates. If available, serve with seafood forks, for removing the meat from the shells. Serve the melted lemon butter on the side for dipping.

Broiled Salmon

Fresh herbs give salmon a delicate flavor. For a different taste, substitute fresh thyme for the dill weed. Choose salmon steaks or ½ of a whole salmon. Garnish with sliced fresh lemon. If you use olive oil, you don't have to heat it first. Serve with Cheesy Asparagus (page 223) and a baked potato (see "Baking Potatoes," page 113).

E

 **Serves 4**

What You Need:
¼ cup butter *or* olive oil
2 pounds salmon fillets
Salt and pepper, to taste
1 tablespoon lemon juice
½ (0.75-ounce) package fresh prewashed dill weed (*or* dried dill weed, as needed)

What You Do:
1. Melt the butter in a saucepan over low heat.

2. Preheat the broiler. Place the salmon skin-side down on the rack of a shallow broiling pan that has been sprayed with non-stick cooking spray. Drizzle the butter over the salmon. Sprinkle with lemon juice, salt, and pepper.

3. Lay sprigs of fresh dill weed diagonal to the length of the fish, evenly spaced about 1½" apart. (Or, lightly sprinkle with dried dill.)

4. Broil for 6 to 10 minutes. Test for doneness. The salmon should be opaque and flake easily with a fork.

Baked Cod

Here's a quick-fix recipe you can serve in minutes. If you can't find cod, you can substitute any white fish in this recipe.

 **Serves 4**

What You Need:
4 cod fillets
1 large white *or* yellow onion
2 tablespoons butter *or* margarine
2 tomatoes

What You Do:
1. Preheat oven to 400°. Place the fillets in an ovenproof baking pan that has been sprayed with nonstick cooking spray.
2. Slice the onion. Layer the slices over the fish. Melt the butter (or margarine) in a saucepan or small frying pan over low heat. Pour over the fish and onion. Bake uncovered for 20 minutes.
3. While the fish is cooking, rinse the tomatoes in cold, running water. Slice the tomatoes. When the fish is done, remove from oven. Layer the tomato slices on top.
4. Return to the oven and bake for 10 minutes more.

Shrimp Pesto Pasta

Even though shrimp can be expensive, this recipe calls for a small enough amount to be affordable and still contribute its seafood flavor. Look for basil pesto sauce in the dairy section of the grocery store.

 **Serves 2**

What You Need:
½ pound raw tiger shrimp
8 ounces uncooked bow tie pasta
2 tablespoons olive oil
½ (7-ounce) package basil pesto sauce *or* ¼ cup homemade Pesto (see page 228)
Grated Parmesan cheese, as needed

What You Do:
1. Rinse the shrimp in cold, running water. Peel off the shells. Remove the veins from the outer edge of the shrimp backs.

2. Cook the pasta according to package directions (boil for about 11 minutes).

3. While the pasta is cooking, cook the shrimp in the olive oil in a frying pan over medium-high heat, stirring constantly to keep them from sticking. Cook for 5 to 8 minutes, until the shrimp just turns pink. (Be careful not to overcook the shrimp, or it will become rubbery.)

4. Drain the pasta and return it to the pot. Stir in the pesto sauce. Spoon the pasta onto serving plates. Top with shrimp. Sprinkle with grated Parmesan cheese. Serve immediately.

Baked Tuna Loaf

Take a break from tuna salad with a tuna dish served warm. Serve with Chilled Pea Salad (page 101) or sliced fresh tomatoes and a steamed green vegetable (see Appendix C).

Serves 6

What You Need:

Shortening *or* vegetable oil, as needed
1 (12-ounce) can tuna
1 stalk celery
3 cups unseasoned bread crumbs
1 egg
1 tablespoon dried minced onion

1 teaspoon salt
¼ teaspoon pepper
½ (7-ounce) can mushroom stems and pieces
1 (10.5-ounce) can condensed cream of chicken soup

What You Do:

1. Preheat oven to 375°. Use a paper towel and solid shortening (or vegetable oil) to grease a shallow ovenproof 9" × 13" baking pan. Set aside.

2. Drain the tuna. Use a fork to flake the tuna into a large mixing bowl.

3. Chop the celery. Add to the tuna along with the bread crumbs, egg, onion, salt, and pepper.

4. Use your hands to squish together all the ingredients, until well blended. Form into a loaf shape. Place in the prepared baking pan.

5. Drain the mushrooms and place in a small mixing bowl. Stir in the soup (do *not* dilute). Pour over the tuna loaf. Bake uncovered for 30 minutes.

Crabmeat Casserole

Here's an economical casserole that provides the flavor of crab-meat without the expense and without the effort of removing the shell. Serve with Cucumber Salad (page 90), Cold Mixed Veggies Salad (page 93), or a steamed green vegetable (see Appendix C).

 **Serves 2**

What You Need:

½ cup milk

¾ cup bread crumbs, plus extra for sprinkling over the top

2 (4.5-ounce) cans cooked crabmeat (*or* 8 ounces imitation crab)

3 hard-boiled eggs (see Boiled Egg, page 9)

¾ teaspoon salt

⅛ teaspoon dry mustard

Dash cayenne pepper

3 tablespoons butter

Shortening, vegetable oil, *or* nonstick cooking spray, as needed

What You Do:

1. In a large mixing bowl, stir together the milk and bread crumbs. Drain the crabmeat (if using canned) or chop the imitation crab. Add to the bowl.

2. Peel the hard-boiled eggs. Cut the eggs in half lengthwise and separate the whites and yolks. Chop whites into small pieces. Add to bowl.

3. Preheat oven to 450°. Place the egg yolks on a saucer or in a separate small bowl. Mash with a fork. Add to the crab mixture along with salt, dry mustard, and cayenne pepper.

4. Melt the butter. Drizzle the butter over the ingredients in the bowl. Gently stir the ingredients together until well mixed.

5. Pour mixture into a greased baking dish. Top with bread crumbs. Bake uncovered for 15 minutes, until heated through.

Garlicky Pasta with Veggies and Shrimp

This simple and delicious pasta has tons of variations. Use your imagination (or whatever leftovers you have in your fridge) to make this quick pasta dish. You can use fresh or frozen cooked or raw shrimp in this recipe. If precooked, thaw first. If raw, thaw and cook in 1 tablespoon of olive oil over medium-high heat just until almost tender. (It will cook more when combined with the other ingredients.) Cremini or button mushrooms are both good choices to use in this recipe.

Serves 4

What You Need:
16 large precooked shrimp (thaw if frozen)
2 fresh plum *or* Roma tomatoes
1 red bell pepper
½ cup fresh spinach *or* frozen chopped spinach (thawed)
½ medium-size white *or* yellow onion
2 cloves fresh garlic *or* ¼ teaspoon dried minced garlic
2 tablespoons olive oil
½ (8-ounce) package fresh sliced mushrooms
8 ounces uncooked penne rigate pasta
1 tablespoon lemon juice
Salt and pepper, to taste
1–2 tablespoons grated Parmesan *or* Romano cheese

Garlicky Pasta with
Veggies and Shrimp (continued)

What You Do:

1. Remove the shells, tails, and veins from the shrimp, if necessary. Rinse the tomatoes and pepper under cold water. Remove the seeds and inner ribs from the pepper. Chop the tomatoes, bell pepper, and spinach. Set aside. Chop the onion and mince the garlic by chopping it into very small pieces.

2. Pour the olive oil into a large frying pan over medium-high heat. Stir in the onion and fresh garlic and cook for 1 minute, stirring constantly. (If you're using dried minced garlic, add it later with the rest of the vegetables instead.) Reduce heat to medium. Add the tomatoes, bell pepper, and mushrooms. Cook the vegetables, stirring constantly, until they are tender but still firm.

3. Cook the pasta according to package directions until tender but still firm. Drain and rinse immediately with cold water. Stir into the vegetable mixture along with the shrimp and spinach. Use 2 table forks to toss until well mixed.

4. Add the lemon juice, salt, and pepper. Stir until heated through. Sprinkle with cheese.

> **Testing Pasta**
> Test pasta for doneness when you have about 1 minute left in the amount of cooking time called for in package directions. Use a slotted spoon or spaghetti server to withdraw several noodles from the pot. Place in a colander and let cool for 10 or 15 seconds. Bite into the noodle. It should be tender but still a bit firm. Be careful not to overcook. Test several times as noodles continue to cook if necessary.

Baked and Flaked Haddock
with Rice Casserole

The smoked flavor of this dish makes it a favorite example of Scottish cuisine. Serve with sliced tomatoes and a steamed green vegetable (see Appendix C).

Serves 4

What You Need:

½ pound smoked haddock fillets
1 cup uncooked rice
1 hard-boiled egg (see Boiled Egg, page 9)
2 tablespoons butter *or* margarine
2 tablespoons lemon juice
2 teaspoons dried parsley flakes
Salt and pepper, to taste

What You Do:

1. Preheat oven to 400°. Place the fillets in an ovenproof baking pan that has been sprayed with nonstick cooking spray. Bake uncovered for 25 minutes. Remove from oven.

2. While the fish is cooking, prepare the rice by cooking it according to package directions.

3. When the fish is done, flake it with a fork. (Remove the skin if present.) Peel and crumble the hard-boiled egg. In a large frying pan, melt the butter (or margarine) over low heat. Add the fish. Cook for 3 minutes, stirring to reheat the fish evenly. Stir in the cooked rice, egg, lemon juice, parsley flakes, salt, and pepper. Serve immediately.

Salmon Casserole

Bring home the flavor of the Pacific Northwest with this salmon and pasta dish. You can substitute angel hair or penne pasta for the egg noodles in this recipe. Serve with steamed asparagus or broccoli (see Appendix C).

 **Serves 2**

What You Need:

4 ounces uncooked egg noodles

1 (10¾-ounce) can condensed tomato soup

1 cup grated Cheddar cheese

2 teaspoons lemon juice

1 tablespoon dried minced onion

1 teaspoon prepared mustard

2 teaspoons Worcestershire sauce

1 (14.75-ounce) can salmon, with liquid

2 tablespoons butter *or* margarine

¾ cup butter cracker crumbs

What You Do:

1. Cook the pasta according to package directions.

2. Preheat oven to 375°. While the noodles are cooking, place the soup, cheese, lemon juice, onion, mustard, and Worcestershire sauce into a 2-quart ovenproof baking pan that has been sprayed with nonstick cooking spray. Flake the salmon, with the liquid, into the pan. Stir until well blended.

3. Melt the butter (or margarine) in a separate saucepan. Stir in the cracker crumbs. When the noodles are done, drain. Add to the baking pan. Gently stir until well mixed. Top with the crumb mixture. Bake for 40 minutes, until the topping has browned.

Crab Tetrazzini

There's nothing like the sweet taste of crabmeat to turn everyone into a seafood lover. Serve with cold spiced peaches and steamed green beans (see Appendix C). Add ½ cup water or milk to the leftover tomato soup and serve for lunch.

🍴 Serves 4 🍴

What You Need:

½ (10-ounce) package spaghetti noodles
Shortening, vegetable oil, *or* nonstick cooking spray, as needed
½ small white *or* yellow onion
1 tablespoon butter *or* margarine
¼ pound fresh sliced mushrooms

½ (10¾-ounce) can condensed tomato soup
¾ cup crabmeat *or* imitation crab
1 cup tomato juice
Salt and pepper, to taste
1 cup shredded sharp Cheddar cheese

What You Do:

1. Break the spaghetti into thirds and cook according to package directions. Drain. Preheat oven to 350°. Grease an ovenproof baking pan with shortening or vegetable oil, or spray with nonstick cooking spray.

2. While the noodles are cooking, chop the onion. Melt the butter (or margarine) over medium heat in a small saucepan. Stir in the onion and mushrooms; cook until tender. Transfer the mixture to the prepared baking pan.

3. Stir in the soup, crabmeat, tomato juice, salt, pepper, and ½ of the cheese. When the noodles are done, drain. Gently stir into the crab mixture. Top with the remaining cheese. Bake for 35 to 40 minutes.

Broiled Orange Roughy

You'll often find orange roughy fillets in the frozen foods section of your supermarket. Thaw before cooking.

 **Serves 2**

What You Need:
1 pound orange roughy fillets
½ cup mayonnaise
½ cup grated Parmesan cheese
1 tablespoon lemon juice
Garlic salt, to taste
Dash paprika
1 medium-size white *or* yellow onion
¼ cup parsley flakes

What You Do:
1. Spray a broiler rack with nonstick cooking spray. Place the fillets on the rack.

2. In a small mixing bowl, stir together the mayonnaise, cheese, lemon juice, garlic salt, and paprika. Spread the mixture onto the fillets.

3. Preheat the broiler. Thinly slice the onion. Arrange the slices on top of the fillets. Sprinkle with parsley. Cover the pan with aluminum foil. Broil for 7 minutes. Remove from oven. Uncover and broil for 5 to 6 minutes more, until golden brown. (No need to turn the fillets.)

Salmon Patties

These tasty patties are a fish alternative to hamburgers. Serve with fresh lemon wedges and Cheesy Asparagus (page 223) or Rice Casserole (page 237). You can buy "plain" or "seasoned" packaged bread crumbs. Seasoned bread crumbs are preferred in this recipe.

 **Yields 6 patties**

What You Need:

1 (14.75-ounce) can salmon

2 green onions

1 egg

½ cup seasoned bread crumbs

Vegetable oil, as needed

What You Do:

1. Drain the salmon. Use a table fork to flake the salmon into a large mixing bowl. Slice the green onions, including the dark green tops. Add to the bowl. Stir with the fork.

2. In a small mixing bowl, use the fork to beat the egg enough to break the yolk and slightly mix it with the white. Stir in 2 tablespoons of the bread crumbs. Place the remaining bread crumbs on a saucer. Set aside.

3. Use your hands to form the mixture into 6 patties, as you would make hamburger patties.

4. Pour the vegetable oil to about ¼" deep in a large frying pan over medium heat. Dip both sides of each patty into the bread crumbs on the saucer. Place the patties in the frying pan. Cook for 4 minutes, until the bottom is crisp and golden brown. Use a pancake turner to flip to the other side. Cook for another 4 minutes.

Jambalaya

You can use any type of poultry, sausage, fish, or seafood in this Cajun favorite. For the best results, use a combination of 2 or 3 of these ingredients. For traditional flavor, choose from andouille sausage, chicken, shrimp, oysters, crayfish, or alligator, but any fish or sausage will work, particularly the spicy and flavorful chorizo sausage popular in Mexico. Common combinations include chicken/sausage and shrimp/oysters.

 **Serves 4**

What You Need:

3 cups cooked poultry, sausage, fish, *or* seafood
1 medium-size white *or* yellow onion
1 green bell pepper
2 stalks celery
2 tablespoons vegetable oil
¼ teaspoon dried minced garlic

1 teaspoon cayenne pepper
Salt and pepper, to taste
1 (14.5-ounce) can chicken *or* vegetable broth
¼ cup water
1 cup uncooked rice

What You Do:

1. Cut the meat and/or fish into bite-size pieces. Set aside. Chop the onion, green bell pepper, and celery. Keep chopped ingredients separate.

2. Pour the vegetable oil into a large frying pan. Cook the meat/fish, onion, and garlic in the oil over medium-high heat for 5 minutes, stirring often. Stir in the green bell pepper and celery; cook 3 minutes more. Sprinkle with cayenne pepper, salt, and pepper.

3. Stir in the broth and water. Bring to a boil. Add the rice. Cover and cook for about 20 minutes, until the rice is tender. Stir occasionally.

Baked Tilapia with
matoes and Olives

..iavorful, farm-raised white fish that is native to ... It is the fastest-growing product of American aquaculture, developed through selective breeding to supplement imported fish. If you prefer, you can substitute any white, flaky fish fillets in this recipe.

Serves 6

What You Need:

6 tilapia fillets (*or* other white fish)
Salt, to taste
3 medium-size tomatoes
¼ red onion
½ cup green olives

¼ cup extra-virgin olive oil
¼ teaspoon thyme
¼ teaspoon dried hot red pepper flakes
¼ teaspoon dried minced garlic
1 tablespoon fresh lime juice

What You Do:

1. Preheat oven to 400°. Place the thawed or fresh fillets skin-side down in a single layer in the bottom of an ovenproof baking pan that has been greased with vegetable oil or sprayed with nonstick cooking spray. Sprinkle the fillets with salt.

2. Chop the tomatoes, onion, and olives and place them in a small mixing bowl. Stir in the olive oil, thyme, red pepper flakes, garlic, and lime juice. Spoon the mixture over the fish.

3. Place the baking pan, uncovered, on the middle rack of the oven. Bake for 15 to 20 minutes, just until the fish flakes easily.

Vegetarian and Vegan Entrées

en Noodles Extreme 🥕

...es from a side dish into a vegetarian meal.
...asty, and full of vitamin C and other nutrients.

🍴 Serves 4 🍴

What You Need:
4 (3-ounce) packages Ramen noodles
1 cup frozen peas
1 (14.5-ounce) can diced tomatoes

1 tablespoon butter *or* margarine
Grated Parmesan cheese, to taste

What You Do:
1. Cook the noodles in a saucepan according to package directions. While cooking, stir in the frozen peas.
2. Reduce heat to low. Drain the tomatoes. Add the tomatoes and margarine to the noodles. Heat until butter (or margarine) has melted and the peas are tender. Spoon into serving bowls and sprinkle with Parmesan cheese.

Vegetable First Aid
You can use bags of frozen vegetables as first aid for headaches, bumps, and sprains. Just grab the bag from the freezer and use it as an ice pack. Don't place the frozen vegetable bag (or any ice pack) directly on the skin. Instead, place a kitchen towel between the injury and the ice. This tip is especially useful if you're babysitting someone's child. When you tell the parents about the big bump on their son or daughter's forehead, smile and say, "Don't worry, I put broccoli on it."

Mac 'n' Cheese

Packaged macaroni and cheese is so easy, you might prefer to make that. However, if you prefer homemade flavor, here's an easy recipe. Serve this vegetarian dish with sliced fresh tomatoes and steamed asparagus (see Appendix C).

Serves 4

What You Need:

3 quarts water

2 cups uncooked macaroni noodles (about 8 ounces)

3 tablespoons butter *or* margarine

½ cup shredded Cheddar cheese

1 cup milk

Paprika, as needed

What You Do:

1. Bring the water to a boil in a saucepan over high heat. Add the noodles. Cook according to package directions (about 8 minutes), until the noodles are tender but still firm. Drain. Return the noodles to the pan and reduce heat to low.

2. Stir in the butter and cheese until melted. Stir in the milk. Cook until heated through, stirring often. Sprinkle with paprika and serve.

Variation:
Nutty Mac

Pecans add a sweet flavor, and sour cream adds body for a main course or side dish. You'll never want plain macaroni and cheese again. In place of butter or margarine, add ½ cup sour cream and ½ cup chopped pecans.

Parmesan Noodles

These cheesy noodles can serve as a tasty lunch, dinner entrée, or side dish. Although fresh ingredients taste better, you can use dried parsley flakes and canned grated Parmesan cheese.

Serves 4

What You Need:

8 ounces medium egg noodles

¼ cup butter *or* margarine

¼ teaspoon garlic powder

2 tablespoons fresh parsley

2 tablespoons grated Parmesan cheese

What You Do:

1. In a large saucepan, cook the noodles according to package directions. Drain and return to the pan.

2. While the noodles are cooking, melt the butter (or margarine) in a separate saucepan. Add the garlic powder. When the noodles are ready, pour the butter over them. Stir until the noodles are well coated.

3. Chop the parsley and sprinkle it over the noodles. Sprinkle with Parmesan cheese. Serve warm.

Measuring Butter

The easiest way to measure butter or margarine in stick form is to look at the markings on the wrapper. Lines indicate 1 tablespoon increments. Here are commonly called for amounts:

¼ cup = 4 tablespoons = ½ stick

⅓ cup = 5 tablespoons plus 1 teaspoon

½ cup = 8 tablespoons = 1 stick

Welsh Rarebit

This tasty cheese dish, a substitute for roasted rabbit, originated among Welsh peasants, who were prohibited from taking game from estates of the aristocracy. Today it's a favorite meatless main course served over toasted bread.

Serves 2

What You Need:
1 tablespoon butter
2 cups shredded Cheddar cheese
$\frac{1}{8}$ teaspoon salt
$\frac{1}{8}$ teaspoon dry mustard
Dash cayenne pepper
1 egg
$\frac{1}{4}$ cup milk
2 slices bread

What You Do:
1. Melt the butter over very low heat. Stir in the cheese, salt, dry mustard, and cayenne pepper. Heat until the cheese melts.
2. In a small mixing bowl, beat together the egg and milk. Stir into the cheese mixture. Continue stirring until the mixture thickens.
3. Toast the bread and place on serving plates. Spoon the cheese sauce on top. Serve immediately.

Baked Ziti

Ziti is a tube-shaped pasta you'll find in the spaghetti aisle in your supermarket. For a nice finishing touch, sprinkle with Parmesan cheese or fresh chopped basil.

Serves 4

What You Need:

8 ounces uncooked ziti

A few drops olive oil, as needed

1 (15-ounce) can tomato sauce

8 ounces ricotta cheese

12 cups shredded mozzarella cheese

1–2 sprigs fresh parsley

What You Do:

1. Cook the ziti according to package directions until tender but still firm. Drain the noodles in a colander. Rinse with cold water and drain again. Leave the noodles in the colander and sprinkle with a few drops of olive oil. Gently stir until the noodles are lightly coated. Preheat oven to 350°.

2. Pour ½ of the tomato sauce into an ovenproof baking pan that has been sprayed with nonstick cooking spray. Place ½ of the cooked ziti in the pan. Layer the ricotta on top of the ziti and sprinkle with ½ of the mozzarella. Use the rest of the ziti to make a new layer. Pour on the rest of the tomato sauce. Sprinkle with the other half of the mozzarella.

3. Bake for 25 minutes or until the cheese bubbles and slightly browns. While the casserole is baking, rinse the parsley in cold, running water. Pat dry with a paper towel. Chop the parsley and sprinkle it over the cooked casserole just before serving.

Eggplant Surprise

No need for fancy dishes with this entrée. The eggplant shell placed on a dinner plate becomes your serving bowl. For a vegan variation, omit the cheese.

 **Serves 2**

What You Need:

1 whole fresh eggplant

1 Roma tomato (also known as plum tomato)

1 green onion

¼ cup sliced fresh mushrooms

¼ teaspoon minced garlic

⅛ teaspoon fresh ground black pepper

½ teaspoon dried basil

2 tablespoons olive oil

½ cup shredded mozzarella cheese

What You Do:

1. Cut the eggplant in half lengthwise, remove the seeds, and scoop out the flesh. Leave ¼" to ½" of flesh attached to the interior of the shell for support. Set aside the shells.

2. Cut the eggplant flesh and tomato into bite-size pieces (about 1" cubes). Slice about 4" of the green onion, including about half of the dark green part.

3. In a frying pan over medium-high heat, cook the eggplant, tomato, onion, mushrooms, garlic, pepper, and basil in the olive oil, stirring constantly until tender but still firm. Remove from heat. Add the mozzarella cheese. Set aside until the cheese melts.

4. With a slotted spoon to drain off the oil, spoon half of the mixture into each eggplant shell half. Serve warm.

Broiled Portabella
Mushroom Caps

M

This colorful, easy entrée looks and tastes like gourmet cooking, especially if you use fresh herbs. You can make this recipe as an attractive side dish by using baby portobellos about 3" to 4" in diameter. Use 1 baby mushroom cap per serving.

Serves 2

What You Need:
2 tablespoons butter *or* margarine
2 portabella mushroom caps (about 4" to 5" in diameter)
2 small tomatoes
2 tablespoons fresh basil (*or* ¼ to ½ teaspoon dried basil)
1 clove garlic (*or* ⅛ teaspoon dried minced garlic)
2 tablespoons olive oil
Freshly grated Parmesan cheese, as needed

What You Do:
1. Melt the butter (or margarine) in a small frying pan over medium-high heat. Place the mushroom caps, rounded-side up, in the frying pan. Move the mushroom caps around during the cooking, until the mushrooms are tender. Remove from frying pan. Place, rounded-side down, in an ungreased pie tin (*don't* use glass).

2. Preheat broiler. Chop the tomatoes, basil, and garlic. Stir together in a small mixing bowl. Spoon the tomato mixture into the mushroom caps. Drizzle olive oil over the tomato mixture. Generously sprinkle with Parmesan cheese. Broil for 5 minutes, until the cheese bubbles. Serve warm.

Stir-Fry Veggie Combo

Chickpeas, also known as garbanzo beans, are high in protein, enabling this dish to be served over rice as a vegetarian main course. Or, you can serve this combo as a side dish for Pot Roast (page 130) or Roast Chicken (page 154).

Serves 4

What You Need:
1 green bell pepper
1 stalk celery
¼ medium-size white *or* yellow onion
3 small zucchini (about 6" long)
1 medium tomato
2 tablespoons olive oil
½ cup chickpeas

What You Do:
1. Cut the green pepper in half and remove the stem, seeds, and inner "ribs." Chop the green pepper, celery, and onion. Place in a small mixing bowl. Set aside. Cut the zucchini in half lengthwise and then slice crosswise into ½"-thick pieces. Keep separate from the celery mixture. Cut the tomato into ½" cubes. Set aside.

2. Pour the olive oil into a frying pan over medium-high heat. Stirring constantly, cook the green pepper, celery, onion, and garbanzo beans in the olive oil for 6 minutes. Reduce heat to medium. Stir in the zucchini and cook for 5 more minutes. Stir in the tomatoes and continue cooking just until the tomato is tender.

Tomato Pie

You can vary the flavor of this tasty pie by substituting Swiss, mozzarella, or your favorite cheese for the Cheddar. Use only Roma or plum tomatoes. Other varieties are too juicy. Cover and refrigerate leftovers. Eat the next day.

M

Serves 6

What You Need:
1 (10") frozen deep-dish pie crust
6 fresh Roma tomatoes
½ (0.75-ounce) package of fresh, prewashed basil
2 cups shredded Cheddar cheese

What You Do:

1. Set out the frozen pie crust to thaw. Rinse the tomatoes under cold, running water. Cut crosswise into slices approximately ¼" thick. Use kitchen scissors to snip the basil into small pieces.

2. Preheat oven to 350°. Layer ½ of the tomato slices in the bottom of the pie crust. Sprinkle with ½ of the basil. Sprinkle 1 cup of the cheese over the basil. Layer the remaining tomato slices on top of the cheese. Sprinkle with the remaining basil.

3. Bake for 40 to 50 minutes. Let cool for 20 minutes before cutting.

Pesto Rigatoni

What could be more delicious than garlicky pesto flavor in a cheesy tomato pasta dish? Serve with a simple mixed greens salad and French bread (page 117). You can substitute linguine for the rigatoni. Just change the name to Pesto Linguine.

Serves 4

What You Need:

3 pints cherry *or* grape tomatoes
1 whole head fresh garlic
½ cup fresh basil (*or* 2 tablespoons dried basil)
½ cup pine nuts

2 tablespoons olive oil
1 teaspoon salt
1 (16-ounce) package rigatoni
½ cup Parmesan cheese

What You Do:

1. Rinse the tomatoes in cold, running water. Slice lengthwise into halves. Mince the garlic by cutting it into small pieces. Roughly chop the basil.

2. Place the pine nuts in a small, dry frying pan over medium heat. Stir until they turn brown. Remove from heat.

3. In a large saucepan, heat the olive oil on low. Add the tomatoes and salt. Cook for 3 minutes. Add the garlic and cook for 1 minute. Stir in the roasted pine nuts and the basil. Stir occasionally until the tomato mixture cooks down into a sauce.

4. Cook the pasta in a Dutch oven according to package directions. Drain. Return the pasta to the Dutch oven. Pour the sauce over the pasta. Stir until well mixed. Cook over low heat for about 2 minutes until heated through. Add the Parmesan and toss to mix.

Lentil Loaf

M Refrigerate the leftover egg yolks in a covered container. Use them the next morning to make Scrambled Eggs (page 10), Huevos Rancheros (page 19), or a breakfast egg casserole.

Serves 4

What You Need:
1 cup uncooked lentils
½ small white *or* yellow onion
2 stalks celery
¼ cup chopped walnuts
5 slices bread (white or whole wheat)

2 eggs
1 (8-ounce) can tomato sauce
½ teaspoon garlic powder
Salt and pepper, to taste

What You Do:
1. Cook the lentils according to package directions. While the lentils are cooking, chop the onion and celery into very small pieces. Place in a large mixing bowl.

2. Preheat oven to 350°. When the lentils are done, drain. Add to the mixing bowl with the onion and celery. Stir in the walnuts. Tear the bread slices into pieces and add them to the bowl.

3. Separate the eggs (see "Chef's Secret: Separating Eggs," page 315) over a small mixing bowl. (Wash your hands and the mixing bowl with soap and warm water after handling raw eggs.) Add the egg whites to the onion and celery mixture. Stir in tomato sauce, garlic powder, salt, and pepper until well mixed.

4. Pour the mixture into a 4" × 8" loaf pan that has been greased with shortening. Bake for 25 to 30 minutes. Test for doneness. A knife inserted into the middle should come out clean. Remove from the oven and let cool for 7 to 10 minutes. Serve.

Spinach Manicotti

A gooey blend of 3 cheeses gives this traditional Italian dish its flavor. Serve with breadsticks or French bread (page 117).

Serves 4

What You Need:

8–10 manicotti shells
1½ cups fresh spinach leaves
1 egg
1 (15-ounce) carton ricotta cheese
½ cup grated Parmesan cheese

½ teaspoon salt
¼ teaspoon pepper
Shortening *or* nonstick cooking spray
1 (15-ounce) can tomato sauce
½ cup shredded mozzarella cheese

What You Do:

1. Cook the manicotti according to package directions. Drain.

2. Rinse the spinach under cold, running water. Remove the stems. Place the spinach in a steamer or a steamer insert in a saucepan. Add about 1" of water. Bring to a boil. Cover and steam about 10 minutes, until the spinach wilts. Drain and squeeze out excess water. Set aside.

3. Crack the egg into a large mixing bowl. Beat with a fork until well blended. Stir in the ricotta, Parmesan, salt, and pepper. Add the spinach and toss with 2 forks until well coated. Preheat oven to 350°. Use solid shortening or nonstick cooking spray to grease an ovenproof baking dish.

4. Scoop the spinach mixture into the shells. Arrange the stuffed shells in a single layer in the baking dish. Pour the tomato sauce over them. Sprinkle with mozzarella. Bake uncovered for 30 to 40 minutes. The dish is done when the sauce in the middle of the pan bubbles.

Quick Vegan Enchiladas

If you don't eat meat, you can still enjoy the fiesta flavor of these enchiladas made with tofu instead of beef. Top with tofu sour cream (see "How to Make Tofu Sour Cream," page 207). Serve with shredded lettuce, black olives, or Easy Guacamole (page 253).

🍴 Yields about 12 enchiladas 🍴

What You Need:
2 baking potatoes
1 (28-ounce) can red enchilada sauce
1 (28-ounce) can water
9 ounces firm tofu
1 medium-size white *or* yellow onion
1 (15.5-ounce) can chili beans
3 tablespoons chili powder
1 tablespoon cumin
2 tablespoons garlic powder
Salt and pepper, to taste
12 (8") flour tortillas

What You Do:
1. Rinse the potatoes under cold, running water. Peel and cut into quarters. Boil for about 20 minutes, until tender. (Check by piercing with a fork.) Drain and let cool. Cut the potatoes into ½" cubes. Place in a large mixing bowl. Set aside.

2. Pour the enchilada sauce and water into a 1-quart saucepan over low heat. Stir often while preparing the rest of the tortilla filling.

Quick Vegan Enchiladas
(continued)

3. Crumble the tofu or cut into ½" cubes. Chop the onion. Add to the potatoes in mixing bowl. Drain the beans. Add to the potatoes. Stir in the chili powder, cumin, garlic powder, salt, and pepper.

4. Preheat oven to 350°. Spray a 9" × 13" ovenproof baking pan with nonstick cooking spray. Spoon in just enough enchilada sauce to cover the bottom of the pan.

5. Dip a tortilla into the remaining enchilada sauce in the saucepan and place in the baking pan. Spoon about ⅓ cup of the filling mixture across the tortilla. Fold the bottom ¼ of the tortilla over the filling mixture. Wrap the right side of the tortilla halfway over the filling (and the already folded bottom section). Wrap the left side of the tortilla over the right side. Carefully turn over the enchilada and place seam-side down in the baking pan. Repeat with the remaining tortillas. Pour the remaining enchilada sauce over the enchiladas. Bake for 20 to 25 minutes.

How to Make Tofu Sour Cream

Use tofu sour cream to top your favorite dishes from Mexico and the American Southwest. In a small mixing bowl, use a wooden spoon or electric mixer to blend together one 12-ounce package silken soft tofu, 2 tablespoons vegetable oil, 1 tablespoon lemon juice, 1½ teaspoons sugar (or honey), and ½ teaspoon salt. Makes about 1½ cups.

Baked Spinach and
Eggplant Casserole

Eggplant takes on the flavors of surrounding ingredients and makes this casserole tasty and filling. A great potluck dish.

Serves 6

What You Need:

3 fresh tomatoes
2 cups fresh spinach
1 tablespoon parsley flakes
1 cup uncooked macaroni noodles
1¼ cups canned stewed tomatoes, with juice
1 eggplant

3 cloves garlic (*or* ⅜ teaspoon dried minced garlic)
⅓ cup olive oil
¾ teaspoon salt
¾ teaspoon pepper

What You Do:

1. Rinse the tomatoes in cold water. Slice them and place in a layer in the bottom of a greased ovenproof baking dish.

2. Rinse the spinach in cold, running water. Drain and chop. Sprinkle the tomatoes with the spinach and parsley.

3. Place the noodles on a cutting board. Cover with waxed paper. Use a rolling pin to crush the macaroni. Sprinkle the crushed macaroni noodles in a layer over the sliced tomatoes. Pour the canned tomatoes and juice over the crushed noodles.

4. Preheat oven to 350°. Rinse the eggplant in cold, running water. Slice in half lengthwise. Remove the seeds. Slice the eggplant crosswise. Place in a layer on top of the stewed tomatoes.

5. Mince the garlic by chopping it into very small pieces. Place in a small mixing bowl. Stir in the olive oil, salt, and pepper. Drizzle the mixture over the eggplant. Bake uncovered for 30 minutes.

Cold Sesame Noodles

Tahini is ground sesame seeds. It has the consistency of peanut butter that's been ground fresh from whole peanuts. Look for it in the gourmet foods section or the Middle Eastern, Asian, or international foods' section of your supermarket. Or, it's sometimes shelved in the peanut butter aisle.

Serves 6

What You Need:

1 (16-ounce) package linguine
½ teaspoon sesame oil
5 tablespoons water
2 tablespoons tahini
¼ cup creamy peanut butter
1 tablespoon vinegar

2 tablespoons soy sauce
1 tablespoon white granulated sugar
½ teaspoon crushed red pepper
Pinch of black pepper
1 green onion, including green top (optional)
1 tablespoon sesame seeds

What You Do:

1. Cook the noodles according to package directions. Drain and rinse with cold water. Drain well. Place in a large mixing bowl. Drizzle the sesame oil over the noodles. Toss until well coated. Cover and refrigerate.

2. Bring the water to a boil in a saucepan over high heat. Stir in the tahini and peanut butter until smooth. Reduce heat to medium.

3. Stir in the vinegar, soy sauce, sugar, red pepper, and black pepper. Stir until smooth and well blended. Set aside.

4. When ready to serve, chop the green onions. Remove the noodles from the refrigerator. Add the green onions to the noodles. Add dressing 1 tablespoon at a time. Toss until the noodles are well coated. Sprinkle with sesame seeds.

Black Bean Burritos

 Cilantro, also called Chinese or Mexican parsley, is an herb with a distinctive flavor similar to sage with citrus. Not everyone likes cilantro. If you've never tasted it, give it a try in a small quantity before adding to the entire recipe. If it's not for you, substitute chopped regular parsley or dried parsley flakes

Serves 4

What You Need:

1 cup uncooked rice
½ medium-size white *or* yellow onion
1 tablespoon vegetable oil
2 medium-size tomatoes
1 ripe avocado
4 (8") flour tortillas
1 (15-ounce) can black beans, with liquid
⅛ teaspoon ground cumin
⅛ teaspoon dried minced garlic
1 cup shredded Cheddar *or* Monterey jack cheese
¼ cup bottled salsa
¼ cup sour cream
½ cup fresh cilantro *or* 2 tablespoons dried parsley flakes (optional)

What You Do:

1. Cook the rice according to package directions. While the rice is cooking, chop the onion. Pour the vegetable oil into a large frying pan over medium-high heat. Add the onions, and cook, stirring constantly, until lightly brown and tender. Remove from heat. Cover to keep warm. Set aside.

2. Preheat oven to 350°. Chop the tomatoes. Set aside. Peel and slice the avocado. Set aside.

Black Bean Burritos 🥕
(continued)

3. Place the tortillas on an ungreased baking sheet. Warm in oven for 10 minutes, until softened. (Or place between damp paper towels in the microwave on high for 40 seconds.) While the tortillas are warming, place the black beans and the liquid from the can into a medium-size saucepan over medium heat. Stir in the cumin and garlic until the mixture is heated through.

4. Remove the tortillas from the oven and place on serving plates. Spoon the onions in a line across the middle of each tortilla. Sprinkle with cheese and top with rice, the black bean mixture, the salsa, avocado, sour cream, and cilantro (or parsley).

5. Fold up the bottom $1/3$ of each tortilla to cover the fillings. Fold side flaps in, over each other. Fold down the top $1/3$ of the tortilla. Place on the serving plate seam-side down. Serve warm.

About Avocados

The avocado's rough skin and pear shape have earned it the nickname "alligator pear." Both ancient Mayan and Aztec written records refer to the tropical fruit. In fact, the Aztecs considered avocados an aphrodisiac and protected all unmarried women during avocado season. The Spanish explorer Hernando Cortés ate avocados with Montezuma II in Mexico City in 1519. Fresh avocados should be stored at room temperature until they are ripe. Test for ripeness by gently squeezing the fruit. It should "give" to slight pressure. Most avocados remain green when ripe, although the lighter the color, the less ripe the fruit. The Hass variety turns black when ripe.

Spinach and Feta Cheese Pie

If you're short on time, use frozen chopped spinach (thawed) instead of fresh.

✨ Serves 8 ✨

What You Need:

1 (10") deep-dish pie crust
4 cups fresh spinach
1 white *or* yellow onion
3 tablespoons olive oil
1 cup grated Swiss cheese
2 eggs
1¼ cups light cream

½ teaspoon salt
¼ teaspoon black pepper
Pinch nutmeg
¼ cup grated Parmesan cheese
6 ounces feta cheese, crumbled
2 medium tomatoes (optional)

What You Do:

1. Preheat oven to 375°. Bake the pie crust for 5 minutes. Remove from oven. Turn off heat.

2. Rinse the spinach under cold, running water. Remove the stems. Place the spinach in a steamer or a steamer insert in a saucepan. Add about 1" of water. Bring to a boil. Cover and steam for about 10 minutes, until the spinach wilts. Drain and squeeze out excess water. Chop and place in a medium-size mixing bowl. Set aside.

Spinach and Feta Cheese Pie
(continued)

3. Chop the onion. Heat the olive oil in a small frying pan over medium-high heat. Cook the onion until golden brown, stirring constantly. Add the onions in the bowl with the spinach. Add the Swiss cheese and toss well. Set aside.

4. In an electric blender, combine the eggs, cream, salt, pepper, nutmeg, and Parmesan cheese. (Or, use an electric mixer in a mixing bowl.) Blend for 1 minute. Preheat oven to 350°.

5. Pour the spinach mixture into the pie crust. Sprinkle with feta cheese. If you're using tomatoes, rinse them under cold, running water. Slice them and arrange in a layer on top of the cheese. Pour the egg mixture over top. Check with your fingers to ensure that it seeps through all the way to the bottom. Bake for 45 minutes. The pie is done when a knife inserted into the center comes out clean.

Types of Olive Oil

If you've tried to buy olive oil, you've likely stared at the labels wondering which type to choose. The 3 main types to worry about are pure, virgin, and extra-virgin. These labels pertain to the olive oil's grade, which is determined by the amount of oleic acid. The less acid, the better. So extra-virgin, which has the least acid—as well as the strongest smell and flavor—is the best quality. If you see "light" olive oil, don't think it's a diet food. The term applies to the pale color and bland flavor, not the calorie count.

Mushroom Tofu Stir-Fry

Hoisin is an Asian sauce. Look for it and sesame oil in the international foods' section close to such Chinese foods as canned water chestnuts. Serve with white or brown rice.

Serves 4

What You Need:
½ pound fresh shiitake mushrooms
4 cups hot water
1 medium-size white *or* yellow onion
1 bunch scallions *or* green onions
1 tablespoon fresh gingerroot
1 clove fresh garlic (*or* ⅛ teaspoon dried minced garlic)
2 tablespoons vegetable oil
3 tablespoons hoisin sauce
½ teaspoon sesame oil
½ teaspoon salt
½ teaspoon vinegar
1 (20-ounce) package silken tofu
1½ teaspoons cornstarch
1 tablespoon water

What You Do:
1. Soak the mushrooms in the 4 cups of hot water for at least 20 minutes. While the mushrooms are soaking, cut the onion in half lengthwise. Slice lengthwise. Set aside. Drain the mushrooms over a small mixing bowl to save the liquid. Remove the mushroom stems and cut the mushrooms into slices about ¼" thick. Set aside.

Mushroom Tofu Stir-Fry
(continued)

2. Chop the scallions. Finely chop the gingerroot and garlic. Heat the vegetable oil in a large frying pan on medium-high. Add the scallions, gingerroot, and garlic. Stir constantly for about 5 minutes, until the scallions are just tender (if using onions, they should be translucent). Reduce heat to low.

3. In a small mixing bowl, stir together the hoisin sauce and sesame oil. Stir into the vegetables along with the salt, vinegar, and 1 cup of the soaking liquid from the mushrooms. Cook for 5 minutes, stirring occasionally.

4. Cut the tofu into 1" cubes. Set aside. Dissolve the cornstarch in the 1 tablespoon water. Stir into the vegetables until well mixed and slightly thickened. Place the tofu cubes on top of the vegetables. Cover and cook for about 5 minutes, until the tofu is heated through.

Cooking Mushrooms

Mushrooms add delicious flavor to many recipes. Some recipes you come across will specify a particular variety of mushroom for a particular cooking style, but in general, you can sauté, broil, bake, and microwave most types. To sauté, place about 1 tablespoon olive oil in a frying pan over medium-high heat, stirring constantly for about 3 minutes until tender. Before broiling, baking, or microwaving, brush the mushrooms with olive oil, butter, or margarine. Broil for about 5 minutes, turning the mushrooms after the first 2 minutes. Bake in a single layer in a shallow baking pan at 375° for 12 to 15 minutes until brown. Microwave uncovered on high for 4 to 6 minutes.

Eggplant Parmigiana

Serve this delicious dish with tomato sauce on the side.

🍴 Serves 8 🍴

What You Need:

1 medium eggplant (about 1 pound)
Vegetable oil, for frying
3 eggs
½ cup milk
1 cup all-purpose flour

3 cups bread crumbs
1 (28-ounce) can tomato sauce
4 cups shredded mozzarella cheese
Fresh Italian parsley *or* whole fresh basil
 leaves, as needed for garnish

What You Do:

1. Rinse the eggplant in cold, running water. Remove the stem. Cut in half lengthwise and remove the seeds. Thinly slice crosswise. Pour the vegetable oil to about ½" deep in a large frying pan. Heat on medium-high. Test for correct temperature by placing a piece of the eggplant in the oil. It will sizzle if the oil is ready.

2. In a small mixing bowl, beat together the eggs and milk. Place the flour on a dinner plate. Place the bread crumbs on another plate. Dip both sides of each eggplant slice first in the flour, then in the egg mixture. Place on the bread crumbs and press so the bread crumbs stick. Fry in the oil for about 3 minutes, until golden brown. Drain on paper towels.

3. Preheat oven to 350°. Layer the eggplant slices in the bottom of an ovenproof baking dish that has been sprayed with nonstick cooking spray. Top each slice with 1 teaspoon of tomato sauce and a rounded spoonful of cheese. Bake for 15 minutes, until the cheese melts and the dish is brown and bubbling. Sprinkle with fresh chopped parsley or fresh whole basil.

chapter 9

Side Dishes

EASY

MEDIUM

HARD

Mashed Potatoes

Serve with your favorite toppings: butter, sour cream, chopped chives, bacon bits, and/or shredded Cheddar cheese. Or try sour cream mixed with ranch or French onion powdered dip mix.

Serves 2

What You Need:
4–6 medium-size red potatoes *or*
  2 large baking potatoes
¼ cup milk

2 tablespoons butter *or* margarine
¼ teaspoon salt
⅛ teaspoon pepper

What You Do:
1. Rinse the potatoes under cold, running water. Peel with a potato peeler or paring knife. Cut into fourths and place in a 2-quart saucepan. Cover with water. Bring to a boil over high heat. Boil for 8 to 10 minutes, until the potatoes are soft when pierced with a fork. Drain in a colander. Reduce heat, and return the potatoes to the pan.

2. Add the milk, butter, salt, and pepper. Using an electric hand mixer (or by hand using a masher), whip the ingredients together until not quite smooth. (Add more milk if needed.) Serve warm.

Variation:
Garlic Mashed Potatoes

Place mashed potatoes in an ovenproof baking pan that has been sprayed with nonstick cooking spray. Sprinkle ¼ teaspoon of garlic powder over the top. Stir in ¼ cup mayonnaise. Top with ½ cup shredded Cheddar cheese. Cover with aluminum foil. Bake at 350° for 30 minutes or until warmed through.

Green Bean Casserole

In a hurry? Here's a quick, easy, and attractive side dish. French-style cut green beans look prettiest in this casserole, but you can use any style of cut beans. You can also substitute canned cut green beans for frozen.

E

 **Serves 4**

What You Need:

1 (10-ounce) package frozen French-style cut green beans

½ (7-ounce) can sliced mushrooms *or* mushroom stems and pieces

½ (10³/₄-ounce) can condensed cream of mushroom soup

⅓ cup milk

⅛ teaspoon pepper

⅔ cup canned French-fried onions (plain *or* Cheddar flavor)

What You Do:

1. Set out the green beans to thaw slightly so you can separate them with a fork. Preheat oven to 350°. Spray a 2-quart ovenproof baking pan with nonstick spray. Drain the mushrooms.

2. Place the green beans and mushrooms in the prepared baking pan. Stir in the condensed mushroom soup, milk, pepper, and ½ of the French-fried onions; mix well. Top with the remaining onions. Bake uncovered for 30 minutes. Or, microwave on high for 3 to 4 minutes, until heated through.

Honey-Baked Golden Acorn Squash

Golden acorn squash looks like a little pumpkin. (Do not confuse it with the small decorative gourds on sale during the same season.) Its peak season is October to December, but you may find it in stores at other times—August through March.

Serves 4

What You Need:

2 acorn squash
Salt, to taste
1 teaspoon ground nutmeg, divided
1 cup honey, divided

¼ cup apple juice, divided
4 tablespoons margarine (*or* butter, for nonvegetarian)

What You Do:

1. Preheat oven to 350°. Rinse the squash in cold, running water. Cut away the stem and cut the squash in half lengthwise. Scoop out the seeds and discard. Use a fork to gently poke holes all over the inner flesh of the squash halves, being careful not to puncture the outer skin. Place in an ungreased ovenproof baking pan.

2. Sprinkle salt and ¼ teaspoon nutmeg on the inside flesh of each half of squash. Pour ¼ cup honey into the "bowl" of each half. Spoon 1 tablespoon apple juice over each half. Cut the margarine into small pieces and put about 1 tablespoon's worth all around the top of each half.

3. Bake uncovered for about 1 hour until most of the honey and butter are absorbed. Serve warm.

Italian Zucchini

Use this casserole as a lacto-ovo vegetarian side dish or as a main course. Use spaghetti sauce from a jar or make your own.

E

🍴 Serves 4 🍴

What You Need:

4 small zucchini (about 6" to 8"long)
½ medium-size white *or* yellow onion
2 tablespoons butter *or* margarine
2 cups spaghetti sauce
¼ teaspoon garlic salt
2 tablespoons canned *or* freshly grated Parmesan cheese

What You Do:

1. Rinse the zucchini in cold, running water. Cut crosswise into ½"-thick slices. Chop the onion. Heat the butter (or margarine) in a frying pan over medium heat. Add the zucchini and onion. Cook, stirring constantly, for 1 to 2 minutes.

2. Reduce heat to medium-low. Stir in the spaghetti sauce, garlic salt, and Parmesan cheese. Cover and simmer for 6 to 8 minutes, until the zucchini is tender but still firm.

> **About Zucchini**
>
> Zucchini, which looks a little like a cucumber, is a type of squash known as "summer squash." Despite its name, summer squash is available year-round. Summer squash, which has a soft shell and edible seeds, is distinguished from winter squash, which has a hard shell. Zucchini has a mild flavor. You can cook zucchini or eat it raw by itself or with dip or in salad. When purchasing, look for firm texture and shiny skin that is free from pits or other injury. Also avoid zucchini with yellowish areas on the skin. Smaller zucchini are more tender than large ones.

Broccoli-Cheese Potatoes

Serve this overflowing side dish with a simple entrée, like Beef Roast (page 112) or Roast Chicken (page 154). If you'd like to add another side, consider sliced tomatoes or Cucumber Salad (page 90).

Serves 2

What You Need:

2 baking potatoes
½ (10-ounce) package frozen chopped broccoli
¼ pound block processed cheese
2 tablespoons butter *or* margarine

What You Do:

1. Bake the potatoes (see "Baking Potatoes," page 113). Cook the broccoli according to package directions until tender but still firm. Drain.

2. Melt the cheese in a saucepan over low heat. Or, heat in a microwave oven on high for 1 minute at a time, stirring after each minute. Stir in the cooked broccoli.

3. Cut an X-shaped slit in the top of each potato. Using potholders, squeeze the ends toward the middle until the potato breaks open.

4. Place 1 tablespoon butter in each potato and top with ½ of the broccoli and cheese mixture.

Cheesy Asparagus

A creamy Cheddar topping adds color and flavor to the aspara-gus for an attractive accent to entrées without sauces. Do *not* substitute canned asparagus—it will be too mushy and too salty.

🍴 Serves 4 🍴

What You Need:

1 pound fresh asparagus
Seasoned salt
2 eggs
¼ cup evaporated milk
½ cup shredded Cheddar cheese
¼ teaspoon salt
⅛ teaspoon pepper
½ cup shredded mozzarella cheese

What You Do:

1. Steam the asparagus (see Appendix C) and sprinkle with seasoned salt. Spray a shallow 9" × 9" ovenproof baking pan with nonstick cooking spray. Preheat oven to 350°.

2. Place the asparagus in the prepared pan. Use a fork to stir together the eggs (break the yolks), milk, Cheddar cheese, salt, and pepper. Pour the mixture over the asparagus. Top with mozzarella cheese. Bake uncovered for 15 to 20 minutes, until the cheese melts.

> ### What Is Evaporated Milk?
>
> Evaporated milk, also called condensed milk, is whole milk cooked until only 40 percent of its water content remains. You can buy evapo-rated milk or evaporated skim milk in 5-ounce or 12-ounce cans, usually found in the baking aisle of the gro-cery store. Do not confuse evaporated milk with *sweet-ened condensed milk*, which has added sugar. And never substitute evaporated or condensed milk for the sweetened variety.

Orange-Glazed Carrots

If you use whole carrots, clean, peel, and slice them before cooking. You can substitute canned or frozen carrots for fresh without precooking them.

Serves 2

What You Need:

1 cup fresh baby carrots
⅛ teaspoon salt
2 tablespoons butter *or* margarine
1½ teaspoons white granulated sugar
¼ cup prepared orange juice
1 tablespoon dried parsley flakes

What You Do:

1. Place the carrots in a saucepan. Add the salt and about ½" of water in the bottom of the pan. Bring to a boil over high heat. Cover and cook for 10 to 15 minutes, until tender. Drain.

2. While the carrots are cooking, melt the butter over low heat in a small frying pan. Add the sugar and orange juice. Stir until the sugar dissolves.

3. When the carrots are done (and drained), stir in the orange juice mixture. Cover and heat over low heat until warm. Sprinkle with parsley.

Spinach and Rice

Nutritious and flavorful, this cheesy side dish can be used as a main dish if you add 1 cup of cooked chicken. For the chicken broth, use canned or 2 chicken bouillon cubes boiled in 2 cups water.

Serves 4

What You Need:
2 cups chicken broth
1 (10.5-ounce) package frozen chopped spinach
1 cup uncooked rice
½ cup shredded Cheddar cheese *or* grated Parmesan cheese

What You Do:
1. Place the chicken broth and spinach in a 2-quart saucepan. Bring to a boil over high heat. Reduce heat to low.
2. Stir in the rice and cover. Simmer for 15 to 20 minutes (5 minutes for instant rice). Remove from heat. Let stand for 5 minutes to allow the rice to absorb the remaining moisture.
3. Stir in the cheese until melted.

Steamed Artichokes

For a vegan variation, you can substitute margarine for the butter.

🍴 Serves 2 🍴

What You Need:
2 artichokes
½ cup (1 stick) butter
Lemon juice, to taste (about 1 teaspoon)

What You Do:
1. To begin (unless you are using a thornless variety), cut off the tips and needles of each petal. For both varieties, cut off the top 1" of the whole artichoke so steam can flow through the inside. Pull off the lowest row of petals, and cut off the bottom ½" of the stem so the remainder is about 1" long. Rinse under cold, running water.

> **Eating Steamed Whole Artichokes**
> To eat a steamed whole artichoke, start from the bottom. Use your fingers to tear off a petal. Hold the tip of the petal between your thumb and index finger. Dip it into the butter mixture, place the petal on your tongue, and pull off the flesh with your teeth. (You eat the larger end of the petal—the end that was attached to the plant.)

2. Set the artichokes in a saucepan or steamer, stem-side down. Steam (see Appendix C) for 20 to 45 minutes, until tender. (Test by sticking a fork into the bottom of the stem. The fork should easily penetrate the stem.)

3. Cool for 2 to 4 minutes. In the meantime, melt the butter in a small saucepan. Stir in lemon juice to taste. Place the butter mixture in a serving dish to share. Serve warm.

Broiled Tomatoes

Instead of slicing fresh tomatoes as an ordinary side, bring them front and center served whole as a featured side dish. For a garlicky variation, serve topped with prepared or homemade Pesto (page 228).

Serves 4

What You Need:
4 medium tomatoes
2 tablespoons margarine *or* butter
¼ cup Italian-style bread crumbs
2 teaspoons fresh parsley

What You Do:
1. Move the oven rack to about 6" from the broiler element. Spray an ovenproof baking dish with nonstick cooking spray.

2. Rinse the tomatoes under cold running water. Cut out the stems. Slice off the top of each tomato and place the tomatoes in the prepared baking dish.

3. Melt the margarine in a small saucepan or frying pan over low heat. Stir in the bread crumbs.

4. Preheat broiler. Use kitchen scissors to snip the parsley into small pieces over the bread crumb mixture. Stir until well mixed. Spoon the mixture onto the tomatoes in equal portions. Broil for 5 to 6 minutes, until lightly browned.

Pesto

Pesto is a green sauce with lots of garlic that tastes good on almost everything. Spoon 1 to 2 tablespoons of the sauce onto Broiled Tomatoes (page 227), Scrambled Eggs (page 10), pasta, or steak. Store covered in the refrigerator for up to 2 weeks. For the best results, use a food processor to make this sauce.

Yields 6 servings

What You Need:

2 cups fresh basil leaves
½ cup olive oil
½ cup grated Parmesan cheese
3 cloves garlic
Freshly ground black pepper, to taste
3 tablespoons pine nuts *or* walnuts

What You Do:

1. Rinse the basil under cold, running water. Drain. Pat dry with paper towels. Place in a food processor. (If you don't have a food processor, cut all the ingredients into very small pieces and blend in an electric blender.)

2. Add the olive oil, cheese, garlic, pepper, and pine nuts (or walnuts). Process until the sauce is well blended. Cover and refrigerate until ready to use.

Sweet Potato–Apple Bake

For the best results, choose McIntosh, Granny Smith, or Jonathan apple varieties for this recipe. For a different flavor, you can substitute unpeeled orange slices for the apples.

Serves 4

What You Need:

2 sweet potatoes
2 apples
4 teaspoons margarine *or* butter
½ cup brown sugar

1 teaspoon salt
Shortening, vegetable oil, *or* nonstick
  cooking spray, as needed

What You Do:

1. Rinse the sweet potatoes under cold, running water. Place in a saucepan and cover with water. Bring to a boil over high heat. Boil for 30 to 35 minutes. Drain and let cool. Slice cross-wise into circles.

2. While the sweet potatoes are cooling, peel the apples and use a knife to remove the cores. Slice crosswise into circles. In a separate saucepan, melt the margarine over low heat. Stir in the brown sugar and salt. Set aside.

3. Preheat oven to 350°. Grease an ovenproof baking pan with shortening or vegetable oil, or spray with nonstick cooking spray. Layer ½ of the sweet potato slices in the bottom of the prepared baking pan. Layer ½ of the apple slices on top. Drizzle ½ of the butter mixture over the apples. Repeat with another layer of sweet potato slices, apple slices, and the remaining butter mixture. Bake for 1 hour.

Mashed Sweet Potatoes

Using fresh potatoes (instead of canned yams) is important in this recipe with a secret. The secret is the white potato added to the mixture. (Don't tell!)

Serves 4

What You Need:

5 large sweet potatoes
2 large baking potatoes
2 tablespoons butter *or* margarine
¼ cup brown sugar
⅛ teaspoon salt
¼ cup whole milk
2 cups miniature marshmallows (optional)

What You Do:

1. Peel and slice the sweet potatoes and baking potatoes. Place in a large saucepan and cover with water. Boil over high heat for about 20 minutes, until tender. Drain.

2. Preheat oven to 350°. Add the butter, brown sugar, and salt to the potatoes. Use a potato masher or electric mixer to mash. Add milk 1 tablespoon at a time until the mixture has the consistency of mashed potatoes. (Add more milk if necessary.)

3. Place the mixture in a 9″ × 9″ ovenproof baking pan that has been sprayed with nonstick cooking spray. Top with miniature marshmallows. Refrigerate to let flavors blend until almost ready to serve. Bake for 20 to 25 minutes, until the marshmallows are melted and slightly browned.

Baked Sliced Potatoes and Onion

This potato side dish is easier and more flavorful than regular baked potatoes—in half the time. Garnish with fresh parsley.

M

🍴 Serves 2 🍴

What You Need:
2 baking potatoes
½ medium-size white *or* yellow onion
2½ tablespoons butter *or* margarine
¼ teaspoon garlic salt
Salt and pepper, to taste

What You Do:

1. Preheat oven to 350°. Rinse the potatoes under cold, running water. Peel and cut crosswise into slices. Place in a 9" × 9" oven-proof baking pan. Slice the onion. Separate into individual rings and mix in with the potato slices.

2. Cut the butter into pats and spread around the top of the potatoes and onions. Sprinkle with garlic salt, salt, and pepper. Cover tightly with aluminum foil. Bake for 30 minutes. Or, cover with baking pan lid or plastic wrap, and microwave on high for about 6 minutes until the potatoes are tender. (Do not use aluminum foil in a microwave oven.)

> **Cooking Terms: Slicing and Dicing**
>
> *Slice* means to cut pieces of food using parallel lines. You can slice foods lengthwise or crosswise. For roasted meat, you want to slice against the grain, or crosswise. If you cut meat *with* the grain, you'll see long lines in the meat. Cutting crosswise makes the meat easier to chew. *Dice* means to cut into cubes. The easiest way to dice is to slice the food lengthwise but keep it in place as if it were still whole; then slice crosswise.

Crunchy New Potatoes

New potatoes are spring favorites, especially with Boiled Corned Beef and Cabbage (page 125) or Pot Roast (page 130).

Serves 4

What You Need:
8 new red potatoes
1 cup cornflakes
¼ cup butter *or* margarine
½ teaspoon seasoned salt

What You Do:

1. Rinse the potatoes under cold, running water. Place in a large saucepan. Cover with water. Bring to a boil over high heat. Cook for about 15 minutes.

2. While the potatoes are cooking, place the cornflakes on a cutting board. Cover with a sheet of waxed paper. Crush with a rolling pin. Place on a dinner plate or in a small mixing bowl.

3. Test the potatoes for doneness. The potatoes should be tender when pierced with a fork. Drain and peel. Leave whole. In a small saucepan, melt the margarine over medium heat. Stir in the seasoned salt. Preheat oven to 400°.

4. Roll each potato in the butter mixture. Use a spoon to move the potato to the plate with the crushed cornflakes. Roll around until well coated. Place in an ovenproof baking dish. Bake uncovered for 20 minutes, until browned.

Asparagus with Almond Sauce

This sauce adds zesty flavor to fresh asparagus. You can substitute 1 teaspoon cornstarch for the 2 teaspoons flour. A wooden spoon works well to stir the sauce to prevent sticking or burning.

 **Serves 4**

What You Need:
¼ cup slivered almonds
1 tablespoon butter *or* margarine
⅓ cup water
2 teaspoons all-purpose flour
½ teaspoon chicken-flavored bouillon granules
2 teaspoons lemon juice
⅛ teaspoon pepper
1 pound fresh asparagus

What You Do:
1. Cook the almonds in the butter (or margarine) in a frying pan over medium-high heat for 3 to 5 minutes, stirring constantly until golden brown. Reduce heat to low.

2. In a medium-size mixing bowl, stir together the water, flour, bouillon granules, lemon juice, and pepper until well blended. Add to the almonds in the frying pan. Cook over medium heat, stirring constantly, until the mixture comes to a boil. Boil for 1 minute. Remove from heat. Keep warm.

3. Steam the asparagus (see Appendix C). Arrange on a serving platter. Pour the sauce over the asparagus. Serve immediately.

Stir-Fry Parsnip Medley

Consider color combinations when planning your menu. This bright orange and white dish offers a nice contrast with green vegetables or salads. You can bake the unused half of the sweet potato and serve with butter and brown sugar. Or, use it in Curried Vegetable Stew (page 62).

Serves 2

What You Need:
1 fresh carrot
1 fresh parsnip
½ raw sweet potato
2 tablespoons olive oil
¼ teaspoon minced garlic

What You Do:
1. Rinse the carrot, parsnip, and sweet potato in cold water and peel. Cut the vegetables into sticks about 3" long and about ¼" wide and ¼" thick.

> **What's a Parsnip?**
> A parsnip is a specialty root vegetable that looks like a white carrot and tastes like a sweet potato. You may have to ask where they are in the produce section of your grocery store, as parsnips don't get the same shelf space allotment as other, more popular vegetables.

2. Coat the bottom of a frying pan with olive oil and heat on medium-high. Stir in the carrots, parsnip, sweet potato, and garlic. Stirring constantly, cook until tender but still firm.

Creamy Broccoli-Cauliflower Broil

You can substitute 1 cup each of frozen cauliflower and broccoli. If you use frozen, you don't steam them. Thaw before chopping.

 **Serves 4**

What You Need:
½ head cauliflower
½ bunch broccoli
⅓ cup sour cream
½ cup shredded Cheddar cheese

What You Do:

1. Rinse the cauliflower and broccoli under cold, running water. Steam them (see Appendix C). Chop and place in an ovenproof baking pan that has been sprayed with nonstick cooking spray. Move the top oven rack into a position closest to the broiler element. Preheat broiler.

2. In a medium-size mixing bowl, stir together the sour cream and cheese. Spoon the mixture over veggies. Broil for 10 to 15 minutes until lightly browned and heated through.

> ### What's Up with Green Cauliflower?
> Lime-green-colored cauliflower is a genetically engineered combination of cauliflower and broccoli. The chlorophyll from broccoli contributes its green color. Green cauliflower tastes sweeter than regular cauliflower. Both types are high in vitamin C and are good sources of folate. Choose cauliflower with firm, compact buds and fresh green leaves. Leaves that protrude through the top of the head are okay.

Twice-Baked Potato Casserole

Hot and cheesy, this yummy side dish goes well with Beef Roast (page 112), Pork Roast (page 139), or Roast Chicken (page 154). It's a popular contribution to a potluck supper.

Serves 6

What You Need:

6 red russet potatoes
1 cup water
2 chicken bouillon cubes
4 green onions

1½ cups sour cream
¾ cup small-curd cottage cheese
2 cups shredded Cheddar cheese, divided

What You Do:

1. Bake the potatoes (see page 113). Let cool. Peel and cut into 1" cubes. Place in a 10" × 15" ovenproof baking pan that has been sprayed with nonstick cooking spray.

2. Preheat oven to 350°. In a saucepan, bring the water to a boil. Add the chicken bouillon cubes. Stir until dissolved. Pour over the potatoes.

3. Chop the green onions, including the green tops. Add to the potatoes, along with the sour cream, cottage cheese, and 1 cup of the Cheddar cheese. Gently stir until well blended. Top with remaining Cheddar cheese. Bake uncovered for 30 to 35 minutes, until the cheese melts and bubbles.

Variation: Baked Mashed Potato Casserole

Instead of baking the potatoes, boil them until tender and mash them. Omit the chicken bouillon cubes and water. Sprinkle with paprika.

Rice Casserole

With cheesy tomatoes and onions, you can serve this rice dish as a side dish with beef, chicken, or pork, or by itself as vegetarian main course. It's especially good as a side dish with Quick Vegan Enchiladas (page 206) and Mexican Corn Bread (page 252).

 **Serves 4**

What You Need:
1 cup uncooked rice
1 medium white *or* yellow onion
½ cup butter
1 (8-ounce) can sliced tomatoes with juice
2 cups shredded Cheddar cheese
1 cup water
Salt and pepper, to taste

What You Do:
1. Preheat oven to 350°. Place the rice in an ungreased 2½-quart ovenproof baking pan.

2. Chop the onion and add to the baking pan. Slice the butter into chunks of about 2 tablespoons each. Add to the pan. Stir in the tomatoes, cheese, and water. Sprinkle with salt and pepper over. Cover and bake for 1 hour.

Hot Beans and Corn

Hot! Too hot! Ya gotta love spicy to enjoy this dish. Serve with something cheesy to balance the meal. Keep a pitcher of ice water handy.

Serves 4

What You Need:
1 medium-size white *or* yellow onion
1 tablespoon vegetable oil
1 (16-ounce) can baked beans
1 (10-ounce) package frozen corn
2 teaspoons vinegar
½ teaspoon hot pepper sauce

What You Do:
1. Chop the onion. Pour the oil into a saucepan over medium-high heat. Add the onion. Cook until the onion is tender, stirring constantly. Stir in the beans and corn, and bring the mixture to a boil.

2. Reduce heat to low. Cover and cook for about 5 minutes, until warmed through. Stir in the vinegar and hot pepper sauce. Serve warm.

Warm Red Cabbage

This tangy side dish goes well with sausages, Hot German Potato Salad (page 110), or other German dishes.

 **Serves 6**

M

What You Need:

1 head red cabbage, shredded
1 small white *or* yellow onion
2½ cups water, divided
2 teaspoons salt, divided
4 slices bacon

2 tablespoons brown sugar
2 tablespoons all-purpose flour
⅓ cup white vinegar
⅛ teaspoon pepper

What You Do:

1. Shred the cabbage using the large holes on the grater. Set aside. Slice the onion. Set aside.

2. Place the cabbage in a large saucepan. Add the 2 cups water and 1 teaspoon of the salt. Bring to a boil. Cover and reduce heat to low. Cook for 5 to 8 minutes, until tender but still firm. Remove from heat. Drain and return the cabbage to the saucepan. Cover to keep warm and set aside.

3. Fry the bacon (see Makin' Bacon, page 6). Drain. Pour off ½ of the bacon fat from the pan. Reduce heat to low.

4. Add the brown sugar and flour to the bacon fat remaining in the frying pan. Stir until well blended. Stir in the onion, remaining ½ cup water and 1 teaspoon salt, the vinegar, and pepper. Cook for about 5 minutes, until the mixture thickens.

5. Pour the dressing over the cabbage in the saucepan. Add the bacon crumbles. Cook over low heat, stirring until well coated and heated through. Serve warm.

French Peas

Leaf lettuce forms a minisaucepan within a saucepan to cook these peas with a distinctive nutmeg flavor. When the peas are done, discard the lettuce.

Serves 4

What You Need:
2 cups frozen peas
Leaf lettuce, as needed
¼ cup butter *or* margarine
½ teaspoon salt
⅛ teaspoon nutmeg
⅛ teaspoon pepper
⅛ teaspoon white granulated sugar

What You Do:
1. Before beginning, set out the peas to thaw. Rinse the leaf lettuce in cold, running water. Place the leaves in the bottom of a medium-size saucepan. Use additional leaves and stand them up against the sides of the pan. Place the peas on top of the bottom lettuce leaves.

2. In a separate small saucepan or small frying pan, melt the butter over medium heat. Stir in the salt, pepper, nutmeg, and sugar. Pour over the peas. Cover the peas with more leaf lettuce. Cover the saucepan with a lid. Cook over low heat for 15 to 20 minutes, until tender. Discard lettuce.

Asparagus Soufflé

Beaten egg whites are the trademark ingredient for soufflés, which may be made with a variety of ingredients to create entrées, side dishes, and even desserts. Cover unused yolks and add to your favorite breakfast casserole. You can substitute frozen cut asparagus for fresh if you let it thaw first.

 **Serves 2**

What You Need:

Shortening, as needed
½ pound fresh asparagus
2 green onions, including tops

½ cup shredded Cheddar cheese
½ cup mayonnaise
1 egg (white only)

What You Do:

1. Grease an ovenproof baking pan with the shortening. Set aside. Rinse the asparagus in cold, running water. Break off the tough ends with your hands, or cut off with a knife. Slice crosswise into pieces about 3" long. Place in a medium-size mixing bowl.

2. Slice the green onions, including the dark green tops. Add to the asparagus. Stir in cheese and mayonnaise.

3. Preheat oven to 325°. Separate the egg (see "Chef's Secret: Separating Eggs," page 315) and pour the white into a separate small mixing bowl. Use an electric mixer to beat it until it forms into soft peaks. Add to the asparagus mixture. Gently stir from top to bottom to combine the egg whites with the mixture. Pour into the prepared baking pan. Bake uncovered for 25 minutes, until lightly browned.

Corn Casserole with Green Chilies

Creamed sweet corn with a twist, this spunky side dish makes a nice alternative to potatoes when you're in the mood for something a bit different.

Serves 8 as a side dish

What You Need:

2 eggs
2 cans yellow cream-style corn
¼ cup cornmeal
¼ teaspoon garlic salt
¼ cup butter *or* margarine
¼ cup grated Longhorn cheese
1 (4-ounce) can chopped green chilies

What You Do:

1. Preheat oven to 350°. In a small mixing bowl, use a table fork to beat the eggs until well blended. In a separate, large mixing bowl, stir in the corn, cornmeal, and garlic salt. Melt the butter (or margarine) in a small saucepan over medium heat. Stir into the corn mixture. Gently stir in the eggs, scraping the mixture from the bottom of the bowl to the top.

2. Grate the cheese into a separate bowl, using the small holes on the grater. Spray a 9" × 13" ovenproof baking pan with nonstick cooking spray. Pour about ½ of the corn mixture into the bottom. Drain the chilies. Spread about ½ of the chilies over the top. Sprinkle with ½ of the cheese. Repeat with the remaining corn mixture, chilies, and cheese. Add more cheese if you like. Bake for 30 minutes.

Snacks and Appetizers

Chapter 10

E

Deviled Eggs

These picnic and potluck favorites also make a quick lunch or snack. Because they contain mayonnaise that can easily spoil, take care to keep them cold until ready to eat—especially on a hot day. If available, use a serving plate with depressions made especially for deviled eggs.

Yields 12 deviled eggs

What You Need:

6 eggs
¼ cup mayonnaise *or* mayonnaise-like salad dressing
½ teaspoon prepared mustard
Salt and pepper, to taste
Paprika, as needed

What You Do:

1. Hard-boil the eggs (see Boiled Egg, page 9). Peel off the shells. Cut the eggs in half lengthwise. Remove the yolks and place them in a medium-size mixing bowl. Place the egg whites, rounded-side down, on a serving plate.

2. Mash the yolks with a fork. Stir in the mayonnaise, mustard, salt, and pepper. (Adjust measurements to taste.) Use a spoon to heap the mixture back into the holes in the egg white halves. Sprinkle with paprika. Refrigerate until ready to eat.

No-Bake Peanut Butter Balls

If you like peanut butter, these treats won't last long. They're delicious! And with niacin, vitamin E, and protein from the peanuts and calcium from the milk, they're nutritious, too. (*Shhh!* Don't tell!)

Yields about 48 (2"-diameter) balls

What You Need:

1 (12-ounce) jar crunchy peanut butter
½ cup honey
1½ cups nonfat dry milk

What You Do:

1. Spoon the peanut butter and honey into a large mixing bowl. Stir until well blended. Stir in the dry milk.

2. Use your hands to form 1 bite-size ball (about 1" in diameter). You should be able to form the ball and place it onto a serving plate without having it stick to your palm. If the mixture is too sticky, keep adding dry milk until you can work with the mixture.

Chocolate and Peanut
Granola Bars ✐

Grab a granola bar for breakfast or when you need a quick snack. Tightly wrap leftovers in plastic wrap until ready to eat.

🍴 Yields 18 bars 🍴

What You Need:
2½ cups crispy rice cereal
2 cups dry instant oatmeal
½ cup raisins
½ cup chocolate morsels
½ cup brown sugar
½ cup light corn syrup
½ cup peanut butter
1 teaspoon vanilla extract (*or* imitation)

What You Do:
1. Place the rice cereal, oatmeal, raisins, and chocolate morsels in a large mixing bowl. Gently stir until well blended.
2. In a saucepan over medium-high heat, stir together the brown sugar and corn syrup until the mixture boils. Remove from heat. Stir in the peanut butter and vanilla extract until smooth.
3. Add the mixture from saucepan to the large mixing bowl. Gently stir until the all the ingredients are well coated. Place in a 9" × 13" baking pan that has been sprayed with nonstick cooking spray. Press into an even layer using the back of a spoon or your fingers. Cool. Cut into bars.

Popcorn Bars

Got leftover popcorn? Don't throw it out. Use it to make this low-fat, nutritious snack. Great for breakfast-on-the-go! A wooden spoon works best for stirring this mixture.

Yields 12 squares

What You Need:

5 cups popped popcorn
3/4 cup sliced almonds
1/2 cup raisins
2 tablespoons butter *or* margarine
1/3 cup honey

What You Do:

1. Preheat oven to 350°. Spray an ovenproof 8" × 8" baking pan with nonstick cooking spray.

2. In a large mixing bowl, stir together the popped popcorn, almonds, and raisins. Set aside.

3. In a small saucepan or frying pan over medium heat, melt the margarine. Remove from heat. Add the honey. Pour the mixture over the ingredients in the mixing bowl. Stir until the popcorn mixture is well coated.

4. Pour mixture into the baking pan. Use a spoon or your fingers to press it into an even layer. Bake for 3 to 5 minutes until warm. Remove from oven and let cool. Cut into squares.

Ranch-Flavored Snack Crackers 🥕

If you're tired of popcorn, here's a tasty snack to share while watching a video, playing cards, or just visiting. Veggies and dip make a nice complement, or offer a dish of chocolate candy. Be sure to keep plenty of beverages and napkins handy.

🍴 Yields about 2 cups 🍴

What You Need:
1 (10-ounce) package oyster crackers
1 (1.25-ounce) package dry ranch salad dressing mix
½ cup butter-flavored popcorn oil

What You Do:
1. Combine the crackers, salad dressing mix, and popcorn oil in a plastic container with tight lid. Shake until the crackers are well coated.

2. Cover tightly and store at room temperature until ready to serve.

Cheese Biscuits

Serve these biscuits as a snack any time of day. They also make a nice accompaniment for Scrambled Eggs (page 10), Breaded Oven-Baked Fish (page 175), or soups and stews. For best results, use ice-cold milk to make the dough easy to work with.

Yields 16 to 18 biscuits

What You Need:
Shortening, as needed
2 cups all-purpose flour
½ cup (1 stick) butter
½ cup milk
1 cup grated Cheddar cheese
Pinch of salt

What You Do:

1. Preheat oven to 400°. Grease the baking sheet with shortening.

2. In a large mixing bowl, use a fork to mix together the flour and butter. Stir in the milk until well mixed.

3. Use your hands to knead in the cheese. Press the heel of your hand into the dough, then fold over the dough onto itself. Repeat until well mixed.

4. Drop heaping spoonfuls of the dough onto the prepared baking sheet in rows. Bake for 10 to 12 minutes, until golden brown.

Preheating an Oven

For cooking times less than 1 hour, you'll want to preheat the oven to ensure even heating. Turn the oven dial to preheat, and turn the temperature selector to the desired temperature. Electric ovens use both the top coil (the one used for broiling) and the bottom coil when set to preheat. Be sure to change the dial from preheat to bake before placing food in the oven if your oven requires it. If you forget, the top of the food will heat too much. Some foods will be crusty, dry, or burned on top.

Trail Mix 🥕

You don't have to be heading out for a hike to enjoy trail mix. It's a nice go-together with a bowl of popcorn while reading or watching a video. You can also take it with you for breakfast or lunch.

🍴 Yields 5 cups 🍴

What You Need:

1 cup dried apples

1 cup dried banana chips

1 cup sunflower kernels

½ cup dry roasted peanuts (without the shells)

½ cup raisins

What You Do:

1. Cut the apples into bite-size pieces. Place in a large mixing bowl.

2. Add the banana chips, sunflower kernels, peanuts, and raisins. Stir until well mixed. Store in an airtight container until ready to eat.

What Is Dried Fruit?

Dried fruits have most of the same vitamins and other nutrients as their full-bodied counterparts. However, vitamin C does not survive heat and light very well, so some of it is lost in the drying process. Some people say that dried fruit is full of iron, but that's because the nutrients are more concentrated. At least 50 percent of the fruits' water is missing in dried fruit. Drying fruits concentrates the fruit's natural sugar—increasing the sweet taste—and concentrates the fruits' calories. So some people think dried fruits are fattening—which isn't true. However, some dried fruit also has added sugar, so read labels. Removing water also makes fruits chewy.

Apple Dip

It takes just a minute to transform an ordinary apple into a tasty snack. This dip tastes best with tart apple varieties like Granny Smith and McIntosh. If you have time, make the dip ahead and let it chill before eating.

Serves 2

What You Need:
1 (8-ounce) package block cream cheese
1 cup dark brown sugar
2 teaspoons vanilla extract (*or* imitation)
2 apples
A few drops lemon juice

What You Do:
1. Let the cream cheese soften at room temperature for about 10 minutes. Place in a small mixing bowl. Add the brown sugar and vanilla extract. Stir until well blended. Chill covered for at least 1 hour to give the flavors a chance to mingle.

> **Keeping Fruits from Turning Brown**
>
> Such fruits as apples, bananas, and pears tend to turn brown after slicing. If you're using these fruits with dips or in salads, you can prevent this browning by sprinkling a few drops of lime or lemon juice on the fruit before serving. You can omit this step if the salad dressing includes lime or lemon juice as an ingredient.

2. Rinse apples in cold, running water. Pat dry with a paper towel. Cut apples in half. Remove cores. Slice apples. (Or use an apple corer.) Sprinkle a few drops of lemon juice on the apples to help prevent them from turning brown. Serve with the dip.

Mexican Corn Bread

Spice up ordinary corn bread to make a tasty snack that you can eat by itself or serve with soups or stews. This is especially good with pork.

Yields up to 12 servings

What You Need:
2 eggs
1 (4-ounce) can diced green chilies
1 cup yellow cornmeal
3/4 cup vegetable oil
1 (14.75-ounce) can creamed corn
1/2 teaspoon baking soda
1 teaspoon salt
1 1/2 cups shredded Cheddar cheese

What You Do:
1. Preheat oven to 400°. Crack the eggs into a large mixing bowl. Beat with a fork until smooth. Drain the chilies and add to the bowl. Stir in the cornmeal, vegetable oil, creamed corn, baking soda, and salt. Pour into a 9" × 9" ovenproof baking pan that has been greased with a few drops of shortening.
2. Top with the cheese. Bake for 45 minutes until the top is golden brown.

E

Easy Guacamole

What would a party be without guacamole? Serve with corn or tortilla chips. Or, serve it as a garnish for Tacos (see page 114), Quick Vegan Enchiladas (see page 206), or other festive Mexican dishes.

Yields 1½–2 cups

What You Need:

2 ripe avocados
2 tablespoons lemon juice
1–2 teaspoons cayenne pepper hot sauce, to taste
1 small tomato
1 small white onion

What You Do:

1. Cut the avocados in half the long way, cutting around the seed. Remove the seed and peel. Place the avocados in a small mixing bowl. Mash with a fork. Stir in the lemon juice. Add the cayenne pepper hot sauce 1 teaspoon at a time to taste.

2. Chop the tomato and onion. Stir into the mashed avocados. Chill for 1 hour before serving.

Yummy Sour Cream Dip

It's party time! Here's a basic cheese dip to serve with raw veggies, potato chips, or crackers. For easy preparation, you can use an electric mixer to combine the ingredients. (Spanish olives are the green ones.)

Yields 2 cups

What You Need:
2 (8-ounce) packages block cream cheese
1 (7-ounce) jar Spanish olives with pimientos
1 cup sour cream
½ cup olive liquid

What You Do:
1. Before beginning, set out the cream cheese for 10 to 15 minutes to soften at room temperature. Drain and chop the olives. (Save the liquid.)

2. In a small mixing bowl, stir together the cream cheese, sour cream, olives, and the liquid from olives in a small mixing bowl until well blended. Serve cold.

Artichoke Parmesan Dip ✏️

The aroma of melting Parmesan cheese will fill the kitchen as you heat this tangy dip. Serve with wheat crackers. Do *not* substitute mayonnaise-like salad dressing in this recipe.

🍴 Yields 2 cups 🍴

What You Need:

1 (14-ounce) can artichoke hearts
1 cup mayonnaise

⅓ cup grated Parmesan cheese
½ teaspoon garlic powder

What You Do:

1. Preheat oven to 350°. Drain the artichoke hearts. Chop into very small pieces (about ¼″ square or less). Place into an ungreased 9″ × 9″ ovenproof baking pan.

2. Stir in the mayonnaise, Parmesan cheese, and garlic powder until well mixed. Bake for 20 minutes or until bubbly.

About Artichokes

If you're unfamiliar with artichokes, don't let their unusual appearance scare you away. Some varieties of fresh artichokes have prickly points, so use the stem as a handle during purchase and preparation. Before steaming, slice off the tip and the thorn from each petal. You can steam artichokes or microwave them in 3 tablespoons water, 1 teaspoon vegetable oil, and 1 teaspoon lemon juice in a covered microwave-safe bowl for 6 to 8 minutes. Prepare several at one time. Cover and refrigerate. Leftovers will store for several days for quick snacks.

Blue Cheese Veggie Dip

For blue cheese lovers only! This dip has a strong flavor that goes well with sliced cucumbers; zucchini; red, yellow, and green peppers; and cool, crisp chunks of celery and baby carrots.

Yields about 1½ cups

What You Need:
1 (8-ounce) block cream cheese
⅛ teaspoon garlic salt
⅛ teaspoon seasoned salt
Milk, as needed
4 ounces crumbled blue cheese

What You Do:
1. Unwrap the cream cheese and place in a mixing bowl. Set aside at room temperature for 10 to 15 minutes to soften.
2. Add the garlic salt and seasoned salt to the cream cheese, and stir in by hand or beat with an electric mixer. Add the milk 1 tablespoon at a time to thin the mixture. Beat until smooth. The mixture should be smooth and thick enough for a spoon to stand up in it.
3. Stir in the blue cheese. Refrigerate for at least 1 hour before serving.

> **Block or Softened Cream Cheese?**
> When purchasing cream cheese for a recipe, choose the block of cream cheese that comes in a box unless otherwise specified. The softened cream cheese that comes in a tub has been whipped. That means processing has added air to the product. If you use that type, your measurement will be inaccurate, especially in recipes that call for heating the cream cheese.

Baked Brie

This is a definite crowd pleaser, and one you don't often see. It makes a fabulous late-night snack on a cold winter night. Serve with sliced apples, red seedless grapes, and slices of French bread.

E

Serves 4–6

What You Need:
1 (6") wheel Brie cheese
2 tablespoons butter *or* margarine
3 tablespoons brown sugar
½ cup chopped pecans

What You Do:
1. Preheat oven to 400°. Unwrap the Brie and cut off the top layer of the rind. Leave the rind in place on the sides and bottom. Place a piece of aluminum foil (big enough to wrap the wheel of Brie) in the bottom of an ovenproof baking pan. Place the Brie on top of the foil.

2. Cut the butter into pieces about ½" square and place all around the top of the Brie. Sprinkle the brown sugar and pecans on top. Close the aluminum foil over the Brie. Bake for 10 to 15 minutes. Unwrap and place on a serving plate.

Tangy Mushrooms

These tangy mushrooms add variety to your party menu. They provide a nice contrast to appetizers with cheese or meat. Provide toothpicks for easy serving.

Yields about 2 cups

What You Need:
2 (7.3-ounce) jars *or* 2 (8-ounce) cans of whole mushrooms
1½ teaspoons minced onion
1½ teaspoons dried parsley flakes
2 tablespoons bottled Italian salad dressing

What You Do:
1. Drain the mushrooms and place in small mixing bowl. Add the onion and parsley.
2. Sprinkle with salad dressing, and stir until heavily coated. (Excess dressing in the bottom of the bowl is okay.) Cover and refrigerate for at least 1 hour to let the flavors blend.

Gouda Goodness 🥕

The aroma of freshly baked dough and warm, creamy cheese will bring your guests into the kitchen before this delightful dish is out of the oven. You can substitute Edam, smoked Gouda, Cheddar, or any wheel-style cheese for the Gouda cheese. Provide a cheese or butter knife for cutting wedges.

🍴 Yields about 8 wedges 🍴

What You Need:
1 (7-ounce) wheel Gouda cheese
1 (8-ounce) can crescent roll dough

What You Do:

1. Preheat oven to 375°. Unwrap the cheese and peel off and discard the wax covering.

2. Open the package of dough and unroll on a cutting board or other flat surface. Use your fingers to mold the dough around the cheese, so it completely covers the cheese.

3. Place the dough-covered cheese in the center of an ungreased baking sheet. Bake for 11 to 13 minutes. Cheese should be warm and gooey, but not runny. Serve immediately.

Krab with a Kick

This dip is not for wimps! You have to like strong, spicy food. Serve with your favorite crackers. Keep emergency ice water handy.

🍴 Yields 3 cups 🍴

What You Need:
³/₄ green bell pepper, divided
3 green onions
2 (4.25-ounce) cans crabmeat
3 cups shredded Cheddar cheese
³/₄ cup mayonnaise
1½ teaspoons garlic powder
³/₄ teaspoon dry mustard
1½ teaspoons ground red pepper

What You Do:
1. Rinse the green bell pepper in cold running water. Cut in half lengthwise. Remove the stem and seeds. Cover ½ of the pepper and refrigerate for another use. Chop the remaining pepper into very small pieces. Place in a large mixing bowl. Remove the outer layer of the green onions. Slice crosswise. Add to the bowl.
2. Drain the crabmeat. Add to the bowl. Stir in the cheese, mayonnaise, garlic powder, dry mustard, and ground red pepper. Stir until well mixed. Cover and refrigerate for at least 2 hours until well chilled.

Cheese Quesadillas

Follow this recipe for a quick appetizer or snack using your favorite cheese. For lunch or a dinner entrée, add ¼ cup cooked chicken. For variety, top with Easy Guacamole (page 253).

Yields 4 slices

What You Need:
1 tablespoon butter *or* margarine
2 (6") flour tortillas
½ cup shredded cheese *or* 2 slices cheese
2 tablespoons bottled salsa *or* picante sauce
2 tablespoons sour cream

What You Do:
1. Melt the butter in a frying pan over low to medium heat. Place 1 tortilla in the pan. Top with the cheese. Place the second tortilla on top. Heat until the bottom tortilla is golden brown.

2. Flip, as you would a pancake, to the other side. Heat until golden brown. Remove from the pan and place on a serving plate. Cut into fourths. Top with salsa or picante sauce and sour cream, or serve on the side.

Bean Chili Cheese Dip

This dip is sure to please the party crowd, or it's great for a case of the munchies. For a lower-fat variation, try using ground turkey instead of beef and low-fat cream cheese.

🍴 Serves 8–10 🍴

What You Need:
1 (8-ounce) block cream cheese
1 pound ground beef
1 packet taco seasoning
1 (10-ounce) jar salsa
About 2 cups shredded cheese (Mexican *or* Cheddar jack)

What You Do:
1. Before beginning, set out the cream cheese to soften at room temperature for 10 to 15 minutes.

2. Spread the cream cheese into the bottom of a cake or pie pan.

3. Brown the meat and add the taco seasoning according to package directions. Drain off the fat. Preheat oven to 350°. Pour the meat over the cream cheese.

4. Pour the salsa over the beef and top with the shredded cheese.

5. Bake until the cheese melts, about 15 minutes. Serve with corn or tortilla chips.

Green Chives Dip

It's not guacamole! But it might fool your guests. Instead, it has a distinctly different flavor of mild onion and garlic. You'll find chives among herbs in the produce section and tarragon in the spice aisle of your grocery store. Serve with corn or tortilla chips.

Yields 2 cups

What You Need:
Fresh chives (enough to yield 2 tablespoons chopped)
1½ teaspoons dried parsley flakes
1 cup mayonnaise
¾ cup sour cream
¼ cup plain yogurt
1½ teaspoons white vinegar
½ teaspoon dried tarragon
1–2 tablespoons lemon juice, to taste
½ teaspoon minced garlic

What You Do:
1. Finely chop the chives. Place in a small mixing bowl along with the parsley flakes.
2. Stir in the mayonnaise, sour cream, yogurt, white vinegar, tarragon, lemon juice, and garlic until well blended. An electric mixer or electric blender makes this dip easier to prepare than stirring by hand, but the flavor will be the same.

Warm Pecan Cheese Dip

Based on appearance, your guests may expect this dip to taste spicy. Instead, it has a creamy-sweet flavor that tastes best with wheat crackers. Because the dip is served warm, prepare and serve it in a slow cooker, if possible. (During the party, stir every 30 minutes or so to keep the surface from hardening.)

Yields about 4 cups

What You Need:
1-pound block processed American cheese   1 (2-ounce) jar diced pimientos
1 cup whipping cream   1 (2.25-ounce) package chopped pecans

What You Do:
1. Cut the processed cheese into 1" to 2" cubes and put in a slow cooker. Add the whipping cream (do *not* whip the whipping cream). Heat until the cheese melts. (If you don't have a slow cooker, you can complete this step in a 2-quart saucepan over low heat or in a microwave-safe mixing bowl in the microwave oven.)
2. When the cheese has melted, drain the pimientos, and add to the mixture. Stir in the pecans. Serve warm.

> **What Is a Pimiento?**
> A pimiento is a red garden pepper often used to stuff green olives. You'll find pimientos in the canned vegetable aisle near the pickles and olives. They come in a small glass jar, so you'll have to look hard! If you can't find it, ask a grocery stocker.

Ugly Blue Cheese Ball

Don't judge this book by its cover. The blue cheese gives this cheese ball an ugly grayish color. But wait 'til you taste it. It's sure to please the blue cheese lovers in your crowd. Serve with your favorite snack crackers. (An electric mixer makes preparation easier.)

1 cheese ball

What You Need:
2 (8-ounce) packages block cream cheese (do *not* used whipped)
½ cup crumbled blue cheese
1 tablespoon Worcestershire sauce
1 cup shredded Cheddar cheese
2 cups chopped walnuts

What You Do:
1. Before beginning, set out the cream cheese for 10 to 15 minutes to soften at room temperature. Place in a medium-size mixing bowl.

2. Stir in the blue cheese, Worcestershire sauce, and cheese by hand or with an electric mixer until well blended.

3. Cover and refrigerate for 1 hour. When the mixture has hardened, place the walnuts on waxed paper or a cutting board. Use your hands to form the cheese mixture into a large ball. Roll in the nuts until the entire ball is covered.

Corned Beef Cheese Ball

 Full of meaty goodness, this cheese ball looks and tastes like it took all day to prepare. To serve, surround the cheese ball with chips, crackers, cut veggies, or slices of party rye bread.

✿ Yields 1 cheese ball ✿

What You Need:
2 (8-ounce) packages block cream cheese (do *not* used whipped)
1 cup fresh parsley
2 (2.5-ounce) packages deli-sliced corned beef lunchmeat
1 (8-ounce) container prepared toasted onion party dip

What You Do:
1. Unwrap the cream cheese and place in a medium-size mixing bowl. Set aside for 10 to 15 minutes to soften at room temperature. Chop the parsley. Place on a salad or dinner plate. Set aside.

2. Chop the corned beef. Stir in to the cream cheese. Stir in the onion dip until all the ingredients are well blended.

3. Use your hands to form the mixture into a single ball. Roll the ball in the parsley. Place on serving plate and refrigerate for at least 1 hour before serving.

Pineapple Pepper Cheese Ball

Use this cheese ball for a delicious spread for club crackers, party rye bread, or melba toast. Garnish the serving plate with a few sprigs of fresh parsley.

Yields 1 cheese ball

What You Need:

2 (8-ounce) packages boxed cream cheese (do *not* used whipped)
¼ green bell pepper
2 green onions
⅛ teaspoon garlic salt
2 teaspoons seasoned salt
1 (8-ounce) can crushed pineapple
1 (2.25-ounce) package chopped pecans

What You Do:

1. Set out the cream cheese for 10 to 15 minutes to soften at room temperature. Place in a medium-size mixing bowl. Chop the green bell pepper. Chop the green onions. Add to the mixing bowl. Sprinkle the mixture with garlic salt and seasoned salt. Stir until well blended. Gently stir in the pineapple. Use your hands to form the mixture into a ball.

2. Place the chopped pecans in a layer on a dinner plate or a piece of waxed paper. Roll the ball in the nuts until the ball is covered. Place on a serving plate and chill for at least 1 hour before serving.

Crab Cracker Spread

Crustacean connoisseurs love this cracker spread. Look for bottled cocktail sauce in the ketchup aisle or near the seafood department.

🍴 Yields 2 cups 🍴

What You Need:
½ cup bottled cocktail sauce
1 (8-ounce) package boxed cream cheese (do *not* used whipped)
1 (8-ounce) package imitation crab
1 sprig fresh parsley

What You Do:
1. Prechill the bottle of cocktail sauce. Unwrap the block of cream cheese and place it in the center of a serving plate. With your fingers or a fork, separate the crab into flakes. Place the flakes on top of the cream cheese, letting some pieces fall over the side. Chill in the refrigerator for at least 1 hour.
2. When ready to serve, pour the cocktail sauce over the crab. Top with parsley. Surround with crackers. Stick a cheese knife into the top for easy serving.

Variation:
Shrimp Cracker Spread

For a shrimp variation, substitute one 6-ounce can of shrimp (drained) for the imitation crab, and add ¼ teaspoon garlic powder. Both variations taste best with club crackers.

Pizza on Rye

Aromatic oregano adds Italian flavor to these easy and delicious party favorites. You may need several baking sheets. Or, heat in "shifts." Remove warm appetizers from the oven. Place on serving tray. Cool and reuse the baking sheet for the next set of "pizzas."

🍴 Yields about 45 appetizers 🍴

What You Need:

1 pound ground pork breakfast sausage
1 pound shredded Cheddar *or* mozzarella cheese
1 loaf party rye bread
Oregano, as needed

What You Do:

1. Brown the sausage in a frying pan (see "Browning Ground Beef," page 115). Drain off fat. Reduce heat to low.

2. Preheat oven to 350°. Cut the cheese into 2" cubes. Add to the sausage. Stir together until the cheese melts.

3. Place the slices of party rye on ungreased baking sheets. Spoon about 1 table-spoon of the mixture onto each slice. Sprinkle with oregano. Bake for 5 to 10 minutes, until the mixture is bubbly. Serve warm.

> **Party Rye Bread**
> Look for party rye in the bread aisle. Loaves are small, and the slices are about ¼ the size of regular bread. For a quick snack, spread with softened cream cheese or spreadable Cheddar cheese. Or, serve with Blue Cheese Veggie Dip (page 256), Corned Beef Cheese Ball (page 266), or Crab Cracker Spread (page 268). Or, make miniature bologna and cheese sandwiches to take to a potluck party.

Sausage Swirls

These appetizers look fancy, but they're easy to make. And they're sooooo good! Refrigerate leftovers and reheat for breakfast.

🍴 Yields about 48 appetizers 🍴

What You Need:

¼ cup butter *or* margarine
½ cup milk
2 cups biscuit mix

1 (16-ounce) package ground pork sausage
Flour, as needed

What You Do:

1. Melt the butter over low heat. In a large mixing bowl, stir together the melted butter, milk, and biscuit mix.

2. Place half of the dough on a floured cutting board. Dust a rolling pin with flour. Roll the dough in each of 4 directions until the dough is about 7" × 10" and about ⅛" thick.

3. Spread ½ of the uncooked sausage in an even layer covering the rolled-out dough. Roll the long edge of the dough over itself until you have formed a roll about 10" long and about 3" in diameter. (The inside will alternate dough and sausage several times as you roll.)

4. Repeat steps 2 and 3 with the other half of the dough and sausage. Place both rolls in the freezer on a piece of waxed paper or aluminum foil for about 30 minutes or until the dough is hard enough to slice easily.

5. Preheat oven to 400°. Slice the rolls crosswise into circles ¼" to ½" thick. (The dough will form a swirl through the sausage.) Lay the circles flat on an ungreased baking sheet. Bake for 15 minutes or until golden brown. Serve warm.

Mexican Potato Cups

You can make Mexican Potato Cups in a regular-size or "mini" muffin tin. (You may need to make several batches if you don't have enough muffin tins.) The smaller size is best for a large party. You can serve the large potato cups as a festive side dish. To serve, top with salsa, sour cream, and 1 or 2 decorative leaves of cilantro.

🍴 Yields 30 mini-potato cups 🍴

What You Need:

2½ cups (20 ounces) frozen hash browns

Shortening, as needed

2 cups shredded Monterey jack cheese

Fresh cilantro (enough to yield 1 teaspoon)

1 egg

What You Do:

1. Pour the frozen hash browns into a bowl to thaw for about 15 minutes. Heavily grease 1 or more muffin tins.

2. Stir the cheese into the potatoes. Rinse the cilantro under cold, running water. Pat dry with paper towels. Use kitchen scissors to snip enough cilantro for 1 teaspoon cut into very small pieces. Add to the potato mixture.

3. In a small mixing bowl or cup, beat the egg until well blended. Stir into the potato mixture. Stir until well mixed. Preheat oven to 400°.

4. Use your hands to fill the muffin tin cups with even amounts of the potato mixture. Press into the cups with your fingers. (If you don't have enough to fill all of the muffin cups at the end, fill empties with water to encourage even heating during baking.) Bake for 20 to 22 minutes until crisp and browned. Remove from muffin tin and place on serving plate or tray. Serve warm.

Hummus

 Here's a tasty high-protein appetizer everyone will love. Serve with warm pita bread or in Hummus Pocket Sandwiches (page 47). For the best results, use a food processor. If you don't have one, use an electric blender, electric mixer, or a potato masher (this will take more elbow grease!) to make the dip smooth.

Yields 2 cups

What You Need:

1 (15-ounce) can chickpeas (also called garbanzo beans)
¼ teaspoon garlic powder
3 tablespoons tahini
½ teaspoon salt
2–3 teaspoons cumin powder

2–3 tablespoons lemon juice, to taste
¼ cup olive oil
Water, as needed (up to ¼ cup)
Additional salt and pepper, to taste
Paprika (optional)
Fresh parsley (optional)

What You Do:

1. Drain the chickpeas and rinse in cold water. Place in a food processor or electric blender. Add the garlic powder, tahini, ½ teaspoon of salt, cumin, and 1 tablespoon of the lemon juice. Process until smooth, gradually adding the olive oil and water (up to ¼ cup) until the hummus reaches desired softness. Sprinkle with salt, pepper, and lemon juice, to taste.

2. Spread into a serving bowl. Drizzle a little olive oil and a few drops of lemon juice over the top. Sprinkle with paprika. Chop the parsley and sprinkle it over the hummus.

Sweet Wings

You can turn this Asian-flavored appetizer into a main dish by serving over cooked rice with a green vegetable or salad (see page 96) on the side. Serve warm with lots of napkins.

Yields about 18 wings

What You Need:

2 pounds chicken wings
¼ cup soy sauce

½ cup honey
1 tablespoon butter *or* margarine

What You Do:

1. Rinse the chicken in cold, running water. Pat dry with a paper towel. Use a knife to separate each wing at the joint into 2 pieces. Set aside.

2. In a large mixing bowl, stir together the soy sauce and honey. Add the chicken wings to the bowl, making sure the wings are well coated with the mixture. Cover and refrigerate for at least 1 hour, or overnight.

3. Preheat oven to 400°. Use the butter (or margarine) to grease a baking pan large enough to allow the wings to cook in a single layer. Remove the wings from the bowl and place in the pan. Spoon 2 to 3 tablespoons of the soy sauce mixture remaining in the bowl over the chicken.

4. Bake uncovered for 15 minutes. Repeat 3 times, using all of the sauce, for a total of 45 minutes cooking time. (To prevent illness, wash hands, bowl, and any surfaces that touched the raw chicken with soap and warm water.)

Spinach-Stuffed Mushrooms

Bubbly Swiss cheese adds zing to these baked appetizers that you serve fresh from the oven. Choose any type or size of mushroom, but larger mushrooms have a more dramatic presentation than small ones. Garnish with sprigs of fresh parsley.

Yields about 24–36 appetizers, depending on the size of the mushrooms

What You Need:
1 (12-ounce) package frozen spinach soufflé
2–3 pounds fresh whole mushrooms
4–6 slices processed Swiss cheese

What You Do:
1. Preheat oven to at 350°. Remove the spinach soufflé from the freezer. Unwrap and place in a small mixing bowl. Thaw for about 15 minutes.

2. Wipe the mushrooms with a damp paper towel to clean. Remove the stems. Cover the stems and refrigerate for another use. Place the mushrooms cap-side down in a 9" × 13" ovenproof baking pan that has been sprayed with nonstick cooking spray.

3. Spoon about 1 to 2 teaspoons spinach soufflé into each mushroom cap. Top with a square of Swiss cheese (about 1" square), big enough to cover the top of the mushroom without hanging over the edge. Bake for 10 to 12 minutes, until the cheese melts.

Potato Skins

You can make this restaurant favorite at home, adding your favorite toppings. Serve with your choice of condiments. Cover and refrigerate scooped-out potato flesh for Mashed Potatoes (page 218) the next day.

Yields 32 appetizers

What You Need:
8 medium-size baking potatoes
Olive oil, as needed (about 2 tablespoons)
Seasoned salt, to taste
Pepper, to taste
2–3 green onions
2–3 cups shredded Cheddar cheese, as needed

What You Do:
1. Bake the potatoes (see "Baking Potatoes," page 113). Cool to room temperature. Cut each potato in half lengthwise and again in half horizontally. (Each potato makes 4 potato skins.) Scoop out the flesh, leaving about ½" of potato flesh on the skin.

2. Preheat oven to 400°. Place the potato skins on an ungreased baking sheet, skin-side down. Use a basting brush or your fingers to spread olive oil on the inside of the potatoes. Sprinkle with seasoned salt and pepper.

3. Slice the green onions as needed. Sprinkle the onion slices on top of the potato skins. Top with shredded Cheddar cheese. Bake for 10 to 15 minutes, until the cheese melts. Serve warm.

Miniature Taco Salads

Great for a Mexican-theme party, these miniature taco salads make attractive crowd pleasers. They're too messy for finger food, so serve on small plates and provide forks and lots of napkins.

⚕ Yields 12 salads ⚕

What You Need:
12 (6") corn tortillas
¼–½ head iceberg lettuce
2 tomatoes
1½ pounds ground beef
1 (1.25-ounce) package taco seasoning mix
⅓ cup salsa
2 cups shredded Cheddar cheese
1 cup sour cream

What You Do:
1. Preheat oven to 350°. Spray a muffin tin with nonstick cooking spray. Cut off the rounded edges of tortillas to make squares and place 1 in each of the spaces in the tin. Spray the tortillas with nonstick cooking spray to help them crisp up. Bake for 5 to 10 minutes until the shells are crisp.

2. Shred the lettuce using the large holes on a grater or by slicing into pieces about ¼" wide and 2" long. Place in medium-size mixing bowl. Set aside. Dice the tomatoes. Place in a separate bowl. Set aside.

Miniature Taco Salads
(continued)

3. Brown the ground beef with the taco seasoning according to package directions. Drain off fat.

4. Spoon about ¼ cup beef mixture into each shell. Top each salad with 1 teaspoon salsa, a layer of shredded lettuce, 1 tablespoon diced tomatoes, a layer of cheese, and 1 tablespoon of sour cream. Serve immediately.

Red Hot Chili Peppers

Chili peppers add distinct, spicy hot flavor to heavily seasoned dishes from Mexico, the southwestern United States, and Thailand. Among fresh chilies, the "King of Hot" title goes to the Habanero Red Savina. Other habanero varieties follow suit. Other very hot chilies include the jalapeño, Scotch bonnet, and pepperoni chilies. Their use in hot climates may have originated from their value as a food preservative. If a chili pepper is too hot for your liking, combine with cheese, sour cream, or other dairy product. A protein in milk called casein neutralizes the burning substance of the pepper.

During food preparation, you can reduce hotness by removing some or all of the ribs, inner membranes, and seeds, or by soaking for 30 minutes or less in cold water with a dash of salt or a little vinegar. When handling fresh peppers, wear rubber gloves, because the same substance that creates the hot flavor can also cause a burning sensation on the skin and in the eyes. Thoroughly wash hands and cooking utensils with soap after use. Chili peppers are high in vitamins A and C.

Spinach Dip

This dip is best served at room temperature, but be sure to cover and refrigerate any leftovers. Serve with corn chips or your favorite tortilla chips.

Yields 2 cups

What You Need:
1 (10-ounce) package frozen chopped spinach
2 green onions
½ cup fresh parsley
1 cup mayonnaise
Garlic salt, to taste
2–3 drops hot pepper sauce

What You Do:
1. Cook the spinach according to package directions. Drain and use your hands and paper towels to squeeze out extra moisture. Place in a medium-size mixing bowl. Remove the outer skin from the green onions. Chop the onions, including the dark green tops. Add to the bowl.

2. Use kitchen scissors to snip the parsley into the mixing bowl. Stir in the mayonnaise, garlic salt, and hot pepper sauce until well mixed.

Spicy Clam Dip

Bring the flavor of New England to your party, no matter where you live. Sliced raw vegetables, French bread, or corn chips all taste great with this "hot" dip you serve warm.

🍴 Yields 4 cups 🍴

What You Need:
4 cups shredded Cheddar cheese
¼ cup all-purpose flour
2 (10¾-ounce) cans condensed New England clam chowder
1 (6.5-ounce) can chopped clams
½ small white *or* yellow onion (enough to yield 2 tablespoons chopped)
4–5 drops hot pepper sauce

What You Do:
1. In a large mixing bowl, stir together the cheese and flour. Set aside.

2. In a large saucepan over medium heat, warm the soup (do *not* dilute), stirring often. When heated through, reduce heat to low. Add the cheese and flour mixture. Stir until the cheese melts and the ingredients are well blended.

3. Drain the clams. Chop the onion. Add the clams and onion to the cheese mixture. Sprinkle with hot pepper sauce. Stir until well mixed and heated through. Serve warm.

Easy Dinner Rolls

Fresh-baked rolls add a homey aroma and flavor to any meal. Make these in a muffin tin for attractive puffy rolls. You can also use this recipe to make Latvian Ham and Onion Treat (page 281).

Yields 1 dozen

What You Need:
1¼-ounce package active dry yeast
1 cup warm tap water
2 tablespoons white granulated sugar
1 teaspoon salt
2¼ cups all-purpose flour
1 egg
2 tablespoons solid shortening

What You Do:
1. Dissolve the yeast in the water in a large mixing bowl. Stir in the sugar, salt, and ½ of the flour. Beat until smooth. Stir in the egg, shortening; then add the remaining flour. Beat until smooth. Cover with a clean kitchen towel. Set aside at room temperature (at least 30 minutes) until it rises to twice its original size.

2. Grease a muffin tin with the solid shortening. Punch down the dough until it reduces in size. Fill the muffin tin cups about ½ full. Set aside for another 20 to 30 minutes. The dough will rise again to the top of the cups. Preheat oven to 400°. Bake for 15 to 20 minutes, until browned.

Latvian Ham and Onion Treat

Here's a traditional Latvian holiday favorite that's good any time of the year. Make the filling the night before to let the flavors mingle. Purchase refrigerated roll dough or double the recipe for Easy Dinner Rolls (page 280).

 **Yields 3–4 dozen rolls**

What You Need:

2½ pounds cooked ham
2 large white *or* yellow onions
Coarse black pepper, to taste

Basic roll dough for 2 dozen rolls
 (see Easy Dinner Rolls, page 280)
Flour, as needed
½ cup butter

What You Do:

1. Cut the ham and onions into very small pieces. Place in a large mixing bowl. Add the pepper. Stir until well mixed. Cover and refrigerate overnight.

2. Make the roll dough and let rise. Dust a cutting board or rolling surface with flour. Also dust the surface of the rolling pin with flour. For each appetizer, use your fingers to pull off a piece of dough about the size of a golf ball. Roll into a ball; then roll the dough flat into a 2½"- to 3"-diameter circle.

3. Preheat oven to 400°. Scoop a heaping teaspoon of the ham mixture onto the middle of the dough circle. Fold one side over the other. Fold the top and bottom over the sides. Pinch the dough together to seal. Turn over and place seam-side down on an ungreased baking sheet. Bake for 10 to 15 minutes, until golden brown. Melt the butter in a small saucepan. Remove the appetizers from the oven and let cool. Brush with melted butter.

Brazilian "Caviar"

There are no fish eggs in this dish, but at least you can afford to make it! Make it by hand even if you own a food processor. Otherwise it will be too runny. This dip is best chilled overnight to give the flavors a chance to mingle. Goes well with tortilla chips.

Yields 2 cups

What You Need:
1 (4¼-ounce) can chopped ripe (black) olives
1 (4-ounce) can chopped green chilies
1 medium-size tomato
2 green onions
1 clove fresh garlic (*or* ⅛ teaspoon garlic powder)
1 tablespoon olive oil
1 teaspoon red wine vinegar
½ teaspoon pepper
Seasoned salt, to taste

What You Do:
1. Drain and chop the olives and green chilies. Place in a colander over the sink to drain again.
2. Peel the tomato. Chop the tomato and drain in a colander.
3. Finely chop the green onions and garlic. Place in a small mixing bowl. Add the drained olives, chilies, and tomatoes. Gently stir in the olive oil, red wine vinegar, pepper, and seasoned salt until well mixed. Cover and refrigerate overnight. Just before serving, drain again.

Chapter 11

Desserts

Caramel Apples

Tart apple varieties work best for this traditional Halloween treat, because the flavor contrasts with the sweet candy.

Yields 5 caramel apples

What You Need:

5 medium apples

5 wooden skewers *or* wooden pop sticks

Shortening, as needed

1 (14-ounce) package caramel candy

2 tablespoons water

What You Do:

1. Rinse the apples in cold, running water. Dry thoroughly with a paper towel. Insert the wooden skewers into the stem end of each apple. Set aside. Set a piece of waxed paper on the kitchen counter or table. Use solid shortening and a paper towel to grease one side of the paper.

2. Place the caramels and water in a microwave-safe bowl. Microwave on high for 1 minute at a time. After each minute, stop cooking and stir. Repeat 2 or 3 times for a total cooking time of 2½ to 3 minutes, until the caramels melt. Stir until smooth. Or, melt the caramels and water in a saucepan or double boiler over medium-low heat, stirring constantly.

3. One at a time, dip the apples into the melted caramels, rolling around until well coated. (You might have to spoon caramel mixture over the apples.) Hold the apple over the saucepan, and let caramel mixture drip off. Place on waxed paper. Wait about 15 minutes for the caramel mixture to cool and set.

Raspberry-Currant
Ice Cream Topping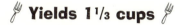

Serve this tangy topping warm over ice cream or a slice of angel food cake. Top with whipped cream if you like. Store any leftovers covered in the refrigerator.

Yields 1 ⅓ cups

What You Need:
1 ¼ cups frozen raspberries
½ tablespoon cornstarch
1 tablespoon water
½ cup currant jelly

What You Do:
1. Before you begin, place the raspberries in a saucepan and set out to thaw for 10 to 15 minutes. In a small mixing bowl, stir together the cornstarch and water until well blended. Set aside.
2. Place the raspberries over medium heat. Stir in the jelly. Cook until the mixture boils. Stir in the cornstarch mixture. Continue stirring for 1 minute. Remove from heat. Let cool slightly. Serve while still warm.

Hot Banana-Cinnamon
Ice Cream Topping

Spoon warm, cinnamon-flavored bananas over ice cream for a yummy hot/cold contrast. You can substitute chopped walnuts for the pecans.

 **Serves 2**

What You Need:
Shortening, as needed
1 banana
1/8 cup honey
1/2 tablespoon lemon juice
1/8 teaspoon cinnamon
1/8 teaspoon nutmeg
1 tablespoon chopped pecans
2 scoops vanilla ice cream

What You Do:
1. Preheat oven to 400°. Use the shortening to grease a 1 1/2-quart ovenproof baking pan. Peel the banana. Slice crosswise into circles. Lay the slices flat in the bottom of a the baking pan.
2. In a small mixing bowl, stir together the honey, lemon juice, cinnamon, and nutmeg. Pour over the bananas. Sprinkle with pecans. Bake for 5 to 10 minutes, until hot and bubbly. Let cool slightly. Serve while still warm over the ice cream.

Blueberry Ice Cream Topping

Jazz up your ice cream sundae with coooool blues. Blueberries, that is. Top with a maraschino cherry for a red, white, and blue dessert for the Fourth of July.

🍴 Yields 1⅓ cups 🍴

What You Need:
2 cups fresh blueberries
¼ cup water
¼ cup white granulated sugar
2 tablespoons lemon juice
2 teaspoons cornstarch
½ teaspoon cinnamon

What You Do:
1. Rinse the blueberries under cold, running water. Drain. Place in medium-size saucepan.
2. Stir in the water, sugar, lemon juice, cornstarch, and cinnamon. Bring to a boil over medium-high heat. Reduce heat to low. Cook for 5 minutes, stirring occasionally. Remove from heat. Cool slightly. Serve while still warm.

Quick and Easy Ice Cream Pie

This dessert looks as good as it tastes. Use any flavor ice cream that goes well with chocolate. Cover any leftover pie with aluminum foil and freeze.

Serves 8

What You Need:

1 quart ice cream
1 (16-ounce) package frozen nondairy whipped topping
1 (9") chocolate cookie pie crust
½ cup chocolate fudge ice cream topping
Chopped candy *or* chocolate sprinkles

What You Do:

1. Let the ice cream soften at room temperature for about 10 minutes. Let the frozen nondairy whipped topping thaw at room temperature for about 5 minutes, until smooth.

2. Spoon the ice cream into the pie crust. Use the back of the spoon to smooth into an even layer. Top with a layer of fudge topping, followed by a layer of frozen nondairy whipped topping.

3. Sprinkle with chopped candy or chocolate sprinkles. Freeze for at least 1 hour. When ready to serve, remove from the freezer and thaw for 5 to 10 minutes at room temperature.

Frozen Chocolate
Banana Pops

Just for fun, bring out the kid in you with these homemade pop-sicles that combine chocolate and banana, two of the world's favorite flavors. You can substitute chopped walnuts or chopped candy for the pecans.

Serves 2

What You Need:
1 banana
2 wooden pop sticks
1 (12-ounce) package semisweet chocolate morsels
½ cup chopped pecans

What You Do:

1. Cut the banana in half horizontally. Cut off the pointed ends (eat). Insert the wooden pop stick into one end of each half. Set aside.

2. Melt the chocolate morsels in a saucepan over very low heat in a saucepan or in a small microwave-safe mixing bowl in the microwave oven for about 1 to 3 minutes on high. Place the chopped pecans on a dinner plate or piece of waxed paper.

3. Dip each banana half in the melted chocolate. Roll around until well coated. Roll the chocolate-covered banana in the pecans. Place on a paper plate or piece of waxed paper or aluminum foil. Freeze for at least 1 hour.

Homemade Brownies

M

You can make brownies from a mix, but homemade are so much better. And they're not any harder to do. Be sure to cool completely before cutting. Serve plain, frost with Chocolate Butter Frosting (page 302), or dust on all sides with confectioners' sugar.

Yields 24 brownies

What You Need:

Shortening, as needed

4 ounces unsweetened baking chocolate

3/4 cup butter *or* margarine

3 eggs

2 cups white granulated sugar

1 teaspoon vanilla (*or* imitation)

1 cup all-purpose flour

1 cup chopped walnuts *or* pecans (optional)

What You Do:

1. Use the solid shortening to grease a 9" × 13" baking pan. Set aside. Preheat oven to 350°. (If you're using a glass pan, preheat oven to 325°.)

2. Place the baking chocolate and butter (or margarine) in a saucepan and melt over low heat. (Or, melt in a microwave on high for 2 minutes.) Stir until well blended. Pour into a large mixing bowl.

3. Lightly beat the eggs and stir them into the mixing bowl, along with the sugar and vanilla until well blended. Gently stir in the flour and nuts until all the ingredients are well mixed. Scrape into the prepared baking pan. Spread the mixture into an even layer.

4. Bake for 30 to 35 minutes. Test for doneness. Insert a toothpick into the center of the brownies and pull it out. The brownies are done if the toothpick has gooey crumbs sticking to it. Cool completely in the pan before cutting.

Shadow Berries

Here's a fun treat to celebrate Ground Hog Day. And you don't need the sun to cast a shadow over these strawberries. Make your own shadow with melted chocolate. You can substitute chunks of banana for the strawberries.

Yields 1 pint

What You Need:
1 pint fresh strawberries
1 tablespoon solid vegetable shortening
1 (12-ounce) package semisweet chocolate morsels
1 (11.5-ounce) bag milk chocolate morsels

What You Do:
1. Rinse and clean the strawberries (see page 86), except leave on the stems to use as little handles for dipping

2. In a saucepan over low heat, stir together the vegetable shortening and both packages of chocolate morsels until the chocolate melts. (Or, heat in a microwave-safe bowl in the microwave for about 2 minutes on high.)

3. Place a cooling rack on top of several thicknesses of paper towel. Use a table fork or fondue fork to "stab" each strawberry. Dip the strawberries in the melted chocolate. Place on cooling rack until the chocolate hardens.

Baked Apples

For the best flavor, choose such varieties as Jonathan, McIntosh, or Granny Smith. Their firm texture is best and their tartness balances the sweetness of the candy. You can substitute 1 tablespoon cornstarch for the flour.

Serves 2

What You Need:

2 fresh apples
3 tablespoons white granulated sugar
1/4 teaspoon cinnamon
1/8 teaspoon salt
1/2 cup water
2 tablespoons all-purpose flour
Red-hot cinnamon candies

What You Do:

1. Preheat oven to 350°. Rinse the apples in cold, running water. Cut the apples in half and remove the cores. Place, peel-side down, in the bottom of a baking pan that has been sprayed with non-stick cooking spray.

> **Using an Apple Corer**
>
> If you like apples, you'll love a kitchen gadget called a corer. A corer is a circular tool with a round space in the middle and pie-shaped holes around the circle. The metal edges are sharp on the bottom side. To use, first rinse the apple in cold, running water. Pat dry with a paper towel. Place the apple on a cutting board, stem-side up. Place the circle of the corer over the stem. Push down in a single thrust. The apple slices will fall away, and the core will be removed.

2. In a saucepan, stir together the sugar, cinnamon, salt, water, and flour over low heat until hot and slightly thickened. Pour the mixture over the apples in the baking pan. Top with cinnamon candies. Bake uncovered for 40 to 50 minutes.

Baked Pears

Because of their spicy, sweet flavor, Anjou or Bartlett pears work best in this recipe. Serve this as a dessert or as a quick, nutritious snack. Place the remaining sauce in a serving bowl and serve with the pears.

Serves 2

What You Need:
2 fresh pears
¼ firmly packed cup brown sugar
2 tablespoons maple syrup
1½ tablespoons water
Dash salt
Dash ginger
¾ teaspoon grated lemon rind

What You Do:
1. Rinse the pears under cold running water. Leave the stems on the pears, but cut off a slice from the bottom so the pears will stand upright without wobbling. Stand the pears in an oven-proof baking dish that has been sprayed with nonstick cooking spray (for easy cleanup).

2. Preheat oven to 325°. In a small mixing bowl, stir together the brown sugar, maple syrup, water, salt, ginger, and lemon rind. Spoon the sauce over the pears. Bake for 1½ hours. After each half-hour, spoon sauce from the bottom of the baking dish over the pears again. Serve warm.

Fruit Pizza

This pizza really is a glorified cookie. But with fresh fruit, it tastes so good, you might forget it's good for you, too.

M

Serves 6–8

What You Need:
1 (18-ounce) tube refrigerated sugar cookie dough
2 (8-ounce) packages cream cheese
½ cup blueberries
½ cup green seedless grapes
½ cup strawberries
2 tablespoons confectioners' sugar

What You Do:
1. Using your hands, shape the cookie dough into a circle on an ungreased cookie sheet. Or, form the dough into a ball and use a rolling pin to form into a circle. Bake according to package directions. Cool.

2. Let the cream cheese soften at room temperature for about 10 minutes. Spread the cream cheese in a thick layer over the cookie.

3. Rinse the blueberries and grapes under cold, running water. Drain. Pick the grapes off the stems. Slice in half lengthwise. Clean the strawberries (see page 86) and slice in half lengthwise.

4. Spoon the fruit over the top of the pizza. With the back of the spoon or your fingers, gently press the fruit into the cream cheese to anchor it in place. Cut into pie-shaped pieces. Sprinkle with confectioners' sugar. To serve, cut into pie-shaped pieces.

Chocolate Drop Cookies

If you're in the mood for something chocolate, whip up a batch of these cookies. Serve with a glass of cold milk or a scoop of your favorite flavor of ice cream.

Yields about 2 dozen

What You Need:
1 (12-ounce) package semisweet chocolate morsels
2 tablespoons butter
1 (14-ounce) can sweetened condensed milk
1 cup all-purpose flour
1 tablespoon vanilla (*or* imitation)
Pinch of salt
1 cup chopped pecans *or* walnuts
Shortening, as needed

What You Do:
1. In a small saucepan over low, melt together the chocolate morsels and butter. Stir in the sweetened condensed milk until well blended.

2. Pour into a large mixing bowl. Stir in the flour, vanilla, and salt until well mixed. Gently stir in the nuts.

3. Preheat oven to 350°. Grease a cookie sheet with solid shortening. Spoon a heaping teaspoonful of the mixture onto the cookie sheet. Repeat in rows. Bake for 8 to 10 minutes.

4. Use a pancake turner to remove from cookie sheet. Cool on a wire rack. Or, eat warm if you can't wait!

Chocolate-Chip Oatmeal Cookies

Chocolate chip cookies should be in every cook's repertoire, and this recipe has the added goodness and texture of oatmeal. You can buy cookies in a package, but they're so much better homemade—especially served warm right out of the oven! You can use either regular or instant oatmeal in this recipe.

Yields 4 dozen cookies

What You Need:
1 cup (2 sticks) butter *or* margarine
1 firmly packed cup brown sugar
½ cup white granulated sugar
2 eggs
1 teaspoon vanilla (*or* imitation)
1½ cups all-purpose flour
1 teaspoon baking soda
2 teaspoons cinnamon
½ teaspoon salt
3 cups uncooked oatmeal
1 (12-ounce) package semisweet chocolate morsels

What You Do:
1. Before you begin, set out the butter (or margarine) for about 20 minutes to soften at room temperature. In a large mixing bowl, use an electric mixer to beat together the butter, brown sugar, and white sugar until creamy. Lightly beat the eggs and add to the bowl, along with the vanilla. Beat until smooth.

Chocolate-Chip Oatmeal Cookies 🥕
(continued)

2. In a separate, medium-size mixing bowl, stir together the flour, baking soda, cinnamon, and salt until well mixed. Slowly add the flour mixture to the large mixing bowl, stirring with a spoon or your hands until well mixed. Stir in the oats. Gently stir in the chocolate morsels.

3. Preheat oven to 350°. Scoop heaping tablespoons of the dough and drop onto an ungreased cookie sheet in 3 evenly spaced rows of 4 cookies each. Bake for 10 to 12 minutes, until golden brown. Remove from the oven and let cool for 1 minute. Use a pancake turner to move the cookies onto a wire rack.

Variation: Chocolate Chip Bars 🥕

You can use the same recipe for chocolate chip bars instead. When the dough is ready, pour into an ungreased 9" × 13" baking pan. Bake for 30 to 35 minutes. Cool in the pan. Cut into twelve 3" × 4" rectangles.

Shopping for Ingredients

What if your recipe calls for a 5⅓-ounce can of evaporated milk, but you get to the store and find only a 5-ounce can? Or, what if your recipe says a 10¾-ounce can of soup, but you find only a 10.5-ounce can? Do you buy 2 cans of evaporated milk and measure out ⅓ ounce? Do you pour out some of the soup? No. Can sizes may vary by brand. If a recipe calls for a certain size can, choose the size closest to what the recipe calls for. For example, vegetables come in sizes that are roughly 8 ounces and 15 ounces. If your recipe calls for 2 cups of green beans, use the 15-ounce can.

Oatmeal Cookies

Here's an old-fashioned treat that's still a favorite with kids of all ages. You can omit the raisins and/or nuts if you prefer. The oats in this recipe are simply uncooked oatmeal.

Yields 24 cookies

What You Need:

1 egg
¼ cup solid shortening
¼ firmly packed cup brown sugar
¼ cup white granulated sugar
¼ teaspoon vanilla (*or* imitation)
1 tablespoon milk

½ cup all-purpose flour
¼ teaspoon baking soda
¼ teaspoon salt
¾ cup oats
½ cup seedless raisins
½ cup chopped walnuts

What You Do:

1. Lightly beat the egg. In a large mixing bowl, stir together the egg, shortening, brown sugar, white sugar, and vanilla. Stir in the milk.

2. In a separate, medium-size mixing bowl stir together the flour, baking soda, and salt. Slowly add the flour mixture to the large mixing bowl, stirring with a spoon or your hands until well mixed. Stir in the oats, raisins, and walnuts.

3. Preheat oven to 400°. Scoop a rounded teaspoonful of dough onto an ungreased cookie sheet. Make 3 rows of 4 cookies each. Bake for 8 to 10 minutes. Use a pancake turner to remove the cookies from the cookie sheet. Let cool on a wire rack.

Peanut Butter Cookies

There's nothing like warm peanut butter cookies straight from the oven. And they're quick and easy to make.

M

Yields 3 dozen

What You Need:

½ cup butter *or* margarine	2 eggs
½ cup solid shortening	1 teaspoon vanilla (*or* imitation)
1 cup peanut butter	2¼ cups all-purpose flour
1 cup white granulated sugar	2 teaspoons baking soda
1 firmly packed cup brown sugar	¼ teaspoon salt

What You Do:

1. Before beginning, set out the butter (or margarine) for 10 or 15 minutes to soften at room temperature. In a large mixing bowl, stir together the butter, shortening, peanut butter, white and brown sugar, eggs, and vanilla until well blended.

2. In a separate bowl, mix together the flour, baking soda, and salt. Stir into the peanut butter mixture, using a spoon or your hands, until well mixed.

3. Preheat oven to 375°. Take 1 to 2 tablespoons of dough and use your hands to form it into balls about 1" in diameter. Place about 2" to 3" apart on an ungreased cookie sheet in 3 rows of 4.

4. Dip a table fork into flour and push down on each ball to partly flatten the cookie. Repeat to form a crisscross pattern. Bake for 10 to 12 minutes. Use a pancake turner to remove from the cookie sheet. Let cool on a wire rack.

Kwik Kake

M You don't even need a mixing bowl for this easy cake you make from scratch. Just mix everything together and bake. And you don't need eggs or frosting, either. It's an almost-instant snack or dessert.

Serves 8

What You Need:
1½ cups all-purpose flour
1 cup white granulated sugar
6 tablespoons vegetable oil
3 tablespoons cocoa
1 teaspoon salt
1 teaspoon baking soda
1 tablespoon vinegar
1 cup cold water
1 teaspoon vanilla (*or* imitation)
1 tablespoon confectioners' sugar

What You Do:
1. Preheat oven to 350°. In an ungreased 9" × 9" baking pan, stir together all the ingredients *except* the confectioners' sugar until well blended. Bake for 25 minutes.

2. Let cool. Sprinkle with confectioners' sugar.

Yellow Cake

Here's a quick and easy cake you can make from scratch. Top with Chocolate Butter Frosting (page 302) or your favorite canned or packaged frosting.

Yields 1 layer

What You Need:
1/3 cup solid shortening, plus extra for greasing
1/2 cup all-purpose flour, plus extra for dusting
3/4 cup white granulated sugar
2 1/2 teaspoons baking powder
1/2 teaspoon salt
1 egg
1 1/2 teaspoons vanilla extract (*or* imitation)
3/4 cup milk

What You Do:
1. Preheat oven to 375°. Grease a round or square baking pan with shortening and dust lightly with flour.

2. Place the 1/3 cup shortening, 1/2 cup flour, the sugar, baking powder, salt, egg, vanilla, and 1/2 of the milk in a large mixing bowl. Beat with an electric mixer or by hand for about 2 minutes. Pour in the remaining milk and beat for another 2 minutes. Pour the batter into the prepared baking pan.

3. Bake for 30 minutes. Test for doneness by inserting a toothpick into the center of the cake. The cake is done if the toothpick comes out clean. Remove from the oven and let cool on a wire rack. Let the cake cool completely before frosting.

Chocolate Butter Frosting

This creamy frosting will satisfy the chocolate lover in you. Use to frost Yellow Cake (page 301), Homemade Brownies (page 290), or your favorite cake or cupcakes.

Yields enough frosting for a 1-layer cake

What You Need:
3 tablespoons butter *or* margarine
1 ounce unsweetened chocolate
2$\frac{1}{3}$ cups confectioners' sugar
$\frac{3}{4}$ teaspoon vanilla (*or* imitation)
1–2 tablespoons milk

What You Do:
1. Before beginning, set out the butter (or margarine) for 10 to 15 minutes to soften at room temperature. In a saucepan over low heat, melt the chocolate. Remove from heat. Set aside.
2. Sift the confectioners' sugar into a mixing bowl or shake through a strainer 3 times. Set aside.
3. In a small mixing bowl, beat the butter with an electric mixer or by hand until fluffy. Stir in the melted chocolate, vanilla, 1 tablespoon milk, and ½ of the sugar. Beat until well blended. Slowly add remaining sugar. If the frosting becomes too thick, add more milk a little at a time until the frosting reaches the desired consistency.

Frozen Chocolate Peanut Parfait

Wow your guests with this frozen dessert that takes only minutes to prepare but needs to be made at least 4 hours before the party to allow for the necessary freezing time. Cover any leftovers with aluminum foil and freeze.

Serves 6

What You Need:
1 quart vanilla ice cream
¼ cup (½ stick) butter *or* margarine
1 dozen chocolate sandwich cookies
6 ounces salted Spanish peanuts
2 cups hot fudge topping for ice cream

What You Do:
1. Remove the ice cream from the freezer and set aside for about 10 minutes to soften. Spray a 9" × 13" baking pan with nonstick cooking spray.

2. In a frying pan, melt the butter over low heat. Place the cookies on a cutting board. Crush between 2 sheets of waxed paper with a rolling pin. Add to the melted butter. Remove from heat and stir. Spoon the mixture into the baking pan. Use your fingers to pack the mixture in the bottom of the pan.

3. Spread the ice cream over the cookie mixture. Add a layer of peanuts. Cover with aluminum foil and freeze for at least 3 hours, until hard.

4. Top with fudge topping. Refreeze for about 1 hour. Serve directly from the freezer.

Apple Crisp

Here's apple pie flavor with half the work. Use such tart apples as Jonathan, Winesap, or McIntosh varieties to balance the sugar and spices. Serve while still warm with a wedge of Cheddar cheese or top with a scoop of vanilla ice cream. You can substitute allspice or apple pie spice for the nutmeg.

Serves 6

What You Need:
1 tablespoon solid vegetable shortening
¼ cup brown sugar
¾ cup white granulated sugar
6 apples
¾ cup all-purpose flour
1 teaspoon cinnamon
½ teaspoon nutmeg
½ cup butter *or* margarine

What You Do:
1. Preheat oven to 375°. Use a paper towel and the solid vegetable shortening to grease a 9" × 9" ovenproof baking pan. Mix together the brown sugar and white sugar in a medium-size mixing bowl. Set aside.

2. Peel and core the apples. Slice or chop the apples into bite-size pieces. Place in the prepared baking pan. Sprinkle with ¼ cup of the sugar mixture. Stir. Set aside.

Apple Crisp
(continued)

3. Add the flour, cinnamon, and nutmeg to the remaining sugar mixture in the mixing bowl. Slice the butter into ½"-wide pieces and add to the mixture. Use 2 table knives to make Xs through the mixture. Work in the butter until the mixture is crumbly.

4. Cover the apples with the crumbly mixture. Let some fall into the spaces between the apples. Bake for 45 to 55 minutes.

How Sweet It Is

You can sweeten foods with corn syrup, honey, maple syrup, and molasses. But the most common sweetener used in home cooking is sugar. Sugar most commonly comes from sugar cane and sugar beet. However, some commercial sugars derive from sorghum, maple, and palm. The 3 types of sugar most often used in cooking are granulated sugar, brown sugar, and confectioners' sugar. Granulated sugar is the sugar you're used to seeing in a sugar bowl. Brown sugar is a mixture of granulated sugar and molasses. Brown sugar comes in light and dark varieties. Confectioners' sugar, also called powdered sugar, is fine granulated sugar mixed with corn-starch. Its texture resembles flour. When cooking, use the type of sugar the recipe specifies. Do not try to interchange them.

Turtle Cake

Chocolate, caramel, and pecan flavors make this cake taste like everyone's favorite turtle candies. Delightful served warm topped with whipped cream or frozen nondairy whipped topping.

Serves 12

What You Need:

1 tablespoon solid vegetable shortening
1 (18.25-ounce) box German chocolate cake mix
1 (14-ounce) package caramels
½ cup (1 stick) butter
1½ cups evaporated milk
1 cup chopped pecans
1 cup semisweet chocolate morsels

What You Do:

1. Preheat oven to 350°. Use a paper towel to grease a 9" × 13" baking pan with the shortening. Dust with about 2 teaspoons of the dry cake mix. Return "extra" dry mix to the package.

2. Mix the cake batter in a large mixing bowl, according to package directions. (Check the box for egg, oil, and water requirements to be sure you have the ingredients on hand.) Pour ½ of the batter into the prepared baking pan. Bake for 15 minutes. Remove from oven.

Turtle Cake 🥕
(continued)

3. While the cake is baking, stir together the caramels, butter, and milk in a saucepan over low heat. Stir constantly until the caramels melt. Be careful not to let the milk scorch the bottom of the pan. After removing the cake from the oven, pour the caramel mixture over the cake. Top with a layer of pecans and a layer of chocolate morsels. Cover with remaining batter. Return to oven and bake for 15 to 20 minutes, until a toothpick inserted in the center comes out clean.

How to Whip Cream

What most people think of as whipped cream actually is sweetened whipped cream. The trick to making fabulous whipped cream is to prechill the whipping cream, as well as the bowl and beaters you will use. Whipped cream is difficult to make by hand. An electric mixer makes the job much easier. Here's what you do. Beat together 3 pints chilled whipping cream and 3 to 4 tablespoons confectioners' sugar. (Start with 3 tablespoons and taste. Add more if you like it sweeter.) Beat until stiff enough to hold a peak when you lift the whisk or beater out of the bowl. Be careful not to beat too long or you'll have fresh butter! Cover and refrigerate until ready to use. You can top a pie with whipped cream as long as 6 hours before serving and refrigerate. If the whipped cream starts to separate while sitting in the refrigerator, whip again for 1 minute.

Pink Lemonade Pie

Served cold, this lemony dessert makes a refreshing treat on a hot summer day. You'll need a portable hand mixer. Also, *do not* substitute frozen nondairy whipped topping for the whipping cream. Cover any leftover pie with aluminum foil and freeze.

Serves 8

What You Need:
1 (6-ounce) can frozen pink lemonade concentrate
1 (8-ounce) package boxed cream cheese
1 (14-ounce) can sweetened condensed milk
3 drops red food coloring (optional)
½ pint whipping cream
1 (9") graham cracker pie crust

What You Do:
1. Thaw the lemonade concentrate (do not dilute). Let the cream cheese soften at room temperature for about 10 minutes.
2. In a large mixing bowl, use an electric hand mixer to beat the cream cheese until fluffy. Beat in the lemonade concentrate, sweetened condensed milk, and food coloring.
3. Whip the cream (see page 307) in a separate mixing bowl. Spoon the whipped cream onto the cream cheese mixture in the large bowl. Gently mix by stirring from the bottom and placing the mixture on top of the whipped cream. Mix until well blended.
4. Refrigerate for 30 minutes or until the mixture mounds slightly when dropped from a spoon. Pour into the crust. Freeze for 6 hours or until firm. When ready to serve, remove the pie from the freezer and let sit for 10 minutes before serving.

Pecan Pie

Sweet and meaty, this pie tastes so delicious, your friends will never guess how easy it is to make. And they'll be back for more. Top with whipped cream if you like.

Serves 6

What You Need:

1½ cups maple syrup
¼ cup white granulated sugar
¼ cup butter *or* margarine
1½ cups pecan halves

1 unbaked 9" pie crust
3 eggs
1 teaspoon vanilla (*or* imitation)
Dash of salt

What You Do:

1. In a medium-size saucepan over medium-high heat, stir together the syrup, sugar, and butter (or margarine) until the mixture boils. Continue cooking for 5 minutes, stirring occasionally. Remove from heat.

2. Place the pecans in an even layer in the bottom of the pie crust. Preheat oven to 375°.

3. In a medium-size mixing bowl, slightly beat the eggs with a fork. Stir in the vanilla and salt. Be sure the syrup mixture has slightly cooled (so it won't cook the eggs). Spoon a little at a time into the egg mixture, stirring until well mixed. Drizzle over the pecans.

4. Bake for 35 to 40 minutes. Test for doneness. A knife inserted in the center should come out clean.

Fresh Strawberry Pie

When luscious fat strawberries come into season in the spring, use some of them to create this popular pie. If strawberries are out of season, you can substitute frozen ones. Thaw them first. Instead of frozen topping, you can make homemade whipped cream (see "How to Whip Cream," page 307).

Serves 6

What You Need:
1 frozen 9" pie crust
2 cups fresh strawberries
1 cup white granulated sugar
2 tablespoons cornstarch
1 cup water
¼ cup strawberry-flavored gelatin (powdered mix)
1 (8-ounce) carton frozen nondairy whipped topping

What You Do:
1. Bake the pie crust according to package instructions. Set aside. Clean the strawberries (page 86). Slice about ½ of the strawberries into halves. Set aside.

2. In a large frying pan over medium heat, stir together the sugar, cornstarch, and water until the sauce is clear and thick. Remove from heat. Stir in the gelatin mix until well blended. Let cool.

3. Gently stir in the sliced and whole strawberries until well coated. Pour the mixture into the pie shell. Chill in the refrigerator. When ready to serve, top with whipped topping.

Chocolate Chip–Cookie Cake

Celebrate a birthday or other special occasion with an easy "cake" you can decorate with an appropriate personalized message. To serve, cut into pie-shaped slices. Serve with your favorite flavor of ice cream.

Serves 6–8

What You Need:
1 tablespoon solid vegetable shortening
1 (18-ounce) tube refrigerated chocolate chip cookie dough
1 (16-ounce) can creamy vanilla frosting
Sprinkles, candies, *or* tubes of gel frosting, as needed

What You Do:

1. Place the cookie dough on an ungreased cookie sheet. Use your hands to spread out the dough in a circle. Or, use your hands to form the dough into a ball, and use a rolling pin to form into a circle. Bake for 5 minutes *less* than package directions, watching to be sure the cookie doesn't overcook. Cool completely.

2. Spread a layer of frosting over the cookie. Decorate with your choice of sprinkles or candies. Or, write "Happy Birthday," "Congratulations," or another message with gel frosting.

Sweetheart Cherry Cheese Tarts à la Chalise

This recipe is responsible for at least one marriage! You can use a 12-cup muffin tin with paper liners. Or, you can use a 9" pie pan instead if you increase the baking time by 5 minutes.

Yields 12 tarts

What You Need:
1 (21-ounce) can cherry pie filling
1 (8-ounce) package block cream cheese (do *not* use whipped)
13 graham cracker squares (7½ rectangles broken in halves)
2 teaspoons white granulated sugar
2½ tablespoons butter
½ cup confectioners' sugar
1 egg
1 teaspoon vanilla (*or* imitation)

What You Do:
1. Chill the pie filling in the refrigerator. Set out cream cheese to soften for 10 to 15 minutes. Place the graham crackers on a cutting board or other rolling surface. Crush with a rolling pin.
2. Place the crumbs in a medium-size mixing bowl. Add the granulated sugar. Melt the butter over low heat in a saucepan. Drizzle over the crumbs. Stir until well mixed. Press the mixture into the bottom of paper cupcake liners placed in a muffin tin.
3. Preheat oven to 350°. In a small mixing bowl, stir together the cream cheese, confectioners' sugar, egg, and vanilla until well blended. Spread over the graham cracker crust. Bake for 10 to 15 minutes. Let cool.
4. Spoon the cherry pie filling over the tarts. Chill for about 1 hour (or even overnight) before serving.

Cherry-Banana-Strawberry-Pineapple Pie

Here's a colorful, tangy dessert that welcomes spring—or makes you feel like spring anytime of the year. Use ¾ cup sugar if you prefer a sweeter flavor. You can substitute one 15-ounce can of bing cherries (drained).

⚘ Serves 6 ⚘

What You Need:

1 (9") frozen deep-dish pie crust

8 ounces frozen cherries

1 (8-ounce) can crushed pineapple, with juice

½ cup, plus 2 tablespoons white granulated sugar

¼ cup all-purpose flour

½ (3-ounce) package strawberry gelatin dessert

1 banana

½ (2.25-ounce) package slivered almonds

4 ounces nondairy frozen whipped topping

What You Do:

1. Bake the pie crust according to package directions until golden brown. Let cool.

2. While the crust is baking, place the cherries into a saucepan to thaw. When partially defrosted, stir in the pineapple with juice, flour, sugar, and strawberry gelatin. Cook over low heat until the cherries have defrosted and the pot is steaming. Remove from heat.

3. Peel and slice the banana crosswise into thin circles. When the pie crust is cool to the touch, place ½ of the banana slices in the bottom of the pie shell. Sprinkle with almonds. Pour the cooled cherry mixture over the almond layer. Top with nondairy frozen whipped topping. Chill in the refrigerator for at least 1 hour.

Coffee Pot de Crème

This sounds hard, but it's so simple! And *mmmm* so good. It's easy enough to make any day, and elegant enough to impress a crowd! Start early, as the dessert needs at least 2 hours to chill. You'll need 6 ceramic, ovenproof coffee mugs. Instead of whipping your own cream, you can use pressurized canned whipped cream. You can use the unused egg whites from the Lentil Loaf (page 204).

Serves 6

What You Need:

5 eggs
½ cup white granulated sugar
½ teaspoon vanilla (*or* imitation)
3 tablespoons instant coffee

½ cup heavy cream
Water, as needed
¼ cup whipped cream (see "How to Whip Cream," page 307)

What You Do:

1. Preheat oven to 350°. Separate the egg yolks and whites (see "Chef's Secret: Separating Eggs," page 315). Cover and refrigerate the egg whites for another use. Wash your hands with soap after handling the raw eggs. In a small mixing bowl, beat together the egg yolks, sugar, and vanilla until smooth. Set aside.

2. In a medium-size saucepan, stir together the instant coffee and heavy cream. Heat over medium-low heat, stirring often until small bubbles form at the sides and a light skin forms on the cream. (Do *not* let the cream boil!)

Coffee Pot de Crème ✎ (continued)

3. Hold a strainer over the yolk mixture and pour ½ of the cream into it to remove any "skin" that forms. Stir until well mixed. Strain the remaining cream into the yolk mixture. Stir until smooth. Divide the mixture into 6 ceramic coffee mugs. Place the coffee mugs in a 9" × 12" baking dish. Fill the baking dish ½ full with water.

4. Bake for 25 to 30 minutes. The dessert is done when the mixture is firm enough not to slosh around when slightly shaken. Remove from oven. Cool to room temperature. Chill in the refrigerator at least 2 hours. When ready to serve, top with whipped cream.

Chef's Secret: Separating Eggs

The easiest way to separate the yolk and the white of a raw egg is to use your hands. (Be sure they're clean!) Hold one hand (palm-side up) over a mixing bowl. Crack the egg into your palm and let the white ooze through your fingers until the yolk is all you have left in your hand. Gently place the yolk in a separate bowl or coffee cup. Be sure to wash hands and mixing bowls with soap and warm water after handling raw eggs.

Another method to separate egg yolks and whites is using a gadget called (ingeniously) an egg separator. Secure the egg separator on the lip of a small mixing bowl (or simply hold it). Crack the egg. Open the shell over the egg separator and let the yolk fall into the depression in the device. The white will run out the sides into the bowl. Place yolk in a separate bowl or cup.

Or use the eggshell itself. Crack the egg over a bowl, being careful to catch the yolk in ½ of the shell. Let the white run into the bowl. Pour the yolk into the empty half-shell, again letting the remaining egg white fall into the bowl. Repeat as necessary.

Honey Cake

Honey cake recipes abound. Here's a recipe to get you started. Look for other variations—or ask your mother or grandmother. Before you begin, let all the ingredients stand on the counter until they reach room temperature (about 70°).

 Yields 1 cake

What You Need:

Shortening, as needed
2 cups, plus 2 tablespoons
 all-purpose flour
½ cup butter (or solid shortening)
½ cup white granulated sugar
2 eggs
½ teaspoon baking soda
1 teaspoon double-acting baking powder
½ teaspoon cinnamon

¼ teaspoon ground ginger
¼ teaspoon salt
½ cup honey
½ cup strong coffee, cooled
½ teaspoon vanilla extract (or imitation)
¾ cup chopped walnuts
1 tablespoon grated orange rind
1–2 tablespoons confectioners' sugar

What You Do:

1. Preheat oven to 350°. Grease a 9" × 9" ovenproof baking pan. Place the 2 tablespoons flour into the pan. Tip, tilt, and gently tap the pan until the flour dusts the sides and bottom.

2. In a large mixing bowl, use a spoon or electric mixer to blend the butter and sugar until soft and smooth. Add the eggs and continue blending until the mixture is light and fluffy. Set aside.

Honey Cake
(continued)

3. Place a piece of waxed paper on the counter. Sift together the 2 cups flour, baking soda, baking powder, cinnamon, ginger, and salt onto the waxed paper. Set aside. In a separate medium-size mixing bowl, stir together the honey and coffee until well blended. Stir in the vanilla extract, walnuts, and grated orange rind until well mixed.

4. Scoop about 1/3 of the sifted ingredients into the egg mixture. Stir. Scoop about 1/3 of the honey mixture into the egg mixture. Stir. Continue alternating 1/3 of each mixture until all the ingredients are well blended. Pour the batter into baking pan.

5. Bake for 30 minutes. Let cool. Sprinkle with confectioners' sugar.

Sifting Flour

Some recipes call for added "air," and sifting flour is the way to accomplish this task. To sift, place a small amount of flour into the top of the sifter. Hold the device over a mixing bowl and pull on the handle several times until all of the flour passes through the screen. One way to mix dry ingredients is to sift them together. Simply place all the ingredients into the top of the sifter at the same time. Sift. If you don't have a sifter, you can create the same effect by placing flour and other dry ingredients in a strainer. Gently shake the strainer until all the ingredients have passed through.

Cupcake Surprise

These easy cupcakes have a nutty cream cheese filling, so you can serve them without frosting if you like. For easy cleanup, use paper cupcake liners.

Yields 12 cupcakes

What You Need:

For the cupcakes:
¼ cup butter *or* margarine
½ cup white granulated sugar
1 egg
½ teaspoon vanilla (*or* imitation)
⅔ cup all-purpose flour
¼ cup unsweetened cocoa powder
1 teaspoon baking powder
½ cup milk

For the filling:
3 ounces cream cheese
¼ cup white granulated sugar
2 tablespoons chopped walnuts *or* pecans
½ teaspoon vanilla (*or* imitation)

What You Do:

1. To make the cupcakes, set out the butter (or margarine) to soften at room temperature for 10 or 15 minutes. In a medium-size mixing bowl, stir together the butter and sugar until fluffy. Stir in the egg and vanilla.

2. In a separate small mixing bowl, stir together the flour, cocoa, and baking powder. Add ½ of the flour mixture to the egg mixture, stirring until well blended. Slowly stir in the milk. Add remaining flour mixture and stir until the batter is smooth. Set aside.

Cupcake Surprise ✎
(continued)

3. To make the filling, set out the cream cheese for 10 to 15 minutes to soften at room temperature. Place the cream cheese, sugar, nuts, and vanilla in a small mixing bowl. Stir until well mixed.

4. Preheat oven to 375°. Grease a 12-cup muffin tin with shortening and dust with flour, or place paper baking cups in the muffin spaces.

5. Spoon 1 tablespoon of the cupcake batter into each cup. Spoon 1 teaspoon of the filling into each cup. Spoon another tablespoon of batter on top of the filling, dividing the batter evenly among all cupcakes. Bake for 20 minutes. Let cool on a wire rack.

Cooking Terms

The term *fold* means to mix ingredients by sliding a spoon or spatula toward you along the bottom of the bowl, then up the side. In effect, you are blending ingredients by gently turning them over on top of each other. The terms *beat* and *whip* refer to rapid, circular stirring motions, using a wire whisk or portable hand mixer. Both methods add air to the ingredients. *Beating* makes ingredients smooth and fluffy. *Whipping* lightens the mixture and increases its volume.

Appendix A
Equipping the Kitchen

f you're new to the kitchen, you may not have the essentials you need to cook for yourself. Here's a list of basic utensils, herbs, spices, and other ingredients you'll want to have on hand. Those marked with an asterisk are recommended for all kitchens. Purchase other items as needed.

Aluminum foil
Appliances:
  Coffee pot
  2-quart slow cooker
  Electric blender
  Electric mixer
  Electric popcorn popper
  Electric skillet
  *Electric (or manual) can
    opener
  *Toaster or toaster oven
*Colander
*Cutting board
Gadgets:
  Apple corer
  Bagel slicer
  Egg slicer
  Kitchen scissors

*Kitchen timer
Meat thermometer
Sifter
Steamer basket
Hand utensils:
  Cheese slicer
  Grater
  Huller
  Ice cream scoop
  *Long-handled fork
  *Pancake turner
  Pizza cutter
  *Potato masher
  Rolling pin
  *Slotted spoon
  Soup ladle
  Spaghetti server
  Spatula (flexible)

*Spoon (large)
Tongs
Wooden spoon

Knives:
Bread knife
*Paring knife
*Potato peeler
*Roast slicer

Measuring cups (oven proof glass)
1 cup
*2 cup

*Measuring spoon set
⅛ teaspoon to
1 tablespoon

*Mixing bowls, set of 3

Muffin tin

Ovenproof pans
Baking pans (2)
9″ × 13″ × 2″
*9″ × 9″ × 1¾″
*Baking sheets (2)
Covered baking dishes (3)
1-quart
1½-quart
*2-quart
Loaf pans
9½″ × 5¼″ × 2¾″
or 8½″ × 4½″ × 2½″

Pie pan
8″ or 9″ diameter, 1½″ deep
Roasting pan
*9″ × 13″ × 2″
Tube pan or bundt pan

*Paper towels

Plastic wrap

Popcorn popper

*Potholders (4)

Stovetop pots and pans (with lids)
Double boiler, 1½-quart
Frying pans (2)
*9″ to 10″ diameter
6″ to 7″ diameter
1-quart saucepan
*2-quart saucepan
*4-quart Dutch oven or stewpot

*Strainer (if you don't have a sifter)

Trivet, 1 or more

Waxed paper

Wire whisk

Herbs, Spices, and Other Ingredients

Baking soda
Basil
Bay leaves
Bouillon cubes, beef, chicken,
  and vegetable
Brown sugar
Cayenne pepper
Cayenne pepper hot sauce
Celery salt
Celery seed
Chili powder
*Cinnamon
Confectioners' sugar
Cumin
Curry powder
Double-acting baking powder
Dry mustard
*Flour, all-purpose
Garlic, minced
Garlic powder
*Garlic salt
Ginger
*Granulated sugar
Honey
Hot pepper sauce (like
  Tabasco)
Ketchup
Lemon juice

Maple syrup
Mayonnaise
Mustard, prepared
Nonstick cooking spray
Nutmeg
*Olive oil
Onion, minced
*Onion flakes, chopped
Onion powder
Onion salt
Oregano
Paprika
*Parsley flakes, dried
*Pepper
Poultry seasoning
Rosemary
*Salt
Seasoned salt (like Lawry's)
Sesame seed
*Solid shortening
*Sugar
Tarragon
*Vanilla extract (or imitation
  vanilla extract)
*Vegetable oil
Vinegar, red wine
Vinegar, white
Worcestershire sauce

Glossary of Cooking Terms

à la mode: The direct translation from French is "in the fashion." Most often, this term refers to a scoop of ice cream served with a piece of pie.

al dente: Tender but still firm. Usually applies to pasta or vegetables.

au gratin: Topped with browned bread crumbs, usually blended with butter or cheese before baking.

bake: Cook in an oven with dry heat.

barbecue: Cook on a grill over hot charcoal.

baste: Spoon liquid or fat over food during cooking.

beat: Stir vigorously to add air.

blend: Mix together.

boil: Cook in steaming water or other liquid. Boiling water has large bubbles that break at the surface.

broil: Like barbecuing, broiling is cooking directly over a fire or directly under the heating element. Heat for broiling is more intense than for baking or roasting.

chill: Cool in the refrigerator until cold.

chop: Cut into small pieces.

coat: Cover with another ingredient, such as coating lettuce with salad dressing or coating a strawberry with chocolate.

colander: A bowl-like pan with holes in the bottom for draining such foods as pasta and steamed vegetables.

confectioners' sugar: Powdered sugar.

cool: No longer warm, but not yet chilled.

corer: A utensil used to remove apple cores.

cream: Stir or beat together 2 or more ingredients until the mixture is soft and smooth. This term usually refers to mixing fat and sugar.

crisp-tender: Food—usually vegetables or pasta—that is tender but still firm.

cube: Cut into little boxes, usually with about ½"-long sides.

dash: An imprecise measurement that means a small amount; less than ⅛ teaspoon.

deep-fry: Cook by submersing in hot fat.

defrost: Thaw.

dice: Cut into little, bitty cubes, usually with sides less than ¼" long.

dilute: Add liquid to make an ingredient thinner or less strong.

drain: Remove liquid or fat; usually done by using a sieve or colander.

dust: Lightly sprinkle, usually with flour or confectioners' sugar.

entrée: The main dish of a meal—usually meat, fish, or poultry, but may be a meat substitute or a casserole.

evaporated milk: Whole milk that has been heated to remove 60 percent of its water; no sugar is added; do *not* substitute for sweetened condensed milk.

fillet: Meat or fish with the bones removed.

firmly packed: A way to measure an ingredient, like brown sugar, by tightly pressing it into the measuring cup or measuring spoon. This method results in more of the ingredient than using the usual measuring method.

flake: Separate into small pieces, often by using a fork; for example, you may want to flake tuna or salmon when you remove it from a can.

fold: A method of stirring from the bottom of the bowl to the top, rather than around in a horizontal circle; start with the spoon in the center of the bowl, then plunge it down to the bottom, and back toward you up the side to the top; turn the bowl and repeat until the ingredients are well mixed together.

freeze: Chill at a cold enough temperature (32° for water) to turn solid.

fry: Cook in hot fat.

garnish: Decorate one food with another. Parsley is a frequently used garnish that improves the appearance of food.

grate: Rub a food against the small holes of a grater.

grater: A utensil with sharp-edged holes used to shred such foods as cheese, carrots, and lettuce.

grease: Coat a baking pan with solid shortening, vegetable oil, or nonstick cooking spray to prevent sticking.

heat: Make food warmer.

hull: Remove stems from fruit.

huller: A utensil used to remove the stem and leaves from strawberries.

invert: Turn upside down.

julienne: Cut into sticks similar in shape to wooden matches. Julienne strips are like long cubes.

marinade: A liquid mixture that contains an acid, seasonings, and, often, oil. Used to add flavor to meats or vegetables before cooking.

marinate: Soak food in a marinade.

melt: Change from solid form to liquid.

mince: Cut into teeny-weeny pieces.

mix: Combine foods, usually by stirring.

mull: Heat, sweeten, and add spices.

pare: Cut off peeling of such foods as apples and potatoes.

peel: The outer skin of a fruit or vegetable; also refers to removing the outer skin of a fruit or vegetable.

pinch: An imprecise measurement term that means the amount you can hold between your thumb and forefinger.

pit: A stone that contains the seed of such fruits as avocados and cherries; also refers to removing such a stone.

poach: Slowly simmer in liquid.

powdered sugar: Confectioners' sugar.

preheat: Heat an oven, frying pan, griddle, broiler, or other cooking appliance to a specific temperature prior to cooking.

rinse: Clean something with water. (Never wash food with soap.)

roast: Cook uncovered using dry heat, usually in an oven. *Roast* usually applies to meat; *bake*, which also means to cook with dry heat, usually applies to such foods as breads, desserts, and casseroles.

sauté: Cook in a small amount of fat in a frying pan, stirring frequently.

shortening: A fat used in baking or frying; often refers to fat in solid form.

shred: Cut into long, narrow pieces; or, rub food across the large holes of a grater.

sift: Add air to a recipe by passing such ingredients as flour through a sieve.

sifter: A utensil used to sift ingredients.

simmer: Cook in water or other liquid that is not quite as hot as boiling; water that is simmering has small bubbles below the surface.

slice: Cut a thin, flat piece of such foods as tomatoes and onions; also refers to cutting meat the same way.

soufflé: A fluffy baked egg dish with a wide variety of other ingredients.

spoon: Scoop using a spoon.

steam: Cook in steam from boiling water rather than cooking in the water.

stew: Cook slowly in liquid over low temperature.

stir: Move a spoon or other utensil in a circle to combine ingredients.

stir-fry: Cook in a small amount of fat in frying pan or wok over high heat, stirring constantly to prevent sticking or burning.

strainer: A sieve used for straining foods; can also be used to sift such ingredients as flour.

sweetened condensed milk: Whole milk that has been heated to remove 60 percent of its water and has been commercially sweetened; *not* a substitute for evaporated milk.

tent: A piece of aluminum foil folded in half and propped open like the roof of a house over such food as turkey to keep the food from getting too brown when baking or roasting in the oven.

thaw: Let warm up from a frozen state to an unfrozen one.

toss: Gently mix such ingredients as lettuce and other vegetables by scooping and lifting them with hands, spoons, or other utensils.

undiluted: Without added liquid; for recipes that include condensed soup, *undiluted* means not to add milk or water to the soup.

whip: Beat rapidly; like beating, whipping adds air.

whisk: A kitchen utensil usually made of wire used to blend such ingredients as eggs, milk, and cream; also used as a verb meaning "to whip."

wok: A large, deep skillet used to stir-fry vegetables.

zest: The outer skin of such citrus fruits as lemons, limes, and oranges. Grated zest is sometimes used as a flavoring.

Appendix C
Cooking Vegetables

f you want to cook fresh vegetables by themselves instead of in a casserole or a fancy side dish, you can boil or steam them. Generally, steaming or boiling in a small amount of water in a covered saucepan works best for cut or small vegetables, while boiling uncovered is preferred for large or whole vegetables.

Here are a few tips:

1. For most vegetables, figure about 2 servings per cup.

2. Before cooking, rinse vegetables in cold running water. Drain. Cut off inedible stems or leaves.

3. You can boil vegetables with about ½" of water in a saucepan. Bring to a boil over high heat. Cover the saucepan. Reduce heat to medium for the prescribed cooking time (see chart following).

4. Steaming is easy if you use a steamer insert that keeps the vegetables up out of the water. Or, use a pot designed as a steamer.

5. For boiling green vegetables, cook uncovered for the first 5 minutes; then cover for the remaining cooking time. For other vegetables, cover as soon as the water boils. Reduce heat to medium. Cook until tender, yet still firm.

Asparagus

You can enjoy dark green asparagus spears topped with butter, lemon pepper, cheese, or special sauces. Although it is available year-round, many people associate slender new spears with spring. In fact, peak seasons stretch from January to June and August to October, depending on the growing area. Before cooking, remove the tough bottom inch or so of the stems by cutting or breaking off as if they were sticks.

Cooking time: Tips, 5 to 8 minutes; 1" pieces, 10 to 15 minutes; whole, 10 to 20 minutes

℣ Yields 1 serving per 5 spears ℣

Broccoli

Choose broccoli with a firm cluster of small flower buds with dark green or sage color. A purplish tone is okay. So is a yellowish tint on the sides of the floret. However, avoid broccoli that has open clusters with greenish yellow color. Before cooking, trim off the bottom of the main stem. Serve with butter, lemon juice, and oregano, or canned cheese sauce.

Cooking time: 10 to 15 minutes

℣ Yields 1 serving per stalk ℣

Brussels Sprouts

Brussels sprouts look like tiny cabbages. Serve with butter or margarine and salt and pepper. Herbs and spices that enhance their flavor include garlic, basil, dill, caraway, or cumin. Before cooking, remove any discolored leaves. Trim stem ends.

Cooking time: 8 to 10 minutes

Yields 1 serving per 4 sprouts

Carrots

Carrots are good for your eyes, but they won't correct your vision. Carrots are high in vitamin A, which promotes good eye health and helps prevent night blindness. Packaged baby carrots that have already been cleaned may also be steamed.

Cooking time: Sliced, 10 to 20 minutes; small (whole), 15 to 20 minutes; large (whole), 20 to 30 minutes

Yields 1 serving per medium-size whole carrot

Cauliflower

Serve cauliflower alone or in combination with broccoli and/or carrots. Tasty toppings include melted cheese, diluted lemon juice, or bottled tartar sauce. Before cooking, cut away leaves and the center core. Cut off any discolored spots. If not cooking whole, separate the florets (the "treetops") with the stems attached.

Cooking time: Florets, 8 to 15 minutes; whole 20 to 30 minutes

Yields 5 servings per head

Corn on the Cob

Fresh corn on the cob is a Midwestern favorite. Do not add salt during cooking, as it will toughen the corn. Serve with butter or margarine and salt and pepper. Before cooking, remove husks and corn silks from the corn. For the best flavor ever, if you live on a farm or have a home garden, wait until the water is boiling before you pick the corn.

Cooking time: 5 to 8 minutes

Serves 1 per ear

Green Beans

Green beans are fat-free and a good source of fiber. They also are low in calories, with just 25 calories per serving. When purchasing, look for clean, tender beans with uniform shape. For added flavor, toss with butter or bacon fat after cooking. Or, season with basil, marjoram, dill weed, or thyme. Before cooking, cut or snap off the ends. Leave whole, or cut crosswise into 1"-long pieces or cut lengthwise (known as French cut).

Cooking time: Cut, 15 to 20 minutes; French cut, 10 minutes; whole, 15 to 20 minutes

Yields 1 serving per ³/₄ cup

Peas

Finding fresh peas in the pod is rare, so most people use frozen. Cook according to package instructions. If you want to shell your own, remove from the pods immediately before cooking. For either frozen or fresh, add 1 teaspoon sugar to the cooking water. You can also use thawed frozen peas in cold salads.

Cooking time: 8 to 15 minutes

1 cup yields 2 servings

Potatoes

The potato is the most popular vegetable in the United States. The easiest way to cook is to bake them. You can boil them for use in mashed potatoes, potato salads, or potato casseroles. You can use any variety, but red and russet potatoes work especially well for boiling.

Cooking time: Bake at 375° for 1 hour or at 350° for 1½ hours; boil, cut 20 to 25 minutes; whole, 30 to 35 minutes

1 serving per medium-size potato

Index

About the Author

Mary-Lane Kamberg is an award-winning professional writer who has published seven nonfiction books and hundreds of articles for magazines, newspapers, and literary and online publications, including *Better Homes and Gardens*, *The Christian Science Monitor*, *Healthy Kids*, *Marriage and Family Living*, *Swimming World*, *TeenAge*, *Current Health*, *Kansas City Star*, and others.

She is listed in *Marquis Who's Who in America* and received the 1996 James P. Immroth Memorial Award from the American Library Association's Intellectual Freedom Roundtable. She has won numerous awards for poetry, humor, newspaper, and magazine writing. Her professional activities and memberships include the National League of American Pen Women, Society of Professional Journalists, Kansas Authors Club, Kansas City Press Club, Sisters in Crime, Missouri Writers Guild, Oklahoma Writers Federation, and Kansas City Writers Group (co-leader).

She was fiction editor for *Potpourri* literary magazine and has taught creative writing workshops for Johnson County Community College, Overland Park, Kansas; Avila College, Kansas City, Missouri; and the Kansas Authors Club.